PROTECTING HISTORIC PROPERTIES

A GUIDE TO RESEARCH AND PRESERVATION
(With Examples from the Delaware Valley)

 Brandywine Conservancy

Protecting Historic Properties

Copyright © 1984
Brandywine Conservancy, Inc.
Chadds Ford, Pennsylvania

ISBN No. 0-940540-03-7

Library of Congress Catalog Card Number 84-72856

For information on ordering additional
copies, contact the Museum Shop, Brandywine Conservancy, P.O. Box 141, Chadds
Ford, PA 19317. Phone: (215) 459-1900.

*The cover and title page photos show the
William Twaddell house in Delaware County,
Pennsylvania, before and after restoration.*

Cover photo: Frank Herzog
Title page photo: George Eisenman

*The old wooden typeface, Antique Light Face c. 1854, used in the book title, appeared
in American Wood Type: 1828–1900, by Rob Roy Kelly. It is used with permission
from Van Nostrand Reinhold Company, New York, New York.*

TABLE OF CONTENTS

Preface

Chapter 1   **1** HISTORIC PRESERVATION

Chapter 2   **5** THREE CENTURIES OF DELAWARE VALLEY ARCHITECTURE: A TOUR
- 17th-Century Precedents
- The 18th Century: A Progression of Styles
- The 19th Century: A Choice of Styles

Chapter 3   **37** RESEARCHING HISTORIC BUILDINGS
- Documenting the House
- Researching the Physical Structure
- Archeological Investigation

Chapter 4   **57** THE NATIONAL REGISTER OF HISTORIC PLACES
- Background
- Benefits and Protections
- How to Nominate a Resource

Chapter 5   **73** THE WAYS AND MEANS OF PRESERVATION
- Survey
- Planning
- Local Regulation
- Negotiation and Mediation
- Funding

Chapter 6   **95** PRESERVATION EASEMENTS
- Alden Park Manor — On a Grand Scale
- Carter-Worth House and Barn
- Legislation
- Benefits
- Criteria — The Three Tests
- The Structure of an Easement
- Financial Considerations

Chapter 7   **119** TAX INCENTIVES FOR HISTORIC BUILDINGS
- An Old House
- Tax Incentives, 1976-80
- Economic Recovery Tax Act of 1981
- What To Do
- Can You Benefit?
- What's Being Done
- Rehabilitating the Old House

134 For Further Reading

Appendix A   **137** Directory of Organizations Concerned with Historic Preservation (National, Pennsylvania, and Delaware Valley)

Appendix B   **141** Research Libraries and Collections (Delaware Valley)

Appendix C   **143** Pennsylvania Historic District Listings; Sample Documents and Forms; Local Ordinances

Hoffman's Mill before reconstruction.

PREFACE

In the past 15 years, the historic preservation movement in the United States has experienced incredible growth in public support and achievements. Membership in the National Trust for Historic Preservation and like-minded regional and local preservation organizations has expanded enormously. During the late 1970s and early 1980s, the U.S. Congress favored direct funding of historic preservation organizations and tax incentive programs; this commitment contributed to the flowering of public and private agencies protecting historic sites and to the development of a historic building renovation and recycling industry that would have been unimaginable in the late 1960s and early 1970s, when many of today's preservationists first became involved.

While the historic preservation movement has its roots in many positive actions of individuals and groups, the great growth of interest and organizations was fired in the late 1950s and 1960s by the negative results of two federal programs: urban renewal and the interstate highway system. The demolition of vast areas of historic buildings and neighborhoods to accommodate "downtown renewal" and "slum removal" and to clear paths in the cities and countryside for expressways to or around downtowns made many people aware of the fragility of our historic heritage and galvanized political action. The National Historic Preservation Act of 1966 and the 4(f) Amendment to the Department of Transportation Act of 1966 (which requires special attention to preserving or protecting National Register sites in transportation corridor construction projects) were specific actions taken in response to the excesses of federal building programs.

The Brandywine Conservancy was founded in 1967 to protect a highly threatened area of southeastern Pennsylvania and northern Delaware: a five-mile-wide corridor along the Brandywine River running from the West Chester area of Pennsylvania to the city limits of Wilmington, Delaware, including the crossroads village of Chadds Ford well known today for its famous artist resident, Andrew Wyeth, and his family. Within this corridor, the state of Pennsylvania was considering two new limited-access highways and Delaware was proposing two, including one along the Brandywine. A new international airport for the Philadelphia region was also being planned for the area. The various highway projects as well as the airport project would have effectively destroyed a majority of the area's most significant 18th- and 19th-century historic structures and desecrated the scenic vistas of an area which had been the inspiration of artists for almost 200 years.

In 1967, with guidance from Dr. S.K. Stevens, Executive Director of the Pennsylvania Historical and Museum Commission, and with assistance from the Chadds Ford Historical Society and other local historical groups, the Brandywine Conservancy undertook National Register nomination programs in Pennsylvania and in Delaware which were among the first in those states. Over a five-year period, nominations were prepared for more than 10 historic districts and 40 individual sites in the two states, and most were placed on the National Register. National Register status for these districts and sites helped thwart both highway and airport plans, the implementation of which would have meant certain destruction of the sites.

The conservancy's founding group had a very large agenda in 1967. In addition to meeting the highway and airport threats and organizing a National Register project, the group had also bought or made commitments to buy several properties in Chadds Ford and was organizing a conservation easement program to protect open lands. One of the properties purchased was Hoffman's Mill, a mid-19th-century grist mill on the Brandywine River at Chadds Ford. The mill property had been a lumber company for a number of years, but the Brandywine's raging flood had washed profits and equity downstream too many times. To save the stalwart brick mill building, it was converted into a museum for the display of works by Brandywine artists. Through the design efforts of an innovative architect, James R. Grieves of Baltimore, aided by artist-founder George A. Weymouth and by organization staff, the mill became the Brandywine River Museum. It opened in 1972 for the preservation and exhibition of the Brandywine's artistic heritage. Essentially the same design team in 1984 completed a $3.5 million addition. Art and history have been brought together in one of the United States' most delightful integrations of historic and contemporary architecture. Sensitive blending of the old with the new has been an objective of all conservancy programs.

Beginning in 1972, the Brandywine Conservancy expanded the scope of its natural and historic resource protection efforts. The conservancy's water resources management study initiated that year was aimed at the 350-square-mile Brandywine watershed. An applied research program to assist local governments in Pennsylvania with the regulation of land development and environmental problems attracted the interest and support of local governments in Philadelphia suburban areas beyond the Brandywine watershed. A major expansion of the conservancy's conservation easement program in 1975 led to increased efforts to perpetually protect the important natural, historic, and scenic resources of vast areas of Chester and Delaware Counties in Pennsylvania and northern New Castle County in Delaware.

The broader focus of these programs and their need to address historic preservation issues led to an expanded vision of the conservancy's historic preservation effort. The historic preservation program was seen as an integral element of water resources planning in the watershed, of the conservation easement and land acquisition programs (to identify important properties deserving protection), and the local government assistance program (to broaden comprehensive planning objectives and provide appropriate regulation of historic sites). The key need of all these programs was for good inventories and evaluations of historic sites within geographical areas of concern. By 1977, only a small percentage of sites had been inventoried in the largest area of concern and the one with the greatest variety and number of historic sites: Chester County. The work of the French and Pickering Creeks Conservation Trust in northern Chester County, the Brandywine Conservancy's efforts in southeastern Chester County, and Bicentennial projects underway in Downingtown and West Chester were the most extensive area efforts at the time.

Under the supervision of the Chester County Historical Society, and with financial support from the Chester County Commissioners' Community Development funds and the Pennsylvania Historical and Museum Commission's federal historic preservation funds, the Brandywine Conservancy organized and managed a survey of almost 10,000 historic buildings and building complexes. The Chester County survey was a three-year effort during 1979–82. Limited funds, as well as a desire to increase local interest and support, suggested extensive use of volunteers for the inventory phase—a decision which also required the development of an easy-to-use inventory form whose illustrations and questions helped the volunteers to identify important historical and architectural details later evaluated by professionals (see this

1742 Square Tavern, Newtown Square, Pennsylvania. Operated in mid-1700s by John West, father of American painter Benjamin West. Now housing the Delaware County Tourist Information Center, the building was restored and is owned by ARCO Chemical Company, a subsidiary of Atlantic Richfield Company.

Delaware County Tourist Information Center

inventory form in Chapter 5). Over 100 volunteers participated in the survey, many of whom have since become more deeply involved in local preservation efforts.

The conservancy and the other individuals and organizations involved in the survey have followed up on the results by pursuing National Register nominations for historic districts, multiple resources (a variety of sites in a municipality's history), and individual properties. These nominations as well as other studies have been used to support municipal land use planning, zoning regulations, and private conservation easement programs as initially intended when the survey was proposed.

This present book was originally conceived in 1976 as one chapter in a larger publication on the preservation of distinctive landscapes and critical natural resources. As various staff members and consultants prepared information for the chapter, it became obvious that a single chapter regarding historic preservation was insufficient for the purposes. In 1977, the idea of a historic preservation primer was born and a new scope of study was outlined. The primer was to contain the most up-to-date information on historic preservation, including federal tax laws and other legislation affecting historic properties. Since 1978, the book has been finished several times only to be made obsolete by changes in tax laws or other critical programs. Undoubtedly, more changes can be expected in coming years, but we believe that this book will have lasting utility.

Support for its preparation has been provided by the National Trust for Historic Preservation, the Catherwood Foundation, Longwood Foundation, Robert J. and Helen C. Kleberg Foundation, and Atlantic Richfield Foundation. For their assistance and forbearance as we postponed publication dates to update text, we are deeply grateful.

In addition to the generous contributors mentioned above, there were countless individuals who helped us as writers, advisors, editors, idea-generators, and morale boosters. Those bearing special mention are listed below; to all the rest, our genuine thanks to you, as well.

Several individuals share primary authorship of the text. Martha L. Wolf, the Brandywine Conservancy's historic preservation specialist, was the principal author of Chapters 4, 5 and 6, was compiler of the appendices, and carried the major responsibility for bringing the book together. Michael Wolf wrote Chapter 1. Margaret Richie did the research for Chapter 2 and was its major author. Chapter 3 was prepared with help from Julia Colflesh, Wick Williams, and Estelle Cremers. (Mrs. Cremers also developed the old-deed terminology found at the end of the chapter.) Michael Schwager researched and wrote Chapter 7.

Many people consented to be interviewed for the book, and to them we express our utmost appreciation. Others also contributed information, materials, photographs, and advice. Special thanks go to:

Berks County Conservancy
Bucks County Conservancy
Bureau for Historic Preservation of the Pennsylvania
    Historical and Museum Commission
Chester County Historical Society
Chester County Historic Preservation Office
Delaware County Planning Department
French and Pickering Creeks Conservation Trust
Historical Society of Montgomery County
John Milner Associates
Lower Merion Township Planning Department
National Trust for Historic Preservation
Preservation Fund of Pennsylvania
West Whiteland Historical Commission

Hoffman's Mill reconstructed as the Brandywine River Museum.

Invaluable assistance came from several Brandywine Conservancy staff members. Claire Murray, Donna Goudie, and Sharon Mitchell saw many drafts through the word processor. Emily Hart contributed her time and expertise to Chapter 6. Stephen Kuter, our graphic artist, created the fine illustrations found throughout the book. Wendy Emrich managed the difficult task of steering the book toward publication (a process begun much earlier by Wick Williams).

Model of Brandywine River Museum with new wing completed in 1984.

Outside consultants played a key role. Bill Hamilton, as design and layout consultant, gave us a magnificent visual product for which we all can be proud. Anne Cook, in charge of marketing, devoted her creative energies to brochure design, mailing lists, and bookstore contacts. And Michael Schwager, as consulting editor, put in tireless hours to ensure a clear, crisp, and highly readable text.

All of these individuals have contributed to a very important Brandywine Conservancy publication, one which we trust will further the cause of historic research and preservation in communities across the United States.

H. William Sellers, *Director*
Environmental Management Center
Brandywine Conservancy
November 1984

What is historic?

Chapter 1
HISTORIC PRESERVATION

No society can call itself civilized if every succeeding generation demolishes the heritage of its predecessors.
—Richard Hughes, Governor of New Jersey, 1967

What is historic? The variety of "historic" things protected or restored under the aegis of preservation seems to defy any unifying logic. Items range from a bus stop sign in Winnetka, Illinois, to a wooden elephant in Margate, New Jersey, to the entire main-street area in Bloomsfield, Ohio. Each has been deemed worthy of preservation, but why?

It may be the presence of a special quality that makes something stand out—quite apart from its age. This quality might be its unusual design features, its superb workmanship and detailing, or the fact that it is a rare or exceptional example of a particular style.

No matter what definition of historic one uses, the lower Delaware Valley is an area of historic resources as rich and varied as any in the United States. Within an hour's travel of Broad and Market Streets, Philadelphia, are outstanding examples of a heritage spanning more than three centuries, a heritage documenting the contributions of English, Irish, Swedish, Dutch, German, French, Swiss, and Finnish immigrants.

The lower Delaware Valley is also home to the Brandywine Conservancy and is therefore the region we work in and know best. Thus it became the model study area for this book. Examples are drawn from the valley to highlight points made in each chapter, but the points have broader applicability. Because the region plays such an important illustrative role in the book, we would like to take a moment to introduce you to its history and its many resources.

The early and continued prominence of the Delaware River and its ports of entry brought to the valley a mixture of cultures and craftsmen with

Chadds Ford Junction in days gone by.

specialized skills and building traditions. The area attracted statesmen, scholars, merchants, industrialists, artisans, blacksmiths, millers, shipwrights, and farmers, generating demand for the array of buildings and facilities needed for an emerging nation.

Whether it was the temperament of the settlers, practical frugality, excellent workmanship, or simply neglect, a wealth of this early history remains intact. It represents a tangible link with the past. Guidebooks and brochures about the region, though, tend to highlight only the most famous historic sites, many of which are publicly owned and associated with the colonial period and the Revolution. Thus, Independence Hall, Carpenters' Hall, the Betsy Ross House, and the battlegrounds and headquarters of military campaigns are well known and teeming with visitors.

Yet many historic places in the region are less known and less appreciated. Besides 18th-century homes of hand-hewn log, Flemish-bond brick, and fieldstone, there are homes of later eras, from distinguished Greek Revival townhouses to the castles and villas of the Main Line built at the turn of the century, to modern residences designed by Louis Kahn, Robert Venturi, and Frank Lloyd Wright. Religious buildings of every description include Quaker, Mennonite, and Schwenkfelder meetinghouses, early synagogues, even a Swedenborgian cathedral. Cemetery headstones in many languages provide insights on the past, and visitors can still discover headstones inscribed by early German settlers. Also instructive are forts and armories, courthouses and jails, hospitals, markets, octagonal schools and barns, opera houses and theaters, libraries, banks, colleges, and art academies that not only survive but are still in use—though sometimes for new purposes.

Thanks to the preservation of numerous grist mills and a number of paper, gunpowder, lumber, cotton, and fulling mills, as well as early iron works and furnaces, the region also serves as a primer on industrial development. Those interested in the history of transportation can find the earliest "turnpikes," with their milestones and their inns and taverns built to serve stagecoaches and Conestoga wagons. Portions of the Schuylkill and Delaware Canals remain, complete with locks and towpaths. Numerous stone-arch and covered bridges survive. Along some of the nation's first railroad routes are splendid Victorian stations. Most of the region's trolleys are now gone, but some amusement parks, built to bolster weekend ridership, remain as testaments to the days of John Philip Sousa and the great brass bands.

Of all the historic places that remain, those in farming areas are perhaps the least celebrated. There are "bank" farmhouses partially built into hillsides and bank barns featuring ground floors of stone for stabling and second-floor haymows. Just as interesting are the outbuildings on some farmsteads, including springhouses, smokehouses, outhouses, root cellars, bake ovens, and summer kitchens. Even some creameries, cider mills, workshops, and family cemeteries remain.

Regrettably, the region has suffered grievous losses. Many farms have been cut up into subdivisions, and countless farmhouses with all their associated buildings have been engulfed by these new developments. Losses also happen in urban areas. One highly publicized disaster occurred in 1969, when the 279-year-old Benjamin Rush House in northeast Philadelphia was accidentally razed. In 1974, after a lawsuit, Episcopal Academy in Merion won the right to demolish the Upper House built in 1899. This French Renaissance building, designed by William L. Price, had exquisite Gothic details, including an inglenook fireplace and oak paneling.

Yet the cycle of destruction can be, and indeed is being, broken. Almost weekly, it seems, come new success stories—clear signs of a rising public consciousness about historic preservation. Preservation is no longer the watchword of a few. Increasingly it is being incorporated in federal and state policy and carried out at the local level. As growing numbers of people are learning, there are many ways to effect preservation: federal tax incentives like the investment tax credit and preservation easement, registration of historic sites, community planning, local regulation, environmental review, and revolving funds.

This book will acquaint you with these techniques and then some. Whether you are a public official, an entrepreneur, or someone just becoming interested in historic preservation, this book will familiarize you with the basics of investigating and preserving historic buildings. Chapter 2 will take you on a tour of prominent architectural styles and design features to help you begin placing buildings in their historical contexts. Chapter 3 will show you how to navigate the research maze and uncover the hidden stories behind historic buildings. Chapter 4 will explain the National Register of Historic Places. The final three chapters will describe a variety of private and public approaches to preservation.

Effective tools for preserving more of the past are now available. It is up to all of us to use them.

Loch Aerie, c. 1865. An outstanding example of one of Delaware Valley's most picturesque styles, High Victorian Italianate.

Margaret B. Richie. All photos in this chapter are credited to Mrs. Richie unless otherwise indicated.

Chapter 2

THREE CENTURIES OF DELAWARE VALLEY ARCHITECTURE: A TOUR

The Delaware Valley boasts some of the finest architecture in the United States. From New Hope to Kennett Square, from Pottstown to Wilmington, the region has buildings representing nearly every architectural style found in the country. Internationally acclaimed architects and unknown carpenters alike have left their mark on the landscape.

This chapter describes the leading architectural styles in the Delaware Valley. It covers styles from the 17th to the end of the 19th century. It discusses some of the region's most important buildings, many of which are open to the public and can be visited for a closer look. It also travels down back roads to some everyday houses that are good examples of local styles.

So sit back and enjoy the tour. There's nothing quite like it anywhere else.

17TH-CENTURY PRECEDENTS

Dutch

Few 17th-century houses in this region have survived, for most were starkly simple and transitory. Documentation about Delaware Valley houses built between 1625 and 1700 indicates a rude and comfortless mode of life.

The Dutch were the first Europeans to arrive, following Henry Hudson, an Englishman in Dutch employ, who discovered the Delaware River in 1609. Over the next 50 years, the Dutch, and then the Swedes, established trading posts. No incontestable traces of Dutch architecture remain. One by one, their houses and forts were destroyed by the ravages of time and man. A written order, dated 1649, for the construction of two wooden houses along the river describes each as being 32 feet long and 18 feet wide, with

PROTECTING HISTORIC PROPERTIES

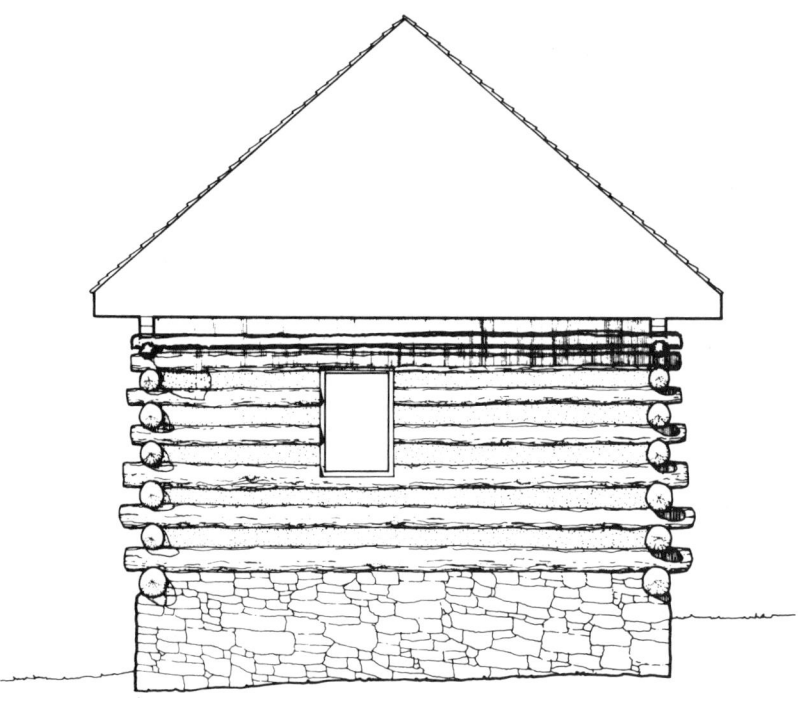

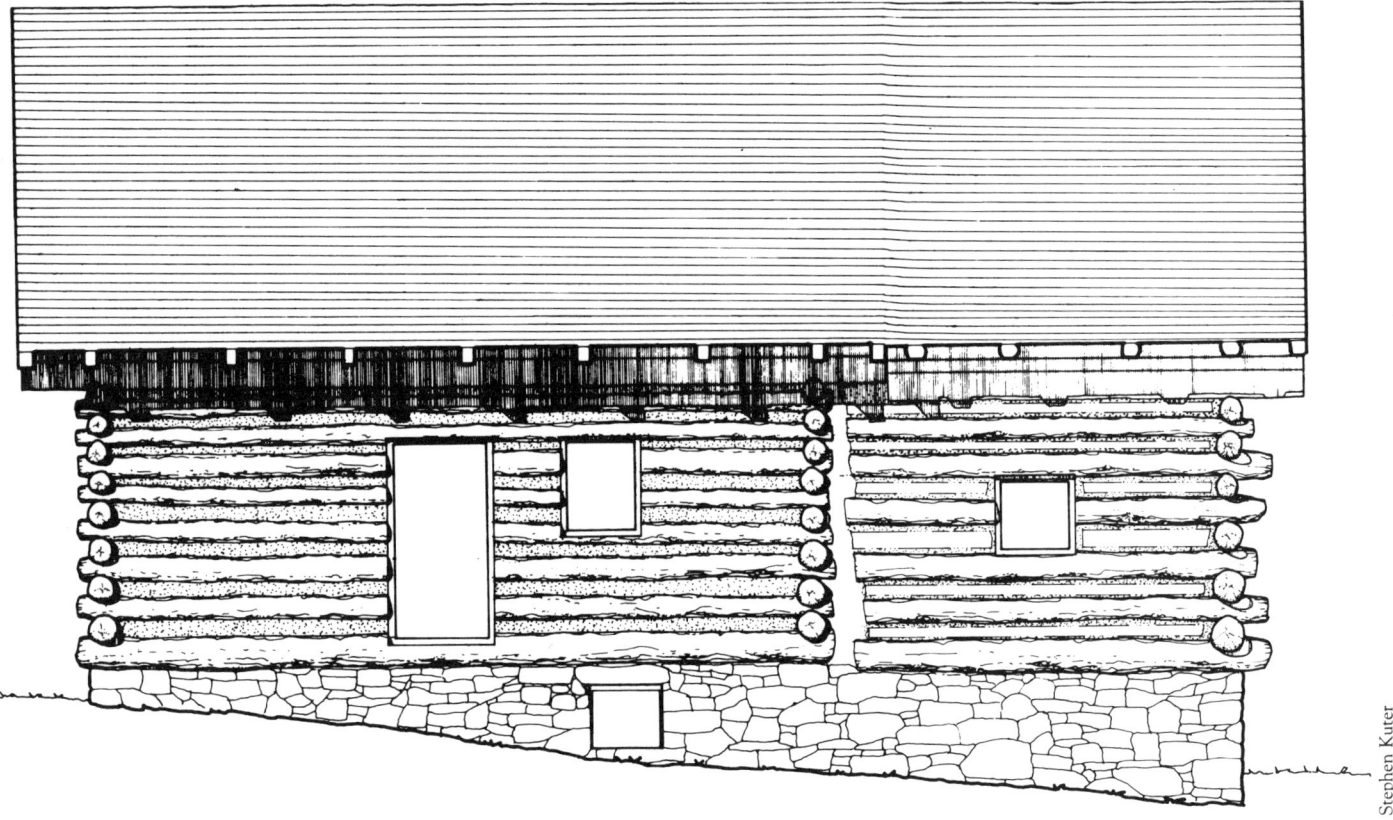

Upper Log House in Delaware County, thought to be of Swedish construction. Destroyed by fire in 1980.

a 9-foot story, the whole to be built of local pine. The order, preserved in volume 12 of the *New York Historical Records,* stipulates that each house have five "outside and inside" doors, three windows, one circular and one TRANSOM WINDOW, a roof to be covered in planking, and a wood-framed double chimney. (See the glossary at the end of this chapter for definitions of terms in SMALL CAPS.) The floor plan was to be divided by three partitions and two planked closets "to be cut off from the square room." This description implies a solid plank house, one story high, with a steeply sloping roof. The builders were Dutch and came south from Manhattan expressly to build these houses.

One survivor from the Dutch settlement may be the ground-hugging "Old Dutch House" (c. 1650) located on Orange Street in New Castle, Delaware. It resembles Dutch examples remaining in Ulster County in New York's Hudson River Valley.

Recent archeological evidence supports the contention that post houses (frame houses built on wooden posts driven into the ground) were built during this early period in the Delaware Valley. Although post houses have vanished, they may have been more commonly used than historians once thought. Many early settlers placed little emphasis on quality or luxury in their houses and thus did not build them to last.

Swedish

The Swedes left more traces than the Dutch. The colony New Sweden was established in 1638 at Fort Christina (part of present-day Wilmington). In 1643, a "capitol," the Printzhoff, was built on Tinicum Island north of Fort Christina on the Delaware River. Both settlements were seized by the Dutch in 1655. Nevertheless, a Swedish culture endured for several decades. A Swedish congregation with an enthusiastic pastor supported the building of Holy Trinity (Old Swedes) Church in Wilmington in 1699, although the church was built by English masons, carpenters, and sawyers, all brought from Philadelphia. Today, no extant building or architectural detail can be identified as particularly Swedish.

The practice of building corner fireplaces, for example, once attributed exclusively to the Swedes, was shared by the English. On the other hand, the Swedes were definitely the first in this region to introduce the log house, a form unknown to the English, Dutch, or French. They brought the tradition with them when New Sweden was chartered in 1638, finding that log structures served well in the American climate. Harold Shurtleff, a leading researcher into the origins of log dwellings, concludes in *The Log Cabin Myth* (1939) that the "Delaware Bay was the principal center from which log construction spread." The Morton Homestead in Norwood Borough, Delaware County, located about a mile from the site of the Printzhoff, is a rare, documented example of Swedish log construction. It was built in the mid-

Caleb Pusey house.

17th century by Morton Mortonson. Now owned by the Commonwealth, it is one of the oldest surviving houses in Pennsylvania.

English

One of the Delaware Valley's few 17th-century houses to survive is the extraordinary Caleb Pusey house at Upland, near Chester in Delaware County, built in 1683. Caleb Pusey, a business partner of William Penn, came to Pennsylvania in 1682 to manage Penn's first proprietary saw and grist mill at Chester. The Pusey house is the only surviving structure that Penn is known to have frequented. The oldest section is the eastern half. It originally appeared as a one-room stone cottage with a GABLE roof. An addition was built to the west in 1696, doubling the size of the early building. In the 1740s the roof of the 1683 portion was raised to a GAMBREL. Although extensively restored, the Pusey house retains much of its late-17th-century character. It features a large walk-in fireplace, low ceilings with exposed BEAMS, small CASEMENT WINDOWS, and a large masonry bake oven with adjacent kettle stand.

Seventeenth-century Philadelphia was an open, planned-town reaching only a few blocks west of the Delaware River. Although William Penn envisioned a city of brick houses, many were initially built of wood. They were patterned after those in London, Amersham, and other English towns from which the settlers had emigrated. The earliest houses had PENT ROOFS and balconies. Later houses, if built of brick, often had FACADES patterned in FLEMISH BOND. By 1700, Philadelphia could count several hundred brick houses, although its streets were unpaved and no church spires glorified the skyline.

THE 18TH CENTURY: A PROGRESSION OF STYLES

English Colonial, c. 1700–50

After 1700, more permanent structures appeared. By 1758, Israel Acrelius, a Swede in charge of Swedish churches in America, could write: "The houses are built of bricks, after the English fashion, without coating, every other brick glazed; or they are of sandstone, granite, etc., as is mostly the case in the country. Sometimes they also build of oak planks 5" thick. To build of wood is not considered an economy, after everything is paid for. The roof is of cedar shingles. Within, the walls and ceilings are plastered, and whitewashed once a year. . . . The windows are large, divided into two pieces, the upper and the lower; the latter is opened by raising and shut by lowering. The woodwork is painted or it does not last long." Acrelius's description makes it clear that by the mid-18th century the English tradition had absorbed the Swedish and the Dutch.

Of the region's many extant structures exemplifying the rural 18th-century English Colonial house, two in Delaware County are of particular interest: the John Chad house in Chadds Ford and the Thomas Massey house in Marple Township. Both are excellent "vocabulary" buildings in the English idiom; that is, they have all the standard details. While the Chad house represents only one step beyond the earliest one-room log or stone cabin, the Massey house, one of the oldest English Quaker–built houses in Pennsylvania, shows the evolution of a simple house into a larger, three-part house, a progression that took place over nearly 200 years. Both were modest structures with more emphasis given to function than to style; both give clues to the dating of 18th-century houses in the Delaware Valley. In addition, both have all the choices of fabric that Acrelius mentioned as being available to the 18th-century builder.

The Chad house (c. 1720) is stone; the Massey house, in its three sections, uses brick (1696), stone (c. 1730), and wood (c. 1860). Except for the central section of the Massey house, the stonework in both houses is of fieldstone laid randomly. The Massey house's central section, having replaced an earlier log house on the site, reflects a slightly more sophisticated treatment, the stone being laid approximately in COURSES. The use of coursed stonework was a refinement introduced about 1750.

The oldest section of the Massey house is built of brick; its facade and END WALLS are laid in Flemish bond. The rear wall, not intended for show, is laid in the plainer ENGLISH BOND. (Occasionally, 18th-century builders achieved highly decorative effects by using glazed bricks in a variety of patterns, even to write a house's date of construction. New Castle Hundred, Delaware, has several of these elaborately patterned brick houses.)

The additive, three-part composition of the Massey house shows the tradition of abutting a new section against an existing one. Large, stabilizing corner stones, called QUOINS, mark the ends of each section of the building.

The Chad house is BANKED into the earth, a technique that provided an easily accessible cellar level for cooking and food storage. It was customary during colonial times to orient the facades of houses and barns toward the south or southeast to obtain the maximum sun in winter; both the Massey house and the Chad house follow that practice.

The Massey house shows a typical room arrangement. Because it lacks a center hall, each room opens directly onto another. Each house has a pent

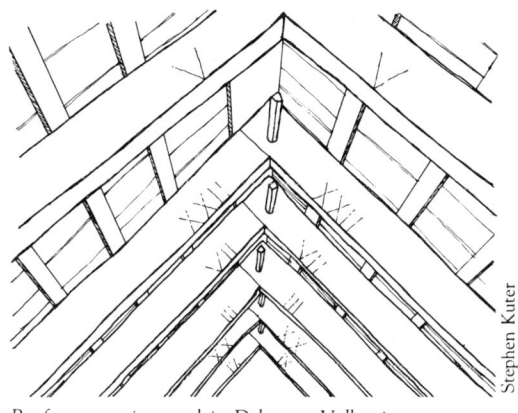

Roof construction used in Delaware Valley in the colonial period and as late as 1850.

Thomas Massey house.

Thomas Massey house, detail of Flemish-bond brickwork.

John Chad house, interior door.

roof, asymmetrical facade, exterior doors placed directly opposite each other, and interior chimneys. In the Chad house, one chimney emerges from the roof near the side of the house, indicating a corner fireplace (a clue to an early house).

Both houses have doors with transom windows, or LIGHTS, above: a row of three lights on the Chad house and the more usual four on the Massey house. Both houses have small, square GARRET WINDOWS; such windows were typically placed in the south-facing gable of rural houses during most of the 18th century.

The brick SEGMENTAL ARCHES over the windows of the Massey house, although not rare for the period, are more decorative than the Chad house's

Barns-Brinton house, detail of stairway.

rectangular window openings, which were commonly used in stone houses. The Chad house also has a typical WINDER (or winding) STAIRCASE. Next to the staircase is a massive chimney, which, on the first floor, features a paneled CHIMNEY BREAST and a built-in cupboard to one side.

Another structure from the colonial period, the Barns-Brinton house in Pennsbury Township, Chester County, is built of red brick laid in Flemish bond. Constructed in 1714, it is a superb example of a building planned as a tavern. On the first floor, most of the space is devoted to public use. The second floor has overnight accommodations for travelers and rooms for the tavern-keeper and his family. In its detail, the Barns-Brinton house has many features similar to those of the Chad and Massey houses, including paneled woodwork and wrought-iron hardware.

German Colonial, c. 1700–60

The Germans who settled Pennsylvania adhered to the building traditions of their Upper Rhine Valley homeland. The early German house differed from the English colonial house in several distinct ways. Whereas the English

Barns-Brinton house.

Peter Wentz Farmstead.

Grumblethorpe.

plan was usually rectangular, being a rod (about 16½ feet) in depth but greater in length, the German plan usually approached a square, about 26 feet on each side. The German house was usually larger than the English. Its greater depth required a heavy "summer" beam stretched from one end of the house to the other as a supplementary weight-bearing member. The house had ample space for two attics: a large, lower one and a small, upper one, which was reached by a stair ladder.

The typical German floor plan consisted of three rooms: a kitchen (*Kuche*), an all-purpose room or parlor (*Stube*), and a small bedroom (*Kammer*). The main door, whose exterior might be adorned with CHEVRONS, led into the kitchen, a narrow room running the full depth of the house. The cooking fireplace was set against the interior wall of the kitchen. The chimney was placed slightly to one side of the center of the house. It was smaller than the massive central chimneys of New England; it served only the kitchen except where an aperture in the back of the fireplace fed heat into a five-plate stove designed to warm the *Stube*.

On the exterior, a pent roof often surrounded the house on three or four sides. (On an English house the pent roof usually went across only the facade.) The main roof of the German house was steeply gabled.

Some of the earliest German houses were built in HALF-TIMBER framing, filled in with brick NOGGING; none of these are known to have survived in the Delaware Valley. Windows were fewer and smaller than in English houses. Also, the Germans were more inclined than the English to build over a spring.

Two examples of German houses in the Delaware Valley are the Mitchell Bunken house and the Peter Wentz house. The Bunkin house, in Tinicum Township, Bucks County, dates from two periods, 1750 and 1815. Its two sections were the product of two generations of the Worman family. The 1750 section, slightly smaller than the later addition, contains a Bible niche, a feature with religious meaning for many German families. Both sections of the house are built of local stone, and each uses the three-room plan discussed above. The larger section exhibits fine chisel work on the *Stube* mantel, a mark of the Federal period (see Federal, below).

The house on the Peter Wentz Farmstead (1758) in Worcester Township, Montgomery County is noteworthy for its combination of Germanic and English Colonial styles. Whereas its plan shows formal Georgian symmetry (see Georgian, below), its decorative features derive from German folk traditions. The colorfully painted walls have designs applied with sponge and brush, expressing the gaudy taste of the Wentz family. Five-plate stoves heat the dining room and the bedroom. That the Wentzes were efficiency minded is shown in their use of PALING under the first floor for insulation. The front door opens onto a STOEP with flanking benches, an arrangement found in another important German house, Grumblethorpe (1744) in Germantown. The balcony on the Wentz house is similar to the two at Grumblethorpe. Balconies, however, were not exclusively German; they are also found on

Grumblethorpe, showing balcony, transom, and 12-over-12 window.

Stenton.

Harriton, an early Welsh-inspired house in Lower Merion Township, Montgomery County.

The Wentz Farmstead's remarkable herb and vegetable garden, which has been restored, is marked off into four separate beds by paths laid in a cross. That form was decreed by Charlemagne, who ruled the Holy Roman Empire from 800 to 814.

Georgian, c. 1725–80

Through most of the 18th century, America looked to England for fashions and standards. Since the English gentry built in the Georgian style, it was natural that wealthy Americans would follow suit.

Three dwellings that exemplify the architectural preferences of affluent Americans of that era are Stenton (1728) in Germantown and the Corbit-Sharp (1773) and Wilson-Warner (1769) houses in Odessa, Delaware. These houses have symmetry, harmony, and classical forms associated with the Georgian style, which was based on the work of Andrea Palladio, a 16th-century Italian architect. All three are brick and feature large (24-light) windows across their facades. The earliest, Stenton, originally the "plantation house" of James Logan, has a simplicity of detail characteristic of early Georgian. Above the front door is a five-light transom that brings light into the hall. Flanking the door are two narrow SIDELIGHTS, probably the first in the area to be incorporated into an early-Georgian-style home.

The two Odessa houses are at the southern end of the Delaware Valley,

Wilson-Warner house.

about 50 miles from Philadelphia. By the mid-18th century, Odessa had become an important grain-shipping port, bringing wealth to its leading citizens and making it possible for one of them, the tanner-merchant William Corbit, to build a Georgian mansion that rivaled those in the city. The Corbit-Sharp house's superb brick masonry, stone window LINTELS and BELT COURSE, arched doorway with PILASTERS, HIPPED ROOF surmounted with a BALUSTRADE of Chinese LATTICE work, and DORMER windows with PEDIMENTS and CONSOLES are all in the finest Georgian tradition.

The interior is equally distinguished. A superb hall and stairway, EARED fireplace panels, Greek FRET decoration, and curved moldings on BASEBOARDS and CHAIR RAILS create a harmony and regularity that are the embodiment of classic gentility. Other architectural elements belonging to the Georgian vocabulary, most of which are incorporated into the Corbit-Sharp house, include CORNICES accented with MODILLIONS and DENTILS, large windows (usually with 12-over-12 lights), BROKEN PEDIMENTS over doors, paired chimneys with CORBELING, graceful staircases with decorated OPEN STRING and three TURNED balusters to a step, central halls flanked by two rooms on each side, and paneled or plastered walls with CROWN MOLDING and WAINSCOTTING.

The Wilson-Warner house, with its simple rectangular front wing, looks like a colonial house with a formal facade. This is a variation of Georgian and appears elsewhere, such as in the mansion Summerseat in Morrisville, Bucks County. The Wilson-Warner house shows proper Georgian balance

Georgian-style broken pediment.

and formality along with large windows, doorway with pediment, cornice with modillions, contrasting stone arches, and brick belt course. Although the familiar hipped roof with balustrade and almost square shape are missing, their absence does not detract from the dignified mien of this substantial house.

Typical Georgian features absent from the two Odessa houses are found in mansions in Philadelphia, such as Mt. Pleasant (1761) and Woodford (1772) in Fairmount Park and Cliveden (1763–67) in Germantown. All three are elevated on high foundations and have projecting center PAVILIONS. Both Mt. Pleasant and Cliveden have DORIC FRONTISPIECES and quoins. Mt. Pleasant has the blank end walls usually seen in city houses and, like Woodford, a PALLADIAN WINDOW.

The above high-style Georgian refinements were based on Renaissance forms imported primarily from Italy into England by way of Holland. In simpler houses, the chief exterior Georgian feature is a symmetrical facade and end walls. Most had exterior shutters. First-floor shutters were paneled and painted white; second-floor shutters were louvered—to admit air into the bedrooms—and painted black or dark green.

Sometime during the 1750s, the four-BAY, twin-door house appeared. This vernacular (homegrown) variation of the Georgian style became one of the most common types of houses in Pennsylvania and is found throughout the Delaware Valley. It had two possible sources of origin: (1) an English-derived

A standard twin-door Georgian facade.

Typical Georgian end wall.

plan containing four rooms, in which the two doors were a matter of expediency, one leading to the parlor and the other to the adjacent kitchen; or (2) a German-derived plan embracing the usual three rooms, but with an extra door opening into the *Stube*, in order to achieve the prevalent Georgian symmetry on the exterior. The end walls of both variations each had six symmetrically arranged windows, clearly following the Georgian mode.

One type of Federal-style doorway has a simple semicircular fanlight.

Another Federal-style treatment has a fanlight with a pedimented roof and columns.

A third type of Federal-style doorway (shown here on the first house to the right) has an elliptical fanlight extending above a pair of sidelights.

Federal, c. 1780–1820

After the Revolution, Georgian architecture gave way to a new interpretation of the classical mode: a less heavy and less imposing style, the decorative elements of which were based on the designs of Robert and James Adam of Scotland, whose *Works in Architecture* was incorporated into popular builders' guidebooks in both Britain and the United States. As with the high Georgian, this Federal style, in its purest form, was generally beyond the means of the average home builder.

It is difficult at first glance to distinguish between typical Georgian and Federal facades; both are symmetrical and show a centered entrance flanked by two windows on each side. On the second level, five windows assume corresponding positions in both styles. The differences lie in detail and in the treatment of doorways and roofs.

Federal-style doorway treatments have three basic types; if found along with supporting details, they place a house in the Federal period. The first type consists of a door with unadorned JAMBS and a simple, semicircular FANLIGHT over the lintel. This form is common in urban centers such as Philadelphia, Wilmington, New Castle, West Chester, and Norristown, and in smaller towns. Another treatment uses an elliptical fanlight extending above a pair of sidelights. The third type has a PORTICO with pedimented roof supported by tapered columns (plain or with fluting) or a pair of such columns at each front corner. The doorway of this third type may retain the fanlight, either elliptical with sidelights or semicircular.

Telltale interior features of the Federal style include curvilinear walls and stairways, more delicate wood and molding, and painted plaster walls.

In some ways, such as its fondness for elliptical rooms, fanlights, curving stairs, and delicate columns, the Federal was more subtle and sophisticated than the Georgian. Favorite decorative devices were LOZENGES, fine chisel work, honeysuckle and garlands carved in mantels, recessed arches, and delicate paint colors such as gray and white. Roofs became flatter, and paired chimneys were usually joined by a PARAPET that rose above the ROOF RIDGE.

Examples of the Federal style are the George Read II house in New Castle, Delaware; Pen Ryn in Andalusia, Bucks County; the Woodlands in West Philadelphia; and the Christopher Dock School near Lansdale, Montgomery County. The elegant Read house was built between 1797 and 1804. The

Fireplace at Fox Heath Farm, Bucks County, showing Federal-style lozenges.

elliptical fanlight over the doorway is the chief clue that it belongs to the Federal, not the Georgian, period. The Woodlands, altered in 1788, features a giant pedimented portico and two recessed Palladian windows. Pen Ryn, built in 1754 and remodeled in the Federal style in the 1790s, has a flat roof, paired chimneys, symmetrical FENESTRATION, Palladian window, and a doorway with lozenge-decorated caps over the pilasters. The Christopher Dock School bears the delicately conceived columns and classical doorway belonging to the Federal style.

In simpler houses the key to Federal designation lies in the fanlights over the doors, flattened roofs, carved FIREPLACE SURROUNDS, and interior design motifs such as ROSETTES. All of these may be applied to a basic rectangular box with gable roof.

In summary, during the 18th century the gradual homogenization of diverse cultures resulted in a similarity of architectural development in the Delaware Valley. As the region prospered, permanent structures appeared and earlier ones were enlarged and improved. Most houses were still conceived traditionally. Gradually, however, architectural books and builders' guides fell into the hands of carpenters and masons and merchants and farmers, prompting a growing awareness of stylistic refinements. The wealthy, having consolidated their position in the New World, aspired to mansions in the English manner. Consequently, the imposing Georgian, followed by the Federal style, came into fashion.

THE 19TH CENTURY: A CHOICE OF STYLES
Roman Revival, c. 1790–1830

When the dust settled after the Revolution, proud new citizens of the United States, beginning with Thomas Jefferson, consciously sought an architectural expression that would speak to the nation's status as a republic. Jefferson liked Roman Classicism and designed buildings using the Roman ORDERS, which he considered suitable for the new republican form of government. Jefferson's predilection did not catch on significantly with his countrymen, although some monumental Roman Revival structures were built, notably (in his home state) the Virginia state capitol, Monticello, and the University of Virginia. Because Jefferson is so closely associated with the style, it is frequently called Jeffersonian Classicism. The style is easily recognized by a massive pedimented portico that dominates the facade. A semicircular window often appears in the pediment. Buildings of this style are generally rectangular and have low-pitched gable or hipped roofs. A rare example in the Delaware Valley is the Fairmount Waterworks on the Schuylkill River, designed by Frederick C. Graff (1744–1847) about 1812.

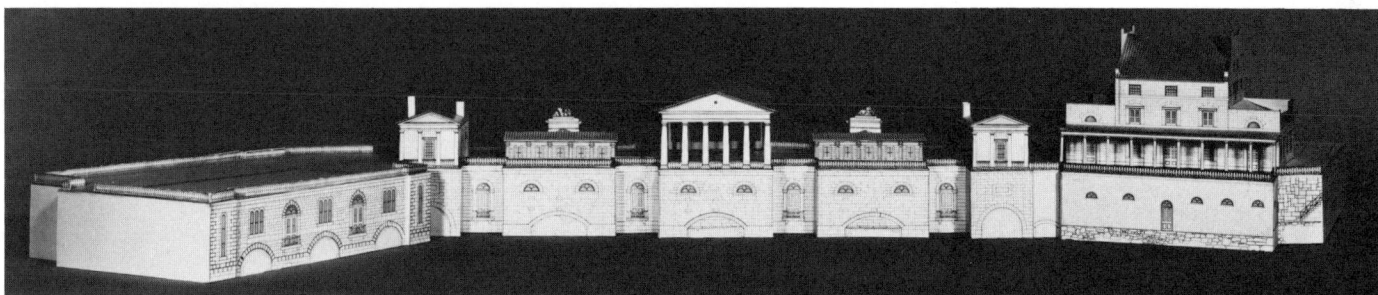

Historic Fairmount Waterworks.

Founder's Hall, Girard College, Philadelphia. A superb example of Greek Revival, by architect Thomas U. Walter.

Greek Revival, c. 1820–60

The style that did win unflagging admiration for some decades was the Greek Revival, which was at its height from about 1825 to 1850. Like the Roman Revival, the Greek Revival was archeologically more accurate than the earlier classical derivations. It was based primarily on Stuart and Revett's measured drawings of classical antiquities. (James Stuart and Nicholas Revett, two Englishmen, had visited Greece and Italy in the mid-1700s and published four volumes of architectural drawings.)

By the early 19th century, Philadelphians could, for the first time, choose from a notable group of architects, among them Benjamin Henry Latrobe (1764–1820) who, although an Englishman with continental training, was considered America's first professional architect. Latrobe and the others, notably William Strickland (1788–1854), Robert Mills (1781–1855), Thomas U. Walter (1804–1887), and John Haviland (1792–1852), left a significant mark on the architecture of the Delaware Valley and elsewhere. They designed public buildings in the Greek Revival style and private houses that were to delight both the rich homeowner and the average American for nearly half a century.

The Greek Revival flourished partly because the Philadelphia banker Nicholas Biddle had made a grand tour of Greece about 1806 and come away imbued with the beauty of its architecture. Upon his return, Biddle engaged Thomas U. Walter to surround his Federal farmhouse, Andalusia on the

Delaware River, with a Doric COLONNADE. A pedestrian farmhouse was thus transformed into a Greek temple. Other Greek buildings followed. Engaging Walter as architect, the town of West Chester in Chester County built a Greek Revival courthouse and other buildings.

In houses found in other parts of the United States, the Greek style was expressed by a templelike front. This aspect of the style did not flourish in rural areas of the Delaware Valley; perhaps the conservative Quakers and other sectarians slowed the spread of these templed homes. Even a thorough investigation will turn up only a few.

Still, the Delaware Valley has many subtle evidences of the Greek Revival. In these houses the doorway treatment assumes a TRABEATED design rather than arches. Horizontal transom lights are placed above the lintel. Along the third story there is frequently a row of short windows, suggestive of the METOPES on a Doric FRIEZE, but colloquially called "lie-on-your-stomach"

Andalusia, interior. Straight balusters are associated with the Greek Revival style.

Wilmar Lapidary house.

The Greek Revival style frequently includes rosettes at the tops of door stiles.

windows. Roofs are flatter than in the Colonial period, and rosettes appear at the tops of window and door STILES and in the corners of fireplace surrounds. Porticoes and porches, supported by heavy square posts or columns, offer protection from the weather. Arched dormers with FLUTING and rosettes spring from roofs. Additional hallmarks of the Greek Revival in the Delaware Valley are heavy SILLS and lintels on windows, visible corner posts or pilasters, stairs with straight-sided balusters, white paint on both exteriors and interiors, and heavy cornices with unadorned friezes. Occasionally, these friezes are decorated with alternating geometric designs that, like the short windows mentioned above, suggest the metopes and TRIGLYPHS of Doric friezes. Often the ENTABLATURE of a portico corresponded proportionately to the entablature under the EAVES. The promotion of the style by architects and builders was assisted by specifications on archeologically correct Greek orders that were added to carpenters' handbooks.

Good residential examples of the Greek Revival style are the Wilmar Lapidary house in Wrightstown Township, Bucks County; a number of imposing houses set among abandoned peach orchards in New Castle Hundred in the environs of Delaware City; innumerable row houses in Wilmington, Norristown, and Philadelphia (such as the south side of the 900 block of Spruce Street); and, above all, Nicholas Biddle's Andalusia. Well-known public buildings in Philadelphia that demonstrate the temple concept are Girard College (1833–47) by Thomas U. Walter, and the Second Bank of the United States (1818–24) and the United States Naval Asylum (1827–33), both by William Strickland.

Gothic Revival, c. 1830–60, 1860–90

Although the Greek Revival was part of the romantic upsurge against the restrictions of the Georgian and the Federal, the Gothic gave even greater scope to the romantic fervor stirring in the hearts of architects, writers, artists, and home builders. It was a movement that spread from novelists such as Sir Walter Scott, who wrote of the medieval period, into other fields of creativity. Under the influence of the English critic A. W. N. Pugin and others, the public associated medieval Christian architecture with morality. The Gothic style led Henry Ward Beecher to say, "The first prop of moral civilization is an upright home."

The Gothic Revival style appeared in the Delaware Valley in two phases. Early Gothic Revival was introduced to Philadelphia with Latrobe's design of Sedgley in 1799, the first American residence with Gothic detail. The style's period of ascendancy, however, did not begin until the late 1820s. It was popularized in a book by the "landscape gardener" Andrew Jackson Downing, *Cottage Residences,* first published in 1842 and reissued a dozen times. The architect most closely associated with the style was Alexander Jackson Davis (1803–1892), whose works appeared in Downing's book. Davis designed a number of major Gothic residences, among them Lyndhurst near Tarrytown, New York, now owned by the National Trust for Historic Preservation.

Gothic Revival is easily distinguished by its use of the pointed arch in windows and doors (above which often appears a LABEL, or DRIPSTONE); a steeply pitched roof; an asymmetrical, extremely flexible plan; towers; CRENELATION; decorative BARGEBOARDS; and elaborate porches. To update an older house, the owner frequently inserted a CROSS-GABLE in the facade; many a Colonial home wears this popular Gothic disguise.

Whereas Gothic architecture of the medieval period was primarily of stone, its 19th-century imitators turned most often to wood, which was cheaper

The Grange, detail of Gothic-style bargeboard trim.

Library on Lake Afton, Bucks County. A choice example of the Late Gothic style.

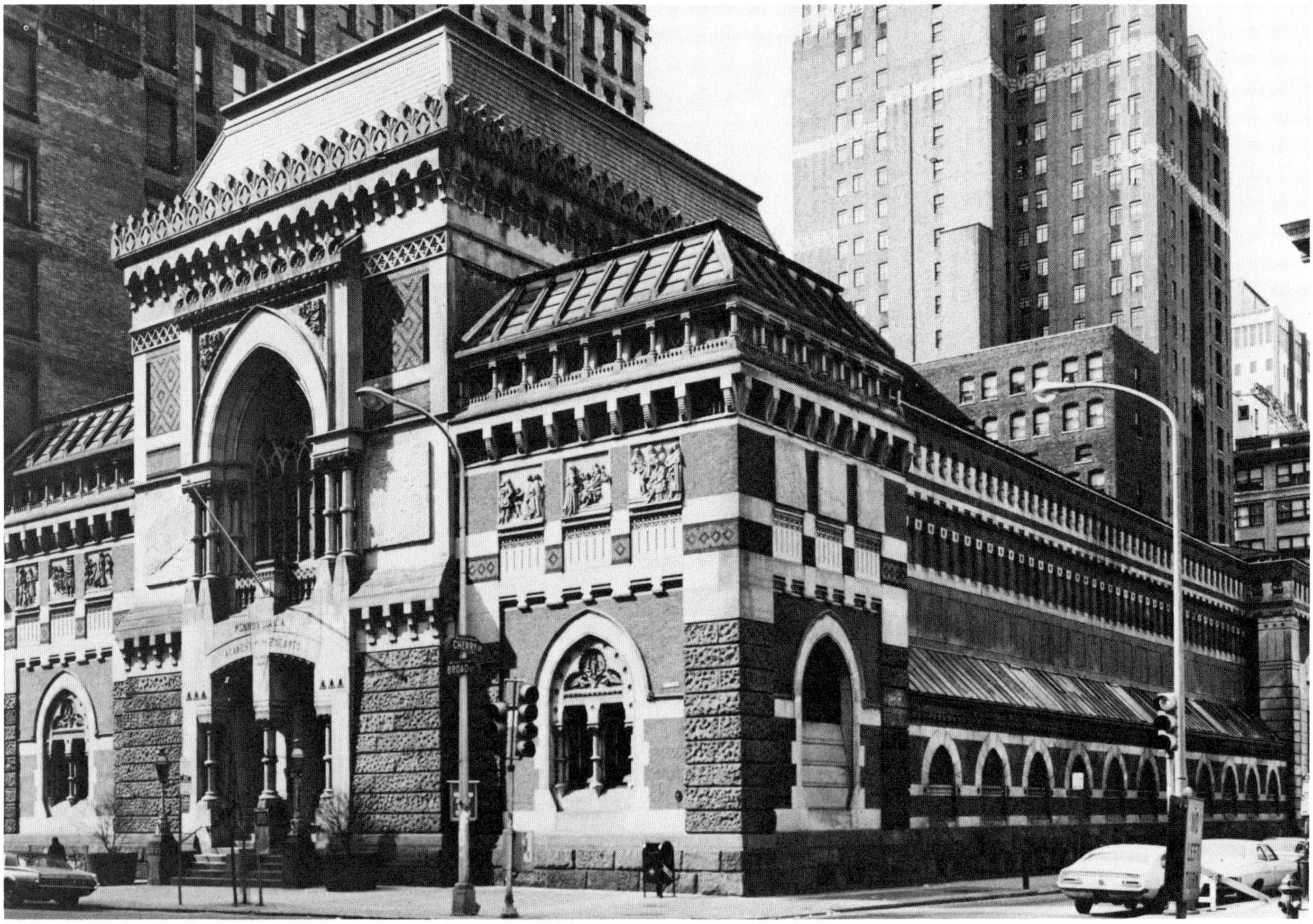

Pennsylvania Academy of the Fine Arts

The High Victorian Gothic style expressed in the Pennsylvania Academy of the Fine Arts.

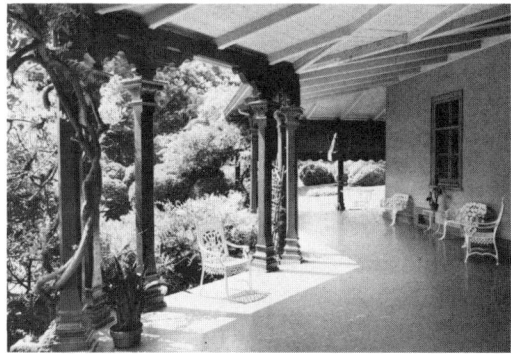

The Grange. This elaborate wraparound porch is typical of the Gothic Revival style.

and easily available. The invention of the jigsaw catapulted woodworkers into a heyday of intricate carving (known familiarly as GINGERBREAD) for porches, SPANDRELS, and bargeboards. The jigsaw was the sine qua non for Carpenter's Gothic. The Gothic style was suitable for many types of structures: cemetery gates, churches, prisons, courthouses, college buildings, and houses.

The early Gothic Revival style never achieved the popularity of the Greek Revival in the Delaware Valley. A good example, though, is the Grange in Haverford Township, Delaware County, lavishly Gothicized in 1850.

The second Gothic Revival occurred toward the end of the century as part of High Victorian Eclecticism (see below). Whereas the early Gothic was a relatively pure interpretation of the English Gothic mode, the High Victorian Gothic drew from a variety of Gothic sources, producing a picturesque eclecticism. The Philadelphia area's most prolific architect of this style was Frank Furness (1839–1912), perhaps best known for his design of the Pennsylvania Academy of the Fine Arts (1876).

Romanesque Revival, c. 1840, 1860–90

Less familiar than the two revival styles described above, the Romanesque Revival appeared in eclectic fashion during the 1840s and again after the Civil War. The round arch, derived from the medieval Romanesque style, used alone or in a series, is the hallmark of both Romanesque Revival phases. The first phase favored broad and smooth wall surfaces, and this style was found particularly appropriate for public buildings. The small Episcopal chapel in Buckingham Village, Bucks County, where the anthropologist Margaret Mead was both married and buried, is an example of the earlier Romanesque Revival.

The second phase was given tremendous impetus by Henry Hobson Richardson (1838–1886), one of America's greatest architects. This revival, in fact, is commonly referred to as Richardsonian Romanesque. Besides the recurring round arch, this style is characterized by the liberal use of ROCK-FACED MASONRY in the foundations, in walls, and as trim, which gives Richardsonian Romanesque buildings an impression of impenetrable mass and authority. The Bucks County Prison in Doylestown, designed in 1882 by the prolific Philadelphia architect Addison Hutton (1834–1916), belongs to this second phase. Richardsonian Romanesque appears in Philadelphia in the house at 1430 North Broad Street (c. 1863) and on the west side of the 1500 block of North 16th Street (particularly at 1530), where there is a much-praised grouping.

Italianate, c. 1830–80

As the 19th century reached its midpoint, the number of architectural styles increased rapidly. One of the most adaptable and popular was the Italianate. This style, in both rural and urban forms, was introduced by a young Scotsman, John Notman (1810–1865). Notman is credited with the design in 1837 of the first Italian "villa" in America, a house in Burlington,

Bucks County Prison in Doylestown, Pennsylvania.

New Jersey, for Bishop Doane. In 1845, Notman designed the Athenaeum at 219 South Sixth Street, Philadelphia, in the Italian Renaissance mode. The Athenaeum helped to launch the Italianate style and to popularize the corresponding suburban and rural house type, the Italian villa.

Generally, Italianate is characterized by wide, overhanging eaves, heavy BRACKETS, a three- or four-story entrance tower, a slightly pitched or flat roof with a CUPOLA or LANTERN, HOOD MOLDINGS or labels over windows, rectangular and round-arched window openings, BAY WINDOWS, VERANDAS, and balustraded balconies or porch railings. A simple version would be a square house with wide, bracketed eaves and a cupola. The style was sometimes known as American or Bracketed, especially when the tower was absent.

Later in the century the perfecting of cast-iron technology to produce elaborately molded and pressed units permitted builders to apply a highly decorative Italianate style to store and office fronts. A portion of Lit Brothers' store on Market Street in Philadelphia is a matchless example. This and other interpretations of the style belong to the High Victorian Italianate, which, like the later Gothic and Romanesque Revival styles, appeared in the architecturally eclectic 1860–90 period. Loch Aerie in East Whiteland Township, Chester County, was designed for the manufacturer William E. Lockwood by Addison Hutton in 1865. It is a High Victorian version of the earlier Italian villa style.

High Victorian Eclecticism, c. 1860–1900

The Victorian era, which technically began with Queen Victoria's ascension to the British throne in 1837, reached its peak between 1860 and 1890. After the Civil War the mood of America changed; the nation underwent a profound technological and social upheaval, which expressed itself, among other things, in architecture. Building technology made giant progress, producing myriad building components and materials that could be ordered from catalogues or local builders. Architects, authors of pattern books, and homeowners drew upon every possible source for inspiration and freely combined disparate stylistic motifs and devices. The houses were generally well built, their quality derived from advances such as portland cement, fireproof ceramic, plate glass, indoor plumbing, and central heating. In the cities, speculative builders added rapidly to the available house supply; Wilmington grew and Philadelphia expanded west. Outstanding among the rich and varied architectural statements of the period, which included High Victorian versions of the Gothic, Romanesque, and Italianate, were the Mansardic, Queen Anne, and Shingle styles.

Mansardic, c. 1860–90

The Mansard or Second Empire style was known primarily for its MANSARD, or double-pitched, roof. Emperor Napoleon III (reigned 1852–70), in glorifying Paris with boulevards and new public buildings, also enlarged the Louvre. To do that, his architects revived the eminently French, 17th-century mansard roof. They thereby launched a craze that quickly spread to America, lodging itself firmly in cities, towns, and countryside. In cities, the Second Empire style included projecting pavilions, sculptural embellishment, paired columns, and elaborately decorated dormer windows protruding from the lower, nearly vertical, slope of the mansard roof. In towns and in the countryside, the style is again recognized by its distinctive roof and also by frequent dormers. It often has a varied combination of eclectically derived elements: towers, balconies, porches, bays, brackets, dentils, modillions, CRESTINGS,

Brick house in Odessa, Delaware, in the American Bracketed style.

and columns. For about 30 years, between 1860 and 1890, the Second Empire style remained popular.

Philadelphia boasts a supreme example of the Second Empire style, City Hall (1871–1901), designed by John McArthur Jr. (1823–1890) with the assistance of Thomas U. Walter. Although City Hall has no main entrance or grand steps, its impact is monumental. The tower, bearing an enormous and handsome statue of William Penn, rises over the city, a symbol of the planning and ideals of the great man surmounting it.

This Mansardic detail shows eclecticism at its height. Note Italianate window, Gothic gable trim, Chinese-pagoda-flared hood.

A frequent Mansardic variation is a reverse curve in the roof.

Dunleigh Castle, c. 1950.

A Queen Anne house in Bucks County, c. 1880s–90s.

Francis Kennedy house, by Frank Miles Day. Featured in American Architect and Building News *in 1889.*

A noteworthy rural residence in the Mansard style is found in East Marlborough Township, Chester County. Here, in 1882, the Quaker farmer Samuel G. Moore built for his new bride a large, multicolored brick house he called Dunleigh Castle. Although it was reported that Moore designed the house himself, he was no doubt assisted by architectural pattern books then readily available. Certainly the inspiration for Moore's use of the Mansard style came from Philadelphia's City Hall, then under construction.

Queen Anne, c. 1870–90

Except for Mansard, the Queen Anne style was the most powerful influence in the late Victorian period. Found chiefly in urban areas, it embraced a complicated yet free-flowing use of space. In the rural parts of the Delaware Valley, examples are stylistically restrained; their builders belong to the simple, provincial school of unnamed carpenter-builders who have always created the bulk of houses in the valley.

The plan is unfailingly asymmetrical, and the building parts vary in texture, design, and color. A Queen Anne building can have many types of fenestration: a Palladian window on the second or third level; SASH windows, each with a large pane on the lower half, and, on the upper half, a series of small, square, colored panes surrounding a larger center pane; and bay, transom, oval, ROUNDHEAD, OCULUS, and SLIT WINDOWS. Porches are conspicuous, as are balconies and TURRETS, which may be round or polygonal. Chimneys are tall, ornate, corbeled, even clustered. End walls are decorated with stickwork or half-timbering.

Structurally, the style is equally eclectic. Whereas the first level can be brick, stone, or stuccoed frame, the upper levels might use patterned SHINGLES, CLAPBOARD, or STUCCO. Roofs sometimes combine a gable with a hipped form.

The interior of a Queen Anne house offered more freedom than any preceding style. A large entrance hall with fireplace and OPEN STAIRCASE was used as a living space inviting sociability, a contrast to the formality of Georgian central halls. At times even an older house, built in some earlier style, was dressed up with a turret, a bay window, a porch, and DIAPER shingles in an effort to keep up with this latest fashion. The Queen Anne style's combination of medieval and classical elements suggested humor, romance, and informality.

Shingle Style, c. 1880–1900

The Shingle style, a derivation of Queen Anne, presented an exterior stripped of the complexities and confusion of the Queen Anne. A shingle covering integrated the lines of a house into a smooth, horizontal form, quiet in color and impact. Shingle was not a dominant style in the Delaware Valley, but a few examples establish it as a transition between the eclectic Victorian and the starker styles of the 20th century. Several Shingle-style residences by distinguished architects can be found in East Bradford Township, Chester County, near the Main Line of the former Pennsylvania Railroad. In the 1880s, the Bradford Hills Land Company attempted to develop this area into a "second Bryn Mawr." Before the company went bankrupt in 1894, six homes were built there. Wilson Eyre (1858–1944) and Frank Miles Day (1861–1918), now recognized as two of Philadelphia's leading architects of the late 19th century, designed two Shingle-style residences.

Green Shadows Farm, Chester County. Designed in 1900 by W. E. Jackson, this Period Revival house combines English Cottage and Chester County vernacular motifs.

Period Revival, c. 1890–1930

By 1890, the exuberance of the High Victorian era was waning. Tastes in architecture turned to colonial and revival styles. They included the Georgian Revival (sometimes called Neo-Colonial), the Spanish Revival, the French Normandy cottage, and the English Tudor. These were modeled on obvious prototypes: the Georgian mansion, the Spanish hacienda, the French chateau or Normandy-style house, and the English Tudor house. The term "period house" is used to distinguish the revival buildings from their prototypes.

Period houses incorporated modern ideas in room arrangement, such as the use of porches, patios, TERRACES, and other details. Rooms were larger than in the prototypes. These houses continued to be widely popular until the 1930s. Well built, many have been in continuous use ever since.

The revival trend, though based on European precedents, was uniquely American. The most popular revival was the Tudor, which maintained a firm hold on American preference through the 1930s. Its main characteristic is half-timbering used in the second-floor exterior. Windows are casement; panes assume small, diamond shapes; chimneys are outsized; and roofs are sharply pitched. Unlike the 16th-century English Tudor house, which required the timber framework for support, the Tudor Revival uses its half-timbering merely for decoration.

A restrained example of the Tudor Revival style, typical of the Delaware Valley.

The Delaware Valley has many Period Revival homes. Examples of one type or another can be found in every city, suburb, and town, be they the houses of bankers, lawyers, or successful merchants. A French chateau tour-de-force in Newtown, now the site of Bucks County Community College, was once the home of the Tyler family. In Doylestown, "Aldie," the former home of William Mercer, brother of the collector Henry Mercer, is a mansion in the Tudor Revival manner. Also in Doylestown, at the Bucks County Historical Society, is the neoclassical Georgian Revival Elkins building, designed by Horace Trumbauer (1869–1933).

It is beyond the scope of this chapter to travel any further into the architectural history of the 20th century, into the era of bungalows, American Foursquares, and skyscrapers. But if the past 300 years are any indication, it will be a tour well worth taking.

GLOSSARY OF ARCHITECTURAL TERMS

baluster. A turned or rectangular spindle supporting a stair rail. A series of balusters is called a **balustrade**, whether along a stair or above the cornice on a building.

banked. Having at least one wall built into the ground.

bargeboard. A board set flush to, or projecting from, the gable end of a pitched roof.

baseboard. A board placed at the base of a wall and resting on the floor; usually treated with moldings.

bay. One of the sections into which the facade of a building is divided.

bay window. A large projecting window. If it is curved or semicircular, it is usually called a bow window.

beam. A heavy, horizontal structural member that spans the area between walls or columns.

belt course. A horizontal projecting row on a masonry wall, mainly for decoration.

bracket. A projecting member to support a weight. When carrying the upper members of a cornice, it is called a modillion.

broken pediment. A pediment that is interrupted at the crest or peak.

casement window. A window hinged at the side to swing in or out.

chair rail. Molding on a wall placed at the height of a chair back to protect the plaster.

chevron. An ornamental motif composed of V-shapes. Also called zig-zag.

chimney breast. The front part of a chimney, which projects into a room.

clapboard. A narrow board, usually under five feet long, and thicker at one edge than the other, that is used for siding. Clapboards are overlapped on the framing.

colonnade. A row of columns usually supporting an entablature and forming part of the design of a corridor or passageway.

console. An architectural member projecting from a wall to form a bracket, or from a keystone for ornament.

corbeling. Courses of brick or stone set in the form of inverted steps.

cornice. A molded or projecting cap on a wall, window, or door opening.

course. A horizontal row of stones or bricks in a wall.

crenelation. An opening, sometimes repeated, along the upper part of a parapet.

cresting. A delicate, repeated ornament, incised, resembling a low fence carried along the top of a wall or roof.

cross-gable. A gable placed across rather than at the end of a roof.

crown molding. The topmost molding in a classical cornice.

cupola. A small structure built on top of a roof or building for ventilation or lookout, or to complete a design.

dentil. One of a series of small blocks, similar to a row of teeth, often used to decorate a cornice.

diaper. A small pattern, such as lozenges or squares, repeated continuously over a wall.

Doric. (See **order**)

dormer. A structure that supports a window and projects from a roof.

dripstone. In Gothic architecture, the projecting molding over windows, doorways, and archways to throw off rain.

eared. Having earlike projections.

eaves. The lower part of a roof projecting beyond a wall.

end wall. The wall on either side of a building.

English bond. Brickwork in which rows of headers alternate with rows of stretchers. Stretchers are bricks laid lengthwise across a wall; headers are bricks laid with the short end across a wall.

entablature. Superstructure carried by columns or pilasters.

facade. The front of a building, usually given special architectural treatment.

fanlight. A semicircular window, with radiating sash bars like the ribs of a fan, placed over a door or window.

fenestration. The arrangement of windows in a building.

fireplace surround. Molding around a fireplace.

Flemish bond. Brickwork whose rows consist of alternating headers and stretchers. Stretchers are bricks laid lengthwise across a wall; headers are bricks laid with the short end across a wall.

fluting. Vertical channeling on a column, pilaster, or fireplace jamb or mantel.

fret. A jigsaw cutout of various patterns used as decoration.

frieze. The central part of a classical entablature; usually a flat surface with ornamental features or carving.

frontispiece. The main facade of a building.

gable. The triangular portion of an end wall above the eaves. Sometimes used to refer to the entire end of a house.

gable roof. A ridged roof forming a gable at each end.

gambrel. A roof with two slopes of different pitch on either side of the ridge.

garret window. Window in an attic.

gingerbread. Pierced curvilinear ornaments on a building. So called after the sugar frosting on German gingerbread houses.

half-timber. Wooden framing of heavy posts and beams, filled in with brick, stone, or plaster.

hipped roof. A roof with slopes on all four sides. The hips are the lines where two adjacent slopes of the roof meet.

hood molding. Molding on top of a window or arch.

jamb. The side of a window or door frame.

label. A projecting molding by the sides and over the top of an opening.

lantern. A small structure placed at the crowning point of a dome, turret, or roof, with openings for light to come through. Frequently its purpose is decorative.

lattice. A framework or structure of crossed wood or metal strips.

light. Pane of glass in a window.

lintel. Horizontal member of timber or stone that spans a doorway or window.

lozenge. A diamond-shaped ornament.

mansard. A roof with a steep lower part and nearly flat upper part.

metope. The space between two triglyphs of a Doric frieze; often adorned with carved work.

modillion. (See **bracket**)

nogging. Rough brick masonry used to fill in the open spaces in a wall.

oculus window. A small, circular window.

open staircase. A staircase not enclosed by walls.

open string. A string (board running along and supporting the side of a staircase) over which the outer edges of the steps project somewhat. In a closed string, the edges of the steps butt against the string and are concealed by it.

order. One of several specific architectural styles. Basic orders are Doric, Ionic, Corinthian, Tuscan, and Composite.

paling. Strips of wood commonly used for fences.

Palladian window. An arched window, flanked by two smaller square-headed windows; always in a group of three.

parapet. A low wall or railing to protect the edge of a platform, roof, or bridge.

pavilion. Part of a building that protrudes from the main part.

pediment. A triangle of wall above an entablature or cornice.

pent roof. An eaveslike feature projecting from a wall to throw off rain and snow.

pilaster. A rectangular or half-round column that projects slightly from a wall.

portico. An entryway or vestibule supported by columns.

quoin. A building corner of heavy stones (or the stones themselves) that are used for stability or sometimes decoration.

rock-faced masonry. Stonework imitating the irregular surface of rocks.

roof ridge. The line where the upper slopes of a roof meet.

rosette. An ornamental motif formed by a series of leaves arranged around a central point.

roundhead window. A window with a rounded top.

sash. A sliding frame that holds the panes of glass in a window.

segmental arch. An arch shaped as a part of a circle that is less than a semicircle.

shingle. A small, thin piece of building material laid in overlapping rows to cover the roof or sides of a building.

sidelight. One of a pair of windows flanking a door.

sill. A horizontal board or strip forming the bottom or foundation member of a structure, especially the board at the bottom of a window.

slit window. A long, narrow window.

spandrel. The triangular space between two adjoining arches and a horizontal line above them.

stile. A vertical strip in a frame or panel.

stoep. German word for step, porch, platform, entrance stairway, or small veranda at the door of a house.

stucco. Plaster or cement used as a coating for walls.

terrace. A relatively level paved or planted area adjoining a building.

trabeated. Supported by post and lintel rather than by arches.

transom window. The upper panel of a window, or a window placed above a doorway.

triglyph. A block with vertical channels in the frieze of a Doric entablature.

turned. Rotated on a lathe and shaped into various forms with cutting tools.

turret. A small tower, sometimes containing stairs, prominent in the Queen Anne style, but harking back to medieval buildings.

veranda. A roofed space alongside a house.

wainscotting. The lower part of an interior wall when treated with a material different from that of the upper part; sometimes called *dado*.

winder staircase. A staircase that turns as it ascends or descends.

Site of the Laurel Iron Works in Chester County. By 1984 the Laurel Iron Works, which was established on this oxbow of Buck Run in the 18th century, had been abandoned for nearly a century. Shells of stone buildings were tantalizing evidence of days gone by, when it was a thriving company town run by ironmaster Hugh E. Steele.

Chapter 3

RESEARCHING HISTORIC BUILDINGS

Researching a historic building is usually the first step toward preserving it. Researching means poring through deeds, tax and census records, newspaper clippings, and other sources. It may mean spending hours in a dusty attic, viewing old photographs, or speaking with longtime residents of the community. For more tangible clues, some researchers also pry off plaster, pull out nails, and scour old trash pits.

Whether you're studying mills, farmhouses, factories, or rowhouses, the techniques are similar. The researching procedures and sources described in this chapter apply particularly to houses—and the illustrations pertain to the site of the Laurel Iron Works in rural Chester County—but the procedures can be used with all types of buildings.

Although there is no hope of finding William Penn's footprint in the house, a persistent search can uncover much useful information: the date of construction, original appearance, architect and builder, or names and occupations of former residents. Research may reveal that the house has enough historical or architectural significance to qualify for the National Register of Historic Places. Or it may reveal a larger picture—a potential historic district, for example, composed of this and related buildings nearby.

Just as important, researching a house teaches respect for its historic fabric. Unintended damage to its integrity during rehabilitation or remodeling is less likely to occur when its historic context is understood.

Research is also fun. The thrill of discovery, of tracking down new leads, of finally understanding how the house came to be, can more than make up for occasionally tedious hours of documentary research.

DOCUMENTING THE HOUSE

Documentary research of a house requires a patient, plodding, almost pedantic strategy that builds on the knowns to uncover the unknowns. It can be a narrowly focused investigation into a house's date of construction, or a comprehensive accounting of its history and physical appearance during various ownerships. Experienced researchers will testify that the comprehensive method is often the only means to arrive at a reliable date of construction.

Although the course of documentary research is unpredictable and largely dependent on locally available resources, it must be structured to yield orderly and useful information. Working within an established framework saves time and effort and produces a well-organized data base that you can easily consult and expand as more information becomes available.

The data base should be constructed of facts uncovered from primary sources. Julia Colflesh (a primary-source researcher from Swarthmore, Pennsylvania, with dozens of cracked cases to her credit) defines primary sources as records created at the time of an event. They include deeds, tax and census records, estate papers, road dockets, sale notices, and some church records. Colflesh considers published histories, prepared genealogies, and obituaries to be examples of secondary sources, that is, sources based on recollections or evidences of an event. "No report should be based solely on one record," she says. "It's the combination of records that gives the full picture. I find secondary sources useful when there seems to be an impasse, or a large body of evidence missing. They might yield a clue as to the direction the research should take from that point."

Generally, primary-source research of old buildings begins with deeds to determine the chain of ownership.

Working with Deeds

Old documents are sometimes tantalizing and oftentimes frustrating. They lead and mislead. Deeds—legal documents used to transfer property—especially mystify the novice researcher. Yet they are the most important primary source material. A thorough deed search is the most direct route to establishing a property's chain of ownership. Not to be confused with a title search, which may involve mortgages, liens, or encumbrances on the title (and which can be provided by a title company), the deed search concerns the names of owners and their dates of tenure. Without this information, it is risky, if not impossible, to move on to other primary and secondary sources.

If all property transfers since William Penn's original patent had been methodically recorded and duly preserved, a deed search would be simple. But every clerk's error, every courthouse fire, every paper moth hatched in the past 300 years has laid a potential obstacle to the search. Nothing is more frustrating than expecting to turn to a critical page in a deed or patent book only to find it missing or illegible. Because the search must proceed step by step through the various conveyances, creativity and resourcefulness are at times your handiest assets in overcoming such hurdles.

Beginning the Search

The deed search begins with the deed of the present property owner and works through previous deeds back to the first one recorded. In some cases (such as when a house dates from the 19th or 20th century) researchers may feel comfortable ending the search with a deed suggesting that a house has been built—that is, when the deed indicates that the property was subdivided into building lots, had increased in price, or had added improvements such as a "messuage" (house). Many researchers, however, see value in taking the

House near the upper Laurel rolling mill. In the 1870s there were two rolling mills in operation at the Laurel Iron Works. This small, banked house sits near the site of the upper Laurel rolling mill. According to an old newspaper account, at one time there were about 17 houses for workers in this vicinity.

search back to the "beginning," to the land grant or patent (in Pennsylvania, when William Penn or his agents were the grantor).

Generally, deeds recorded since each county's establishment are on file at the recorder of deeds office in the county courthouse. If the county was originally part of another one, earlier records may be located in the seat of the original county (for example, Delaware County's deeds executed before its separation from Chester County in 1789 are in the Chester County, not the Delaware County, Courthouse) or in the state archives. Many of southeastern Pennsylvania's earliest land records remain in Philadelphia.

Mastering the Deed Index

Sometimes, reading the deed is less trouble than *finding* it. You can find the deed by consulting the deed index or tax records.

If you know the name of the present property owner, a quick way to get to the deed is to look in the "tax duplicates" at the appropriate county's board of assessments office. The tax duplicates, which are arranged by municipality and then alphabetically by property owner, list the deed book and page where the most recently recorded deed can be found. (Deeds are bound in books and arranged chronologically, according to the "date of record." They are located in the county recorder of deeds office.)

If you don't know the name of the property owner but do know the location, you can look up the property on tax maps. Tax maps are also located at the board of assessments office. They show the boundaries of each property, its acreage, sometimes its dimensions, and a number (part of the "tax parcel number," which will lead you to the deed). The complete tax parcel number consists of a municipal number (found in the margin of the map), the map number (there are usually several maps for each municipality), and the specific number shown for the property.

Deeds, tax records, and other primary sources can be found at county courthouses.

Molly K. Morrison/Public Information, Chester County Courthouse

For example, East Fallowfield Township (Chester County) has municipal number 47 and currently takes 19 maps to show all the properties in the township. The maps are numbered 47-1, 47-2, and so forth. Let's say you find the property you're looking for on map 47-8. The number shown for that property is 23. The complete parcel number, then, is 47-8-23.

Now look in the "tax number index" at the board of assessments. Entries appear in numerical order (47-8-23 comes after 46-1-5 and before 52-7-16.4). Next to the parcel number, 47-8-23 in our example, are notations showing the deed book (H-22) and page (162) where you'll find the present deed. Go to the counter in the recorder of deeds office and ask for deed book H-22. Page 162 shows the deed you want.

117					**GRANTEE S**									
		A	B	C	D	E	F	G	H	I	J	K	L	M
		1	26	33	51	65	90	98	115	138	146	227	229	242
INST.	GRANTEE			GRANTOR				DATE OF IN	DATE OF RECORD	BOOK	PAGE	LOCATION			
	Smith	Henry		Jesse Brooks				1836	1841	U 4	315			
	Smith	Henry		Matthew Law ux				1841	1841	U 4	356			
	Stiles	Hopkins		Saml. A. Whitehill ux				1842	1842	Y 4	484			
	Shingle	Henry al		John Dingler ux				1839	1842	W 4	24			
Rel	Shingle	Henry		Sarah Dingler				1834	1842	W 4	26			
	Still	Henry		James H. McClear ux				1843	1843	W 4	297			
	Sloan	Hugh		Edmund Griffith				1843	1843	W 4	419			
	Schofield	Hannah		James Yearsley Trus				1843	1843	X 4	283			
	Steele	Hugh E.		John D. Steele				1844	1844	Z 4	55			
	Steele	Hugh E.		Joseph pyle ux				1844	1844	Z 4	75			
	Suplee	Horatio J.		John Clemson Exr				1844	1844	Z 4	61			
	Smith	Henry		Joseph Dolby ux				1843	1844	Z 4	378			
	Sims	Henry		Jacob George				1844	1844	A 5	290			

Excerpt from Grantee Index, Chester County Recorder of Deeds. In 1844 Hugh E. Steele was the purchaser (grantee) of property from Joseph and Mary Pyle (grantors). The deed index indicates that this transaction is recorded in deed book Z4 on page 75.

Another way to get to the deed is through the deed index. Deeds are indexed twice: once by the name of the grantor (seller) and once by the name of the grantee (buyer or recipient). These indexes (which are at the recorder of deeds office) are arranged chronologically—a given volume may cover all deeds recorded between 1750 and 1825—and are alphabetized by the first letter of the last name and then by the first letter of the first name.

To find the deed book reference for a property that, say, Hugh E. Steele purchased in 1844, look in the grantee index that includes 1844 and that contains the letter S. Among the S's, the first batch you'll see are people whose last names begin with S and whose first names begin with A. Next will be people whose last names begin with S and whose first names begin with B. Go down to people whose first names begin with H. Look in the last-name column for Steele. When you find one, look in the first-name column. If the name is Hugh, you've got your man. If the name is Harold, look for other Steeles until you find Hugh.

Besides the name Hugh E. Steele, the entry will include the seller's name, the date of record, the municipality in which the property is located, and the book and page number where you'll find the deed. Knowing the approximate date of purchase will help narrow the search, although the chronology of the indexes is not completely reliable. Many a deed was recorded years after execution, often to clear the title, on the very day the property was sold again. Also, if Steele purchased several properties in 1844, you may not have the right entry. The seller's name and the municipality listed in the entry may be all you need to ascertain that; if not, you'll have to look through all of Hugh Steele's deeds for the year until you're sure you've got the one you want. In the case of Hugh E. Steele, the deed index shows that he bought the Laurel Iron Works from Joseph Pyle and wife in 1844 and that the deed is located in book Z4 on page 75.

Mastering the indexing system is not done quickly or easily. Confusion arises over multiple buyers and sellers (whose names will be indexed?), sheriff and estate sales, miscellaneous and corporate transfers, and archaic spellings and letters. Eventually you get a feel for the system's idiosyncrasies and, if necessary, can make educated stabs in the dark.

Once you locate the deed—whether by the tax parcel number, the deed index, or quiet pleas for help—you can begin work on the chain of ownership.

① _____ ② _____
  Property name   Location
③ _____   ⑥ _____
  Source   Date executed
③a _____   ⑥a _____
  Book/Page no.   Date recorded

④ _____ to ⑤ _____
  Grantor(s)   Grantee(s)

  _____   _____
  _____   _____

⑦ _____   ⑧ _____
  Acreage/Description   Consideration

  _____   _____

⑨ _____
  Key words

  _____
  _____
  _____

⑩ _____
  References to prior deeds

  _____
  _____

① Property name. Use the property's historic name (such as Laurel Iron Works), if known. Otherwise use the name the property currently goes by.

② Location. First, note the municipality in which the property is located, that is, the township, borough, city, whatever. The current street address can follow.

③ Source. Deeds are the most common form of property conveyance, but patents, wills, and estate papers are also used.

③a Book/Page no. Volumes are generally identified by letters and numbers. Note both and don't forget the page number(s).

④ Grantor. Record the full name of the grantor (remember the index system?). If there are several grantors, write their names in the order given. Note any additional information concerning the grantor's place of residence, occupation, or relationship to others mentioned in the document. ("Ux," short for the Latin *uxor*, refers to the wife.)

⑤ Grantee. Again, write the first and last names of the grantee(s), and look for other clues, as suggested in item 4.

⑥ Date executed. Record the date as it appears in the deed. (In the "Old Style" calendar, which was used in Britain and its colonies until 1752, March was the first month of the year.)

⑥a Date recorded. This date appears at the end of the deed and, as noted earlier, could be years after the actual transfer.

⑦ Acreage/Description. The acreage is given in the "containing" clause following a metes-and-bounds description of the property. Any variation here warns of some form of subdivision where the chain might deviate. (See below for a full discussion of metes and bounds.)

⑧ Consideration. This means the price of the transaction. A dramatic price difference from one deed to the next may indicate the construction (or demolition) of a house or a subdivision of the original parcel. If the price seems inappropriate or nominal, note the tax stamps for clues of real value.

⑨ Key words. Check the deed terminology at the end of the chapter for the meaning of such key words as "messuage" and "appurtenance."

⑩ References to prior deeds. The "being" clause indicates how the grantor obtained the land and in what deed or will book it is recorded. Occasionally, a lengthy summation of the property's chain of ownership is included. Use deed referrals to continue tracing the property back through previous owners.

Figure 3–1

Extracting Useful Information

Few experienced deed researchers take the time to read each deed thoroughly. Besides being wordy and labored, deeds are repetitive. They are, after all, legal documents certifying a standard transaction and must be specific, perhaps overly so. Identical long-winded phrases, tedious format, and archaic terminology appearing in deed after deed actually simplify the search, because they can be ignored. Even 18th- and 19th-century handwritten deeds are readily deciphered once the standard format, oddities of old script, and usage are understood. (For an expert's definitions of old-deed terminology, see the end of this chapter.)

With all their complexity, deeds contain important primary information that can be extracted with little difficulty. Organizing this information to construct the chain of ownership is essential. One way to organize this information is presented in Figure 3-1. Most deeds will yield facts for each line, and possibly additional information. You can take notes on 5"x7" (or larger) cards, which, when arranged chronologically, show the chain of ownership. After you have closed any gaps in the chain, you can summarize the information on standard-size paper for quick reference.

Being meticulous in accumulating this information will save a lot of time later, when pieces begin to fit together. It will also provide some handles and clues (names, dates, and so on) that will be helpful in getting past the pitfalls that may be ahead.

Plotting the Metes and Bounds

Item 7 of Figure 3-1 mentions metes and bounds, the legal description of a property's boundary lines. Written in courses, degrees (°), minutes ('), seconds ("), feet, rods, perches, and even chains and links, metes and bounds tend to overwhelm and confuse the first-time deed researcher. Although it is tempting to bypass them in favor of such "hard" information as ownership and sale price, metes and bounds must be noted, perhaps sketched, and certainly comprehended to construct an accurate account of the property's

Deed, Chester County Recorder of Deeds. The 1844 deed from Joseph Pyle and his wife (ux) to Hugh E. Steele shows that Steele paid $12,500 for 104 acres of land including "all those messuages, rolling mill, nail factory, water rights, and plantation or tract of land known as the Laurel Iron Works."

history. If, as is frequently the case, the metes and bounds vary from one deed to the next, the property may have been subdivided or a wrong deed included in the search.

A typical metes-and-bounds description could read in part: ". . . thence leaving said spike of beginning south 03 degrees, 09 minutes, 59 seconds east, 355.75 feet to an iron pin marking the southeasterly . . ." Metes and bounds, Julia Colflesh points out, are a form of legal shorthand that traditionally omits key phrases for the sake of brevity. Take the phrase ". . . beginning south 03 degrees, 09 minutes, 59 seconds east, 355.75 feet . . ." She suggests mentally inserting words to fill it out: ". . . beginning *from the* south, *proceed* 03 degrees, 09 minutes, 59 seconds *toward the* east *for a distance of* 355.75 feet . . ."

To add to the confusion, metes and bounds are based on the surveyor's compass, which reads 90 degrees in either direction from points north and south, rather than the more widely known mariner's compass, which reads 360 degrees clockwise from north.

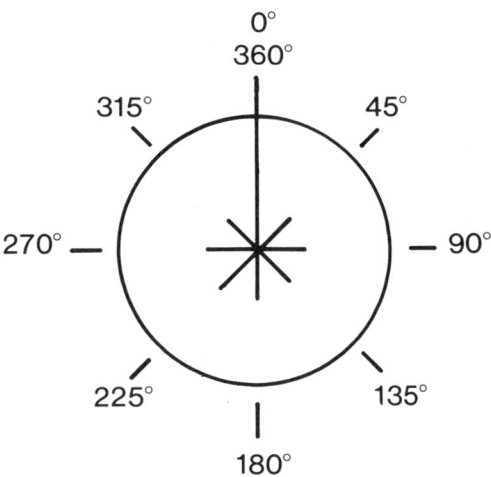

MARINER'S COMPASS

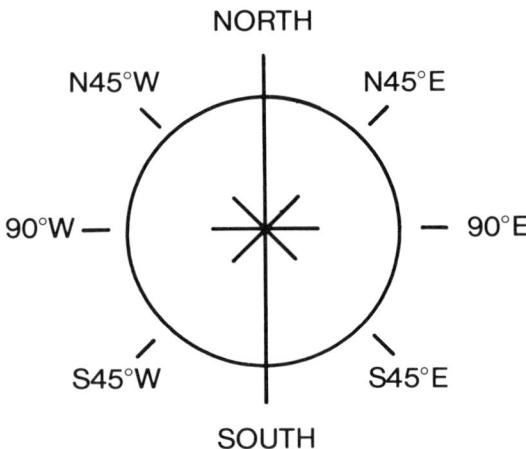

SURVEYOR'S COMPASS

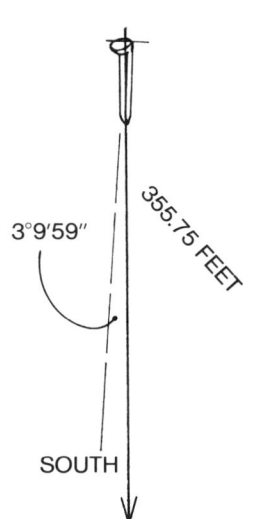

Using the surveyor's compass system, "south 03 degrees, 09 minutes, 59 seconds east" would be sketched as shown to the left.

A deed usually mentions points of reference such as spikes, iron pins, roads, corner and adjacent landowners, streams, and trees (oaks, hickories, and walnuts were common). You may want to record all this information on a sketch or "plot," as shown in Figure 3-2, so that you can later compare it with similar information in other deeds pertaining to the property.

You can draw a fairly accurate plot plan using 10-squares-to-the-inch graph paper, a surveyor's compass (or protractor), and an engineer's rule.

When possible, photostat the deed to avoid a return trip to the courthouse.

Other Sources

If, in continuing the deed search, you find no referrals to prior deeds or the next step is unclear, it is time to analyze the information and think creatively. The land might have been inherited and no deed recorded. Decades could have passed without the usual links in the chain being left. But the deed might "recite" earlier "devises" that could be investigated—that is,

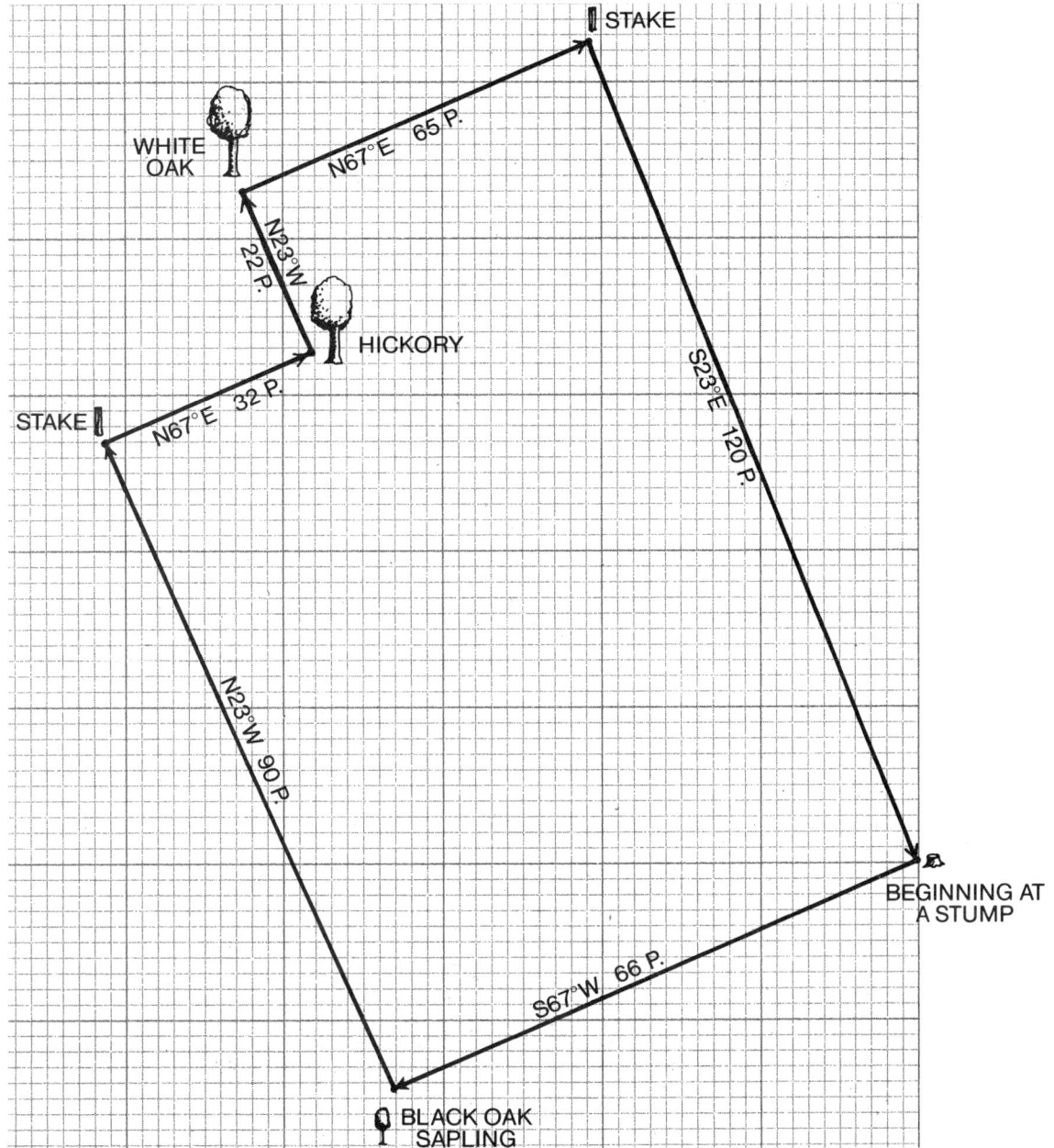

Figure 3–2

Hiram Pennyweather may say he inherited the property from his father, George, who inherited it from *his* father, Samuel. Or the land may have passed through an executor. If Edward Morrison owned a property and wanted to leave equal parts of it to his three children, an executor—named in the will or appointed by the Orphans' Court—would have to carry out the deceased's wishes. Consequently, in such cases, the executor's name (rather than Edward's) would appear on documents to settle the estate. For more about wills, see Estate Papers, below.

If a deed seems to be "missing," it might be found in the sheriff's or prothonotary's office. When the sheriff was given the responsibility of selling

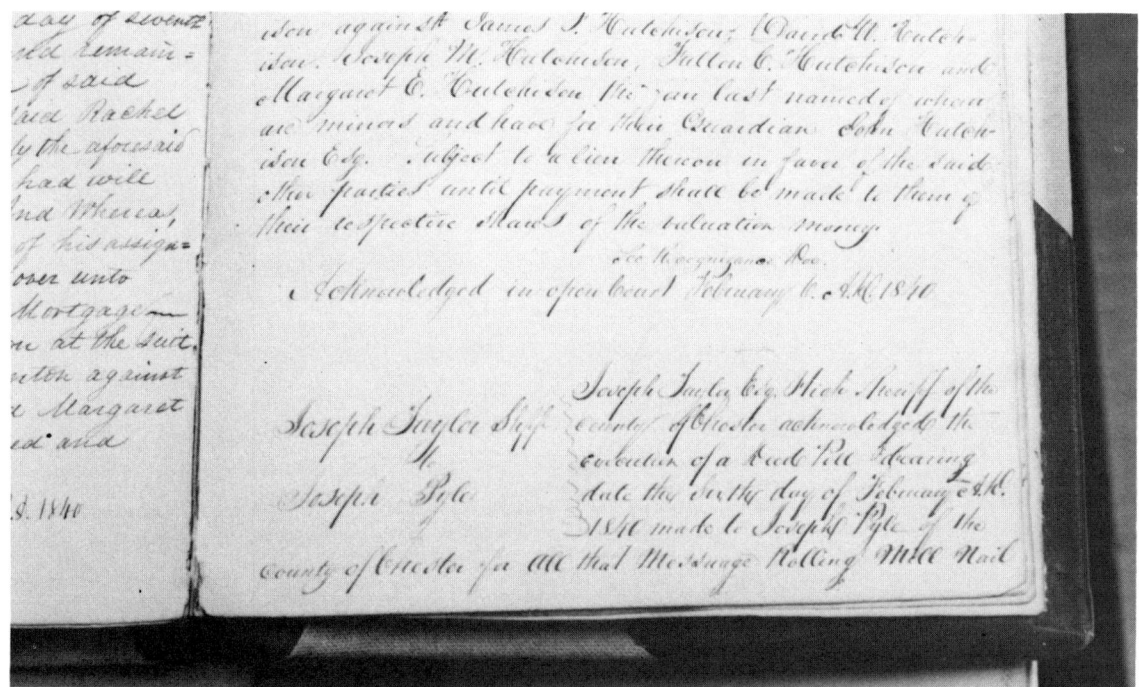

Deed Docket, Chester County Recorder of Deeds. Joseph Pyle obtained the Laurel Iron Works through a sheriff's sale in 1840. In this deed docket Joseph Taylor, High Sheriff of Chester County, sold Joseph Pyle "all that messuage, rolling mill, nail factory, and tract of land called 'Laurel Works.'"

a property, the ensuing transaction was, for various reasons, not always recorded in the deed office. Sheriff sales are both a bane and a blessing to the researcher. If the deeds were indexed improperly (as happened frequently), finding them requires luck and persistence. On the positive side, sheriff sales were advertised at length in old newspapers, and the land and improvements were usually described in some detail. These very informative sale notices are preserved in some historical societies' collections.

Estate Papers

No matter how complete it is, a chain of ownership constructed from deed research is really a bare outline needing a story. Additional digging will turn up information about the people who occupied the site and how it was used.

Resourcefulness will lead you to other documents, the most intriguing of which are estate papers: wills, inventories, Orphans' Court records, and letters of administration. Like deeds, estate papers are recorded with the county and are readily located if the indexing systems are understood. Wills are filed with the register of wills office and indexed, like deeds, by the deceased's first and last names. Besides recording the writers' wishes for the disposition of their estates, wills can yield valuable information about family members (such as names, marital status, place of residence) and properties (which may be described in great detail). Some old wills bequeathed rooms and furnishings individually. It was common in the 18th century to leave a widow the use of certain rooms—perhaps the cellar, a bedroom, and the kitchen—and to grant her various rights and privileges, such as access to a well or the delivery of firewood. The will may contain clues about outbuildings by mentioning, for example, "hay in the barn" or "carpenter tools in the shed." Occasionally, a will recites a history of the property, concluding with a statement of how the deceased took possession. This recital is especially helpful when a property was frequently transferred by inheritance or when some deeds are missing.

A will is generally accompanied by an inventory that lists and sets a value upon every important item in the estate. Inventories frequently describe the possessions room by room. This information can help determine a house's early appearance and floor plan and aid in its restoration. Not surprisingly, most house museums are guided by an early owner's inventory of its furnishings. The furnishings of the 1704 House in Birmingham Township, Delaware County, for example, are based on items listed in the 1751 and 1756 inventories of William Brinton (its builder) and his wife. Wills and inventories, then, are not only useful for filling in the deed search; they can give important clues to the use and development of the historic house.

Not everyone has the opportunity or foresight to prepare a will. Since the early 18th century, the estates of those dying intestate (without a will) have been handled by the Orphans' Court. The court does serve orphans, as its name suggests, but its focus is estates at the time of death. For example, the court grants letters of administration authorizing a particular individual to settle the estate of a property owner who died intestate. Records of such settlements—which may show the names of people who bought the property, how the property was subdivided, and to whom it was sold—are included in the minutes of the court. Orphans' Court proceedings are arranged chronologically, according to session. An estate may have been discussed at several of the court's sessions over a period of months. Unfortunately, unless an index to the court records has been prepared, you will find it difficult to use them.

Road Dockets

Although somewhat tricky to locate and work with, county road dockets are a primary source not to be overlooked. They touch on a number of road-related matters, including survey, construction, relocation, abandonment, and reopening. In conjunction with a road's legal description, dockets recite landowners and properties along its path. Occasionally, a docket will include a sketch of the road's courses and distances and some buildings along the way. Road dockets are usually found in the county courthouse or archives.

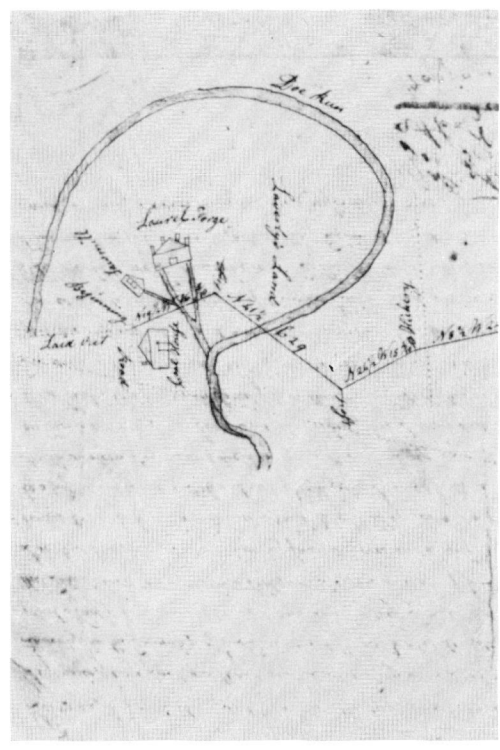

Original Road Papers, vol. 19, Chester County. One of the earliest records of an iron industry at Laurel is a road docket dated 1797, now found in the Chester County Archives. The docket petitions for a road to be laid out from the Laurel Forge to the Strasburg Road and is particularly helpful in locating the forge, a coal house, and a saw mill.

An example of old lettering and spelling from Chester County Court Records, 1681–1697. Translation: "Robert Wade made over a deed unto John Bristow his heires and assigns for ever dated ye 8th day of ye 10th moneth for a parcell of land lying and being in the Township of Chester."

Old Tax Records

Though a strain on the eyes (you have to look through roll after roll of microfilm), old tax records can be especially helpful for information on when a house was built or added to. But old tax records can be misleading. For example, early Chester County taxes were paid by the land occupant, not the landowner, providing problems for the researcher trying to tie certain deeds together with the tax records. By the 1800s, most county tax systems were based on uniform assessments paid by landowners. These records are particularly useful when you examine the assessments of a property over the years. A significant increase in assessments can indicate a new structure or the enlargement of an existing one. (It can also mean a uniform increase in assessments throughout the area.)

Rarely was property assessed as specifically as in the Direct Tax of 1798. This was a federal tax based on land value, number of slaves, and type of house. For each property that existed then, the tax list cites a house's dimensions, number of stories, number of windows and "lights" (panes) in each window, materials (wood, brick, stone), outbuildings, and owners and occupants. The exterior dimensions given in this list, and the number and type of windows, can help pinpoint a house's construction date as before or after 1798. Portions of this list have been lost; however, if a property you're researching is on it, you're lucky indeed.

Most tax records after 1900 can be found in county courthouses. The earlier records have been distributed among various historical collections. Generally, records are indexed according to the municipality and then chronologically within the municipality.

Census Records

You may be able to learn something about the people who lived in the house by looking at census records. The first federal census of population was taken in 1790, and subsequent ones in every succeeding decade. Information recorded by the censuses varies considerably. From 1790 to 1840, for example, the census gives only the name of the head of the household and the total number of other family members. Beginning in 1850 and continuing through 1900, the census was more specific. It gives the name, age, and place of birth of every free person in the household. Slave owners and slaves are listed in a separate schedule in 1850 and 1860. Censuses taken after 1900 are even more detailed.

Census records from 1790 to 1910 (except for 1890's, most of which were destroyed in a 1921 fire) are available to the general public. Post-1910 censuses are not yet published because, by law, they must remain confidential for 70 years. The National Archives in Washington, D.C., is the official respository for original census records. Microfilm copies may be viewed at the regional branches of the National Archives or at certain historical libraries.

Secondary Sources

Once you've constructed an accurate chain of ownership using data from primary sources, you can move with some confidence to secondary sources. Information obtained from historic maps, old photographs, drawings and paintings, history books, genealogies, newspapers, neighbors, and sages can help tighten loose connections in the deed search and tell a fuller story. To find out something about previous owners, look at genealogies and obituaries. They may tell you that an owner was a merchant or farmer or, if the property was held only as an investment, that he never even lived there! Knowing when the family expanded or a parent died can help you reach conclusions about the physical structure, such as when a bedroom wing, kitchen, or additional story may have been constructed. Old photographs are especially helpful, not only in determining the house's earlier appearance, but also by the clues they give about the family then living there—their clothes, furnishings, pets, and so on.

Not to be overlooked are previous occupants or their children, if still

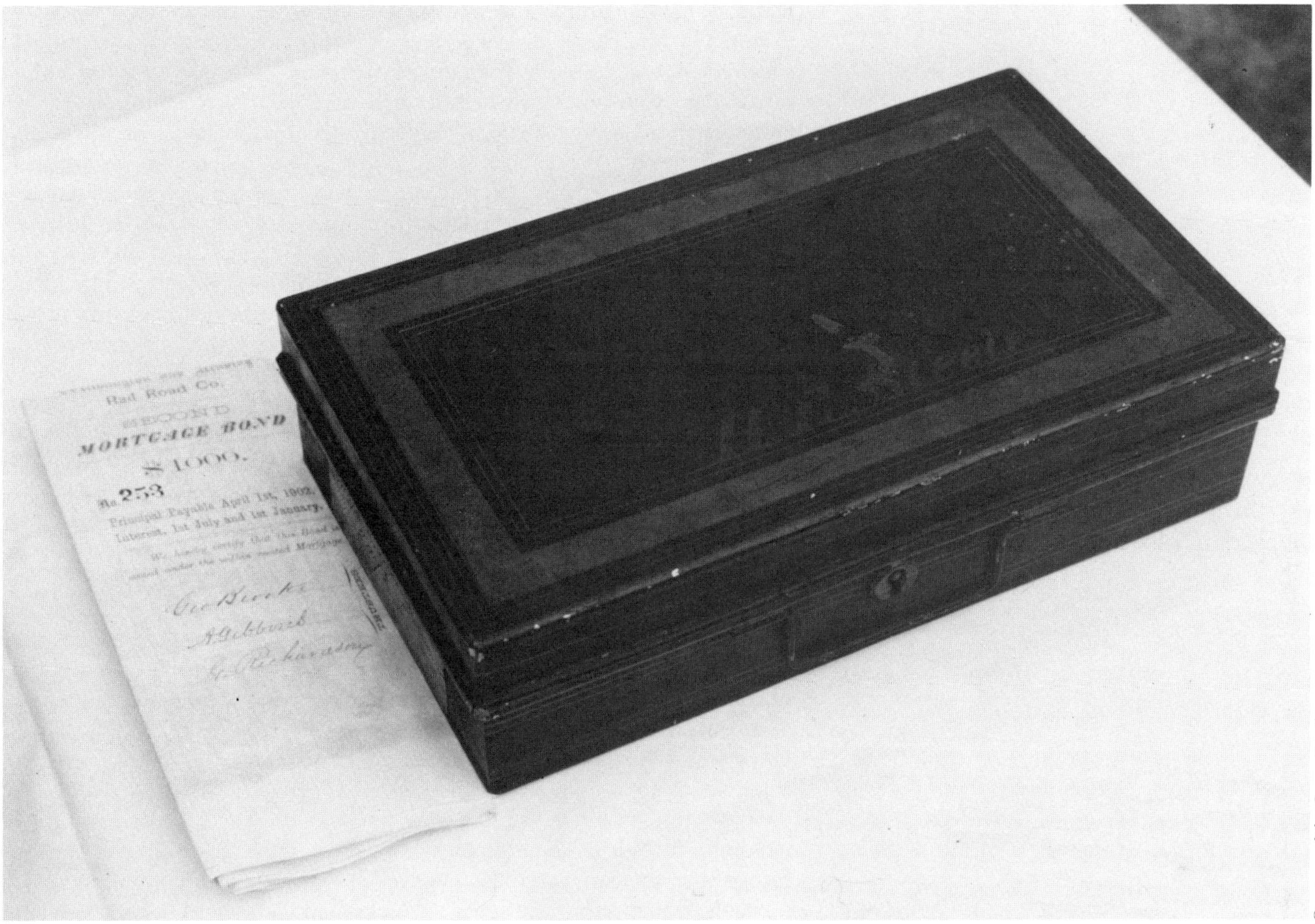

Courtesy of the Stone Family

Hugh Steele's money box and one of the bonds he purchased for the Wilmington & Reading Railroad Company. This bond, which should have been redeemable on April 1, 1902, became worthless soon after it was issued in 1873. Steele's losses in the railroad company led to the collapse of his iron works in the next decade.

Courtesy of the Stone Family

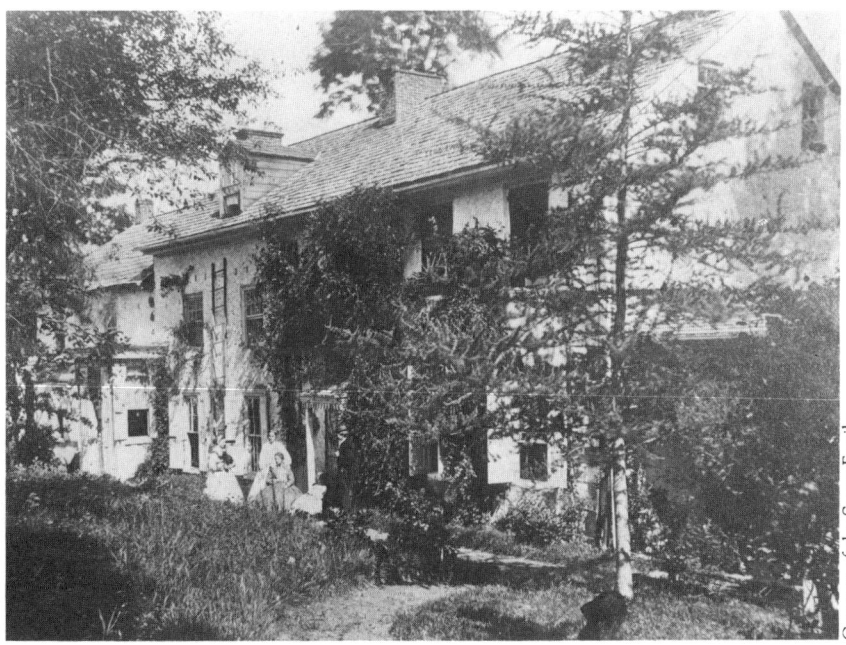

Hugh E. Steele house, c. 1867. This photograph of the Steele homestead at Laurel was made from a glass negative still in the possession of one of his descendants. A close look at the photograph shows that a portion of the house was log and that the roof was raised on another part. Seated and standing in front are some members of his family.

living. A baffling problem was solved in West Whiteland Township (Chester County) by one phone call to a previous owner (located by looking through a current *Social Register*). For months the local historical commission had searched in vain for the identities of the architects who had designed two particularly handsome country residences located on adjacent tracts. Although somewhat startled by the call, the previous owner, who by then lived in a different area, gladly provided the names of the two architects involved, one for her in-laws' former house, Chesteridge (1908), and the other for hers, Autun (1928).

Although it is wise to evaluate a source's credibility critically, none should be overlooked as too mundane. Sometimes seemingly insignificant facts help answer perplexing questions.

RESEARCHING THE PHYSICAL STRUCTURE

At some point during your research, you should supplement documentary inquiry with physical analysis. Logically, the extent of this analysis is governed by your goals, expertise, and endurance. Many find researching their own properties particularly enjoyable and invigorating, for they are putting together a story in which they are the latest chapter.

Examine the house as an artifact having a story to tell. Although you cannot undertake a detailed architectural analysis without extensive training, you can glean a great deal of information if you have a basic understanding of your area's architectural development and use some common sense.

Architect Ed Hinderliter of Media, Pennsylvania, says that the key to visual research is anomalies. Any feature that looks out of place tells something about the building and the people who have used it. A plastered-in doorway, a seam in the stonework, a break in the floorboards, a gap in the molding—all tell of some change from the house's original condition. By recognizing as many of these changes as you can and determining their probable sequence of occurrence, you can build a framework for the history of the building, just as the chain of ownership established the framework for the general history of the site.

Documentary research often fills in the information you need to back up any assumptions you may have about construction or alteration. For example, let's say that the type of nails used in construction leads you to date a frame addition to a stone house as before 1840. Wills might pinpoint the date to the early 1830s by showing that 11 family members lived in the house, easily justifying a new addition.

You should constantly go back and forth between the records and the physical structure, letting one corroborate the other.

Here are the kinds of things to look for. (Bear in mind that the goal is to seek out structural anomalies or inconsistencies.) After you have surveyed the entire building and noted all the inconsistencies, ask "why?" about each, then "when?" or "in what order?"

The Exterior

Structural openings: Check the alignment and uniformity of doors and windows. Variations could indicate additions or alterations.

Roof: A seam or sag in the roof suggests an addition. Scars in the outside walls may show where a roof has been raised or lowered.

Appendages: Telltale signs of former porches, sheds, or projecting eaves

Porch or pent roof? Metal support brackets and a drip course would indicate a porch, but the rectangles above the windows indicate that outlookers (floor joists) once extended through the wall to support a pent roof.

A log house in Chester County losing its stucco disguise.

visible from the exterior include exposed ends of joists, differences in a wall's color or surface, drip courses, and hardware remaining in the walls.

Wall surface: Additions can be discerned from seam lines and differences in surface treatments. Many an old house, however, was enlarged and then resurfaced in a uniform material. Frequently, stucco was applied to give an enlarged house a uniform, "modern" appearance. (Options may have to be weighed here. Although chipping off the stucco can answer your questions about sequence, it may also result in huge restoration problems.) If the house has aluminum or plastic siding, chances are there is something older, if not original, underneath. Hundreds of log houses wear an aluminum or clapboard disguise.

The Interior

Floors: Differences in flooring, patched areas, and the supporting joists are worthy of careful inspection. Generally, the best places to look for original material are the basement and the attic.

Walls/floor plan: Interior walls were frequently moved or removed, altering the original floor plan. Check for wear marks indicating old doorways and passages, nail patterns, or seam lines in the walls and ceilings.

Fireplaces/chimneys: The best place to start is in the basement, where the original supporting structure might remain. In the 19th and 20th centuries, many old fireplaces were made smaller, covered up, or ripped out.

Ceilings: Very old ceilings seldom remain unaltered, thanks to modern plumbing and wiring, relocations of stairways, and shifts in aesthetics. Not all, of course, had exposed joists; those that did are beaded and blackened with age or smoke.

Stairways: Generally, a stairway's original location is easy to spot by patches in the floor or ceiling.

Trim: Note any disparities in the trim around doors, windows, fireplaces, walls, and ceilings. Follow the baseboard around the house, checking for breaks and inconsistencies.

Paint: You can carefully chip away layers of paint to determine the sequence of application. Samples can be taken for further analysis to date them or to reproduce them.

Hardware: If original, hardware can be the key to determining dates of construction and alteration. In addition, evidence of old hardware, such as

Door hinges and other hardware can be clues to a building's history.

Occasionally a fireplace will even include the house's date of construction, as shown in this residence in Paoli, Pennsylvania.

nail patterns or hinge scars, can tell almost as much as the hardware itself. Types of nails and screws can date a house as before or after the mid-19th century. (Several publications listed under For Further Reading are good guides to this kind of detective work.)

Roof: Although the roofs of many old houses have been replaced or rebuilt, it is wise to check the attic for the type of rafters and framing and any variations. Check the saw marks on the rafters. If they are circular (curved), they were made after 1830 (when the circular saw was introduced to this area); up and down (vertical) marks usually indicate an earlier date.

Observations of a house's physical structure are best recorded on floor plans, whether roughly measured by you or prepared by an expert. Photographs and measured drawings documenting significant features are useful for closer scrutiny and comparison with standard models.

Documentary research coupled with physical examination provides a nearly complete picture. Some people, however, will want to go further.

ARCHEOLOGICAL INVESTIGATION

If you have the time and the inclination, you can find many clues to a house's history in the ground around it. Although archeology is an exact science usually left to experts, a novice can undertake some basic archeological investigation, following proven procedures, at almost any site.

First, look around for abandoned wells or trash pits, where previous inhabitants discarded items that can tell a great deal about how they lived. (A word of caution: while exploring a well, don't take needless chances; don't dig alone, and be wary of unstable well walls.)

In digging out a well or trash pit or in excavating around a fireplace, a bake oven, or an outside entrance, don't remove artifacts before documenting them. Otherwise you will lose their context forever. For any item or artifact found in the ground, precisely describe its location in relation to given

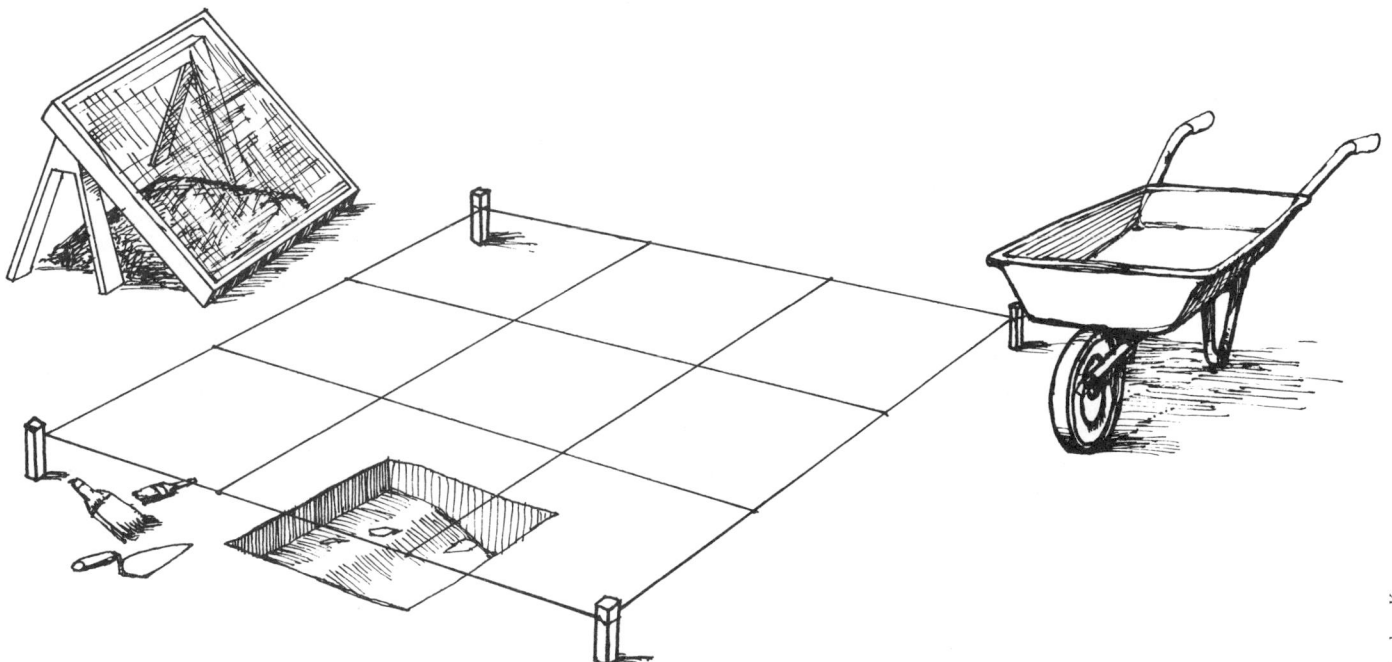

Laying out a grid is an important first step in any archeological dig.

A dig undertaken at Chester County prison to comply with the "Section 106" review process (see Chapter 4) prior to installation of a sewage disposal system. Indian arrow points dating from 6000 B.C.–1000 A.D. were discovered with the help of 91 volunteers.

reference points. Particularly, note the depth and the position of the artifact when found. You can then clean it and bag it with an identification number.

Perhaps the most efficient system for mapping the locations of artifacts is to lay out a master grid covering the entire area to be surveyed. Wherever there will be digging, rope off smaller grids (perhaps five by five feet) conforming to the master grid. Record your findings grid by grid. Photography is also essential. Be sure each photograph includes a visual scale, such as a person or an easily recognized object (such as a trowel) and a rough indication of north.

The steps described here are merely an introduction to archeological research. You may wish to consult your local library or the Pennsylvania Historical and Museum Commission's Section of Archeology for the names of organizations in your area. Some consulting firms and universities have archeology departments, and there are also local chapters of national archeology organizations.

During the research, the joy of discovery and inquiry can make a sometimes monotonous, tiring, and even dirty job thrilling. After the data and artifacts have been collected, however, it all becomes headwork. The conclusions you draw should complement those you developed through the documentary and architectural examinations. Each line of research should enrich the others, so that you can reach well-formulated, solidly based conclusions.

Researchers in Chester County Historical Society's well-equipped library pore over historical records and documents.

OLD-DEED TERMINOLOGY

alien. To make over to another; to transfer or convey.

all and singular. The whole, without exception, including each of the parts.

appurtenance. An adjunct to something more important, such as a right of way to land, or an orchard to a house.

collier. One who works in a coal mine (in early Pennsylvania, one who made charcoal).

conveyance. A transfer of legal title by deed, lien, mortgage, or assignment.

cordwainer. Leather worker.

covenant. A contract or a clause within a contract.

covenant of non-claim. Used in Pennsylvania in deeds terminating ground rents; for example, "that neither the vendor nor his heirs, nor any other person shall claim any title in the premises conveyed."

covenant of seisin (or seizin). An assurance to the purchaser that the seller has the very estate in the quantity and quality that he purports to convey.

deed of release. A document releasing property from the encumbrance of a mortgage, lien, etc., by payment or performance of certain conditions.

deed poll. A deed made by one party, and ordinarily used only when there were no covenants obligating the grantee. It was replaced by the indenture, except as used in the sheriff's deed poll. Before 1700, the proprietors of Pennsylvania allowed no one to locate and survey more than 300 acres. To evade this rule, speculators customarily made application in the names of third persons, and, having obtained a warrant, took from them what was called a "deed poll," or a brief conveyance of their claim.

demesne. Domain, held in one's own right; not allotted to tenants.

devise. To bequeath real property by will. (*Device* is the property bequeathed.)

enfeoff. To invest with an estate.

estate. The interest anyone has in land, real property, real estate; everything a man owns.

feoffment. Originally the grant of a "feud" or "fee" (a barony or knight's fee) for which certain services were due; later a grant of a free inheritance to a man and his heirs.

freeman. In early Pennsylvania, not holden to any lord or superior; a bachelor.

grantee. Purchaser; a person to whom a grant is made.

grantor. Seller.

hereditaments. Originally things capable of being inherited: not only lands and everything thereon, but also heirlooms and certain furniture that, by custom, could descend to the heir together with the land; generally used as the widest expression for real property of all kinds and therefore employed in conveyances after the words "lands" and "tenements" to include everything in realty that those words did not cover.

indenture. A deed signed by two or more parties in counterpart, but on a single sheet of paper or parchment. The counterparts were then separated by cutting or tearing along a line containing indentations; hence the term "indenture." Each party kept one of the counterparts, which could be matched if its authenticity were questioned.

inmate. In Pennsylvania tax usage, a married man; one who lodges in the same house with another, but not in the same room.

liberties. Privileged districts exempt from the sheriff's jurisdiction; in colonial times, laws or legal rights resting upon them (Massachusetts's ordinances were called "laws and liberties"); in Philadelphia, early political subdivisions, as "Northern Liberties."

messuage. Dwelling house.

parcel. A piece of ground, usually part of a large acreage or estate.

patent deed. The very first deed for a given property, given from the proprietors to the first owner.

perch. Measure of land equal to $5^1/_2$ yards (also called rod or pole); early measurement of distance equal to $5^1/_2$ yards used in conjunction with degrees (angles) to give the metes and bounds on surveys and descriptions.

public vendue or outcry. Public sale or auction, under authority of law, as by constable, sheriff, tax collector, administrator, etc.

quit-claim deed. A deed clearing the title of old encumbrances.

relict. Widow or widower.

remainder. Remnant of the whole estate after a preceding part has been given away; arises through act of the parties.

reversion. The residue of an estate left to the grantor or his heirs during the continuance or termination of an estate; arises through act of law.

seisin. The right to immediate possession.

tenement. In its original, proper, and legal sense, everything that may be holden (held), provided it is of a permanent nature, applicable not only to lands and other solid objects, but also to offices, rents, commons, franchises, peerages, etc.; vernacular usage applies only to houses and other buildings; not used in modern deeds. (In old deeds, the first definition is applicable.)

weaver. One who weaves cloth. (Beware the designation. In the early 18th century, many men listed themselves as weavers because as such they were taxed less.)

yeoman. In England, a commoner, a freeholder under the rank of gentleman; in America, a farmer.

"Old Rivets," or GG1 4800, built in 1934 by the Baldwin Locomotive Works and the General Electric Company, was the prototype for the Pennsylvania Railroad's legendary GG1 fleet of 139 units. As a class, the GG1 served longer and recorded more miles than any other locomotive. In 1983 No. 4800 was registered as a National Historic Mechanical Engineering Landmark. She has been on display in the Railroad Museum of Pennsylvania since 1980.

Ken Murry

Chapter 4

THE NATIONAL REGISTER OF HISTORIC PLACES

The National Register of Historic Places occupies a central position in the nation's preservation program. It is both a list of resources and a tool for preserving them. As a list it is unsurpassed in quantity, quality, and variety; as a tool, whether used alone or in conjunction with other preservation techniques, it can be highly effective.

Dubbed the "Super List" by Steve Weinberg in the July-August 1982 issue of *Historic Preservation*, the National Register is the official (and ever-growing) national record of cultural resources worthy of preservation. Between 1968 and 1981 the number of entries jumped from 1,241 to nearly 25,000, of which 2,500 were historic districts containing more than 250,000 buildings. Despite its year-long closing in 1980–81 to permit the development of new regulations, and despite criticism of its standards, procedures, and powers, the register continues to be the cornerstone of the preservation movement.

The National Register recognizes the most significant and representative resources of America's history, architecture, archeology, engineering, and culture. It divides them into five categories: districts, sites, buildings, structures, and objects. Resources can be nominated individually, thematically, in groups, or as historic districts. As a result, the list encompasses a spectrum of resources in American history: from Philadelphia's Old City to Miami Beach's Art Deco Historic District; from the Strickler Susquehannock Indian Village Site in rural Lancaster County (Pennsylvania) to the site of William Penn's landing in the city of Chester; from the ancient Gila cliff dwellings in New Mexico to Frank Lloyd Wright's "Fallingwater" in western Pennsylvania; from the celebrated Brooklyn Bridge to scores of covered bridges; from Lucy, the Margate (New Jersey) elephant, to the last operating GG1

"CEDARCROFT."
RESIDENCE OF THE LATE BAYARD TAYLOR,
EAST MARLBOROUGH.

From the History of Chester County, Pennsylvania by Futhey and Cope, 1881.

streamlined electric locomotive. Despite its relentless growth and seemingly unbounded diversity, the register is a carefully regulated federal program.

BACKGROUND

The National Register program was created in 1966 by the National Historic Preservation Act (NHPA). This act established a comprehensive national preservation policy and program under the direction of the Secretary of the Interior. The act empowered the secretary to "expand and maintain a register of properties of national, state, or local significance." This provision, both a continuation and an expansion of existing law, led to the immensely successful National Register program, which, despite some "mid-course corrections," is little changed in intent from the 1966 program.

Neither the assignment of the nation's preservation programs to the Department of the Interior nor the creation of an official list of historic resources originated in the NHPA. The authority for both came from much earlier legislation, the Historic Sites Act of 1935. This act, which declared it "national policy to preserve for public use historic sites, buildings and objects of national significance," authorized the Secretary of the Interior, through the National Park Service, to implement the policy by surveys, research, restorations, and other means. Besides fostering the popular Historic American Buildings Survey (see Chapter 5), the act gave rise to the National Historic Landmark Program (NHL), implemented in 1960 to give federal recognition to properties of exceptional national significance. Well-known Delaware Valley buildings designated as national historic landmarks include Old Swedes Church in Wilmington, Cedarcroft (Bayard Taylor House) in Kennett Square, and the Academy of Music, John Bartram House, and Pennsylvania Hospital in Philadelphia.

The National Historic Landmark Program had been in effect only six years when the National Register of Historic Places was authorized. Unlike national historic landmarks, which must possess exceptional national significance and which are selected according to prescribed historic themes, National Register properties may be significant at the local, state, or national level and are not subject to the rigid nominating procedures of the landmark program. (See Constance M. Greiff, *The Historic Property Owner's Handbook*, listed in For Further Reading for a discussion of procedures for designating landmarks.)

Whereas the somewhat esoteric purpose of the NHL program is to study themes in American history and to search out and mark outstanding representations of those themes, the National Register was created as a planning tool. This official list of the nation's "cultural property . . . worth saving" was to be used by federal, state, and local governments, private groups, and citizens in identifying, certifying, and protecting historic sites. Despite the "higher" significance and national importance of landmarks, no built-in benefits or protections are attached to the designation as they are with national registration. To compensate, landmarks are automatically listed in the National Register of Historic Places, from which flows eligibility for certain federal tax incentives, grants, and protections. If a building listed in the National Register is also a National Historic Landmark, the letters "NHL" are shown at the end of the official entry in the National Register. Likewise, "HABS" is added to National Register entries for buildings also included in the Historic American Buildings Survey. Some entries show both "NHL" and "HABS." By the end of 1982, after 22 years of existence, the National Historic Landmark Program had designated 1,574 buildings and districts; the National Register of Historic Places, after 16 years, had more than 25,000 individual buildings and more than 2,500 historic districts. A Super List indeed!

The National Register's benefits and protections basically have not changed since 1966. Conceptually, it is still a planning tool. Increasingly, however, the register has become linked with other preservation opportunities, programs, and techniques, the most visible being federal income tax incentives. Because of the incentives' success (see Chapter 7), there is a tendency to gloss over some of the less tangible benefits of being listed in the register.

BENEFITS AND PROTECTIONS
Loans and Grants

The National Register has played a key role in preservation by certifying the significance of selected resources and affording them a degree of protection. Resources listed in the register are prime candidates for acquisition by historical groups, government agencies, and individuals interested in preservation. Since they are certified to be important, they are in a strong position

Collins Mill as it appeared in 1972.

The mill with shingle roof construction underway, 1984.

to attract funding and other forms of support. The experience of the French and Pickering Creeks Conservation Trust with the Collins Mill is a case in point.

The existence of a small, unaltered, stone 18th-century grist and flour mill along Pickering Creek in West Pikeland Township, Chester County, Pennsylvania, was brought to the attention of the trust in the early 1970s. Established in 1967 as a nonprofit organization to preserve open space and historic buildings in northern Chester County, the trust has run an aggressive registration program, which has resulted in the listing of 42 buildings and districts in the National Register. Impressed by the architectural integrity of this rare survivor dating from 1747, the trust sponsored its National Register nomination. The Collins (Lightfoot) Mill was officially listed on April 13, 1973. Complete with its wooden gearing, mill stones, and sifting reel, the mill had been owned since 1919 by O. Ernest Collins, a miller and country mechanic who operated it as a mill until the late 1940s. It was put high on the trust's "wish list" of acquisitions.

After Mr. Collins's death in 1982, the trust purchased the mill with the help of a loan from the Endangered Properties Fund of the National Trust for Historic Preservation. The same year, the Bureau for Historic Preservation of the Pennsylvania Historical and Museum Commission awarded the trust a planning and survey grant for an inventory and feasibility study. The necessary match for this grant was contributed by the Chester County Commissioners through the redevelopment authority. The trust was awarded another grant from the bureau through the federal Emergency Jobs Act of 1983. The matching share for this grant came from a private gift. These latest funds have enabled the trust to undertake phase 1 of the preservation of the mill buildings, including new roofs and repair of water damage.

Further phases are planned to complete restoration to operational condition. Thus the long-term preservation of the mill as an educational site is virtually assured. According to Eleanor Morris, president of the trust, "The great attention the mill has attracted reflects a growing interest in our industrial heritage and early forms of economic development."

Section 106 Review

Had federal matching grants for the acquisition and development of nationally registered sites not been terminated, the trust might have applied to that source for funds, as it did for its acquisition of the Coventry House in 1977, now trust headquarters. Similarly, had the Collins Mill stood in the path of a federally assisted project, such as sewer or dam construction, bridge replacement, or subsidized housing, it would have qualified for the protection offered to nationally registered resources under Section 106 of the National Historic Preservation Act (NHPA). According to Section 106, federal agency "undertakings" that may have an "adverse impact" on nationally registered resources are subject to review by the Advisory Council on Historic Preservation, established by the NHPA as an independent agency of the executive branch to advise the President and Congress on historic preservation. As a result of a 1976 amendment to the NHPA, the Section 106 protections were extended to buildings determined to be eligible for the National Register but not listed in it. Determinations of eligibility (DOE) are made by the Keeper of the National Register upon request by a "concerned" federal agency.

In the opinion of some, the story of the Thompson Building in Coatesville, Pennsylvania, concluded unfortunately, but it illustrates the strengths and weaknesses of Section 106 protections. Public concern about the large, somewhat shabby building on Coatesville's main street surfaced in 1978. The city

Thompson Building (in center), c. 1910.

Thompson Building during demolition.

was about to embark on its Action Plan to revitalize its central business district. One aspect of the plan called for the Chester County Redevelopment Authority, administrator of the federal Community Development Block Grant program, to acquire and demolish three downtown buildings, among them the 1901 Romanesque Revival–style Thompson Building. While one of the doomed sites was intended for parking, no use was specified for the other two. The Coatesville Historical Commission registered its opposition to the plan, found no sympathy in city council, and contacted the Bureau for Historic Preservation for advice. A bureau staff member visited the building and found it to be structurally sound and a significant component of the main street. The redevelopment authority was pressured as a "concerned" agency to request a determination of eligibility. The authority complied, and in 1980 the Thompson Building received a DOE. That triggered Advisory Council review of its proposed federally funded demolition. As a result of the council's review, the authority was required to aggressively market the building for 90 days. In its "Memorandum of Agreement," the council detailed the marketing procedures, which included the preparation of a sales brochure and advertisements of the property in newspapers of state and local circulation. Despite this effort, no offers were made for the building. To the relief of some and to the bitter disappointment of others, it was demolished in August 1981, more than three years after its destruction was proposed.

As illustrated with the Thompson Building, Section 106 protections may not be strong enough to avoid or mitigate all federally funded "adverse impacts"; but they tend to create a climate for the resolution of conflicts, give preservationists more time to develop strategies, and focus public attention on endangered historic resources.

Besides the Section 106 process, nationally registered (or eligible) properties receive special consideration in projects affected by the National Environmental Policy Act and the Department of Transportation Act.

National Environmental Policy Act

The effect of federal agency undertakings on historic properties can also be considered in the environmental impact statement (EIS). For every federal action "significantly affecting the quality of the human environment," Section 102 (2)(C) of the National Environmental Policy Act of 1969 (NEPA) requires the preparation of a detailed study of the undertaking's impact on the environment, including historic resources. Besides analyzing the proposed action's impact, the statement should consider unavoidable adverse environmental effects, alternatives, short- and long-term results, and "irreversible and irretrievable commitments of resources."

Although the NEPA Section 102 and NHPA Section 106 procedures are legally independent of each other, in some projects the reviews are coordinated to save time. EIS's may also be prepared to meet the requirements of Section 4(f) of the Department of Transportation Act.

Section 4(f)

Enacted in 1966, the Department of Transportation Act contains a provision that has spared hundreds of historic properties from thoughtless destruction.

Arguably one of the strongest protections for registered historic properties, Section 4(f) discourages the use of federal funds for highway construction that encroaches on historic properties, as well as on public park land, recreation areas, and wildlife and waterfowl refuges. State highway departments may condemn or expand a right of way onto historic properties only if "there is no feasible or prudent alternative" and they have done "all possible planning to minimize harm" to the resources. Properties listed in or eligible for the National Register receive consideration under Section 4(f). As Gary W. Wilburn noted in the March 1983 issue of the *Preservation Law Reporter*, the Section 4(f) protections have been vigorously upheld by the courts.

Private Actions

Although resources on the National Register receive considerable protection from government actions, those that are privately held are not protected from actions taken by their owners. Privately owned registered buildings can be burned, demolished, moved, or drastically altered with no fear of federal repercussion, other than the risk of losing their National Register status and thus the benefits and protections described above. Indeed, this lack of federal control over the actions of the private sector is viewed as one of the program's strongest attractions. Contrary to popular belief, restrictions on privately owned registered buildings are generally imposed at the local level—for example, by deed restrictions, easements, or ordinances—not by the federal government and the National Register program.

For the Community

The National Register is effective in catalyzing local preservation efforts. The research and certification of historic resources can stimulate a broadened appreciation of the resources' (and the community's) history. The prospect of a historic district may, for example, be the impetus to form a local historical

Leiper house, Delaware County. Since it lies near a proposed Interstate highway route, this historic property came under both the 4(f) and EIS review processes.

commission. Registration of a number of properties in the community may promote a review of its planning policies and ordinances.

All things considered, a listing in the National Register of Historic Places is worth pursuing, especially for the benefits and protections it offers the private property owner. Getting on this Super List, however, can be a long process for which there is no guarantee of success. Professionals in historic preservation would probably agree on the best advice for would-be applicants: Only the determined and highly motivated need apply.

HOW TO NOMINATE A RESOURCE

Even the most resolute of applicants will not succeed if the historic resource does not meet the National Register's standards for significance and integrity. Before beginning the formal registration process, an applicant is well advised to question whether and how the resource could qualify.

Although some changes in the National Register program have occurred since 1966, the criteria against which all nominations are evaluated have remained remarkably intact. The criteria are worded to embrace a diversity of resources whose level of significance may be local, state, or national. (See criteria in Figure 4-1.) In addition, the National Register has established more than 25 "Areas of Significance"—such as architecture, economics, and transportation; a resource should hold some importance in at least one of them. Despite this apparent latitude, however, only a fraction of all historic resources will be listed in the National Register.

One reason is that along with satisfying at least one of the National Register criteria, a resource must have integrity. Integrity (not to be confused with physical condition) is, according to the National Register, "the authenticity

Even though a house may be well maintained and have interesting features, it does not necessarily have architectural integrity. As shown in this example, a Gothic Revival house has undergone a number of changes—replacement of front door, addition of bay windows and exterior chimney—which detract significantly from its integrity.

of a property's historic identity, evidenced by the survival of physical characteristics that existed during the property's historic or pre-historic period. If a property retains the physical characteristics it possessed in the past then it has the capacity to convey association with historical patterns or persons, architectural or engineering design and technology, or information about a culture or people."

In evaluating nominations, the National Register Division assesses resources' integrity of location, design, setting, materials, workmanship, feeling, and association, taking into account their areas of significance. Integrity is perhaps best explained by citing a few examples of what it is not.

> A house (nominated under architecture) designed in 1888 by a famous architect, but modernized inside and out in the 1960s.
>
> The birthplace (nominated under politics) of a well-known early-20th-century politician, recently restored to its 18th-century appearance as a log cabin.
>
> A 1795 grist mill (nominated under industry) converted to apartments featuring skylights and patios with sliding glass doors.

Assessing integrity and significance is often best left to professionals. They will advise not only whether a resource should be nominated, but also how.

Categories

Underlying the seeming confusion of National Register entries, which range from carousels to skyscrapers, is a strict classification system. It is essential to nominate the resource in its most appropriate category. A resource ineligible in one category, such as a nondescript storefront nominated as an individual "building," may prove eligible in the "district" category.

The National Register recognizes five categories of significant properties:

District: "a geographically definable area, urban or rural, possessing a significant concentration, linkage, or continuity of sites, buildings, structures, or objects united by past events or aesthetically by plan or physical development."

Site: "the location of a significant event, a prehistoric or historic occupation or activity, or a building or structure, whether standing, ruined, or vanished, where the location itself maintains historical or archeological value regardless of the value of any existing structures."

Building: "a structure created to shelter any form of human activity . . ."

Structure: "a work made up of interdependent and interrelated parts in a definite pattern of organization. Constructed by man, it is often an engineering project large in scale."

Object: "a material thing of functional, aesthetic, cultural, historical, or scientific value that may be, by nature or design, movable yet related to a specific setting or environment."

Most resources can be nominated in the building or district category. Examples from the other categories include (structures) bridges and carousels; (objects) trains and ships; and (sites) Indian villages and burial grounds.

Format

Another variable in the registration process is format. Along with submitting nominations for individual buildings, structures, or objects, there is the option of multiple submissions. Most owners of historic properties find the individual nomination the most effective route to registration. Com-

Great Valley Mill, Chester County. Nominated to the National Register in the "building" category.

munity or group efforts, however, often elect to use the historic district, thematic resource, or multiple resource format.

Historic districts, as described above, consist of groups of buildings related by location, history, and significance. They range from tiny crossroad villages, such as Dilworthtown in Chester County, to portions of university campuses, as at West Chester University and the University of Pennsylvania, to large urban concentrations, as in the Society Hill and Spring Garden areas of Philadelphia. As of February 1983, 102 National Register districts were listed in Pennsylvania. Some of these are regulated by local ordinances (authorized under Pennsylvania Act 167 of 1961) providing architectural controls. (See Local Regulation, Chapter 5.) Appendix C lists the registered and the Act 167 historic districts in the four-county area surrounding Philadelphia.

The thematic resource format was developed by the National Register Division in 1977 "to expedite the recognition and protection of historic resources identified through thematic surveys" and to encourage further use of the National Register as a planning tool. Thematic resources must be related to one another in a clearly distinguishable way, such as by historic person or event, or by architect or building type. All eligible resources of the thematic type must be nominated within a specified area, such as county or state. The most extensive thematic resource effort thus far in Pennsylvania was undertaken in 1978–80 by the Bureau for Historic Preservation and concerned the covered bridges of each county. As a result of that nomination, 225 of Pennsylvania's covered bridges are listed in the National Register.

At the same time it recognized thematic groups, the National Register also provided for multiple resource nominations. Like the thematic format, the multiple resource nomination was designed to implement the findings of surveys. The two formats differ, however, in their organizing principles. Whereas thematic resources are related to one another in a certain way, multiple resources are linked only by geographic study area. A multiple resource nomination is described by the National Register as "all or a defined

The 1881 Mary Ann Pyle bridge, in Chester County. Listed in the National Register of Historic Places in 1980 in a thematic resource format.

The National Register of Historic Places / 67

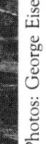

Photos: George Eisenman

Views of the Dilworthtown Historic District, submitted with its National Register nomination in 1970.

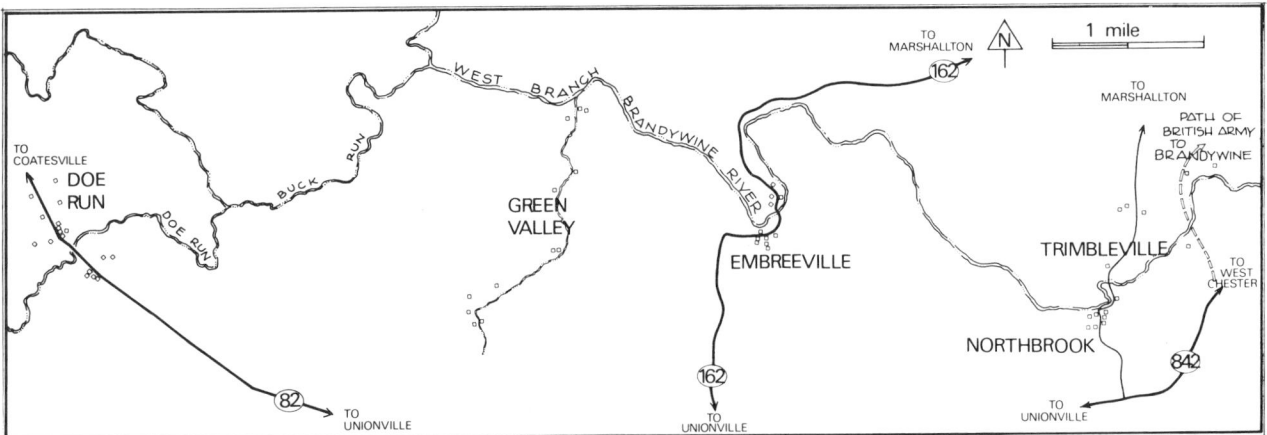

Located along the Brandywine River's West Branch, these five districts as well as a number of individual properties are being researched for nomination to the National Register under the multiple resource format.

portion of the historic resources identified in a specified geographical area." Although municipal boundaries usually define the multiple resource area, a nomination may span several communities or an entire county, or may be limited to a portion of a large city or town. Relatively few of these nominations have been developed, a major reason being the need for a comprehensive survey to precede the nomination. By the end of 1983, only three multiple resource nominations had been submitted in Pennsylvania (Newtown Borough in Bucks County, and East Fallowfield and West Whiteland Townships in Chester County). As this format becomes better understood and as more surveys are completed across the state, its use is expected to increase substantially.

Despite their complexities, historic district, thematic resource, and multiple resource formats tend to save time and money compared with nominating resources individually. In addition, they maximize the beneficial effects of registration. The use of multiple registrations is unfortunately limited by the sometimes difficult task of garnering sufficient community support. Most areas with these registrations in place, though, would probably agree that they were well worth the effort.

The Process

Whatever the resource or its significance, integrity, and category, most nominations to the National Register follow the same basic procedure. The process is determined by laws and regulations emanating from Washington; the state programs adjust their procedures to incorporate the federal regulations.

Two noteworthy publications describe the process in detail. *How to Complete National Register Forms*, published by the National Register Division of the Department of the Interior, first appeared in 1977 and is considered the bible of registration manuals. Especially useful to Pennsylvanians is a manual produced by the Bureau for Historic Preservation, *The National Register Process in Pennsylvania*. It describes from start to finish how the National Register process works in Pennsylvania and includes pertinent "how to" guidelines from the National Register Division. Neither book gives much detail about procedures for thematic and multiple resource nominations. Guidelines for these may be obtained from either agency upon request.

Understanding how to nominate a resource to the National Register is the first step in a successful application. Placing a resource in the register is a test of skill, determination, and patience. The process can take a year, sometimes longer.

What follows is a summary of how the process works in Pennsylvania. Each state's preservation agency has its own procedures, but they must be in accordance with federal law. Hence, any differences reflect only the variations in each state program; the basic process is the same across the country. The summary below applies particularly to nominations of individual buildings, sites, structures, and objects. Multiple registration procedures—for districts and for thematic and multiple resources—are slightly more complex. In these cases, at least, the applicant will want to work closely with the Bureau for Historic Preservation.

The Steps

1. Historic Resource Form: If the resource appears to satisfy at least one of the National Register criteria and possesses integrity, the applicant can fill out a Pennsylvania Historic Resource Form and submit it to the Bureau for Historic Preservation (BHP). This form and the instruction sheet for completing it can be obtained from the BHP and from many local preservation organizations and agencies. (See Appendix C.)

2. Eligibility and Priority: Within 30 days of receipt, the BHP will review the form for completeness, eligibility, and priority.

   A. Incomplete or technically deficient forms will be returned to the applicant for correction. Properly completed forms will proceed to Step 2B.

   B. The resource is reviewed for integrity and significance against National Register criteria. The applicant will be notified in writing if the resource is deemed ineligible. The applicant may appeal this decision to the BHP. Applications for resources found eligible will proceed to Step 2C.

   C. Eligible resources will be reviewed against "Pennsylvania Priorities for the Processing of National Register Nominations" (see Appendix C). The priorities were developed in 1982 to help make the nomination process more efficient; in recent years, nomination activity in Pennsylvania has mushroomed, partly because of the federal tax incentives for registered properties. The priorities enable the BHP to respond to applications in a timely manner. If the resource has no or low priority, the application may be placed on an indefinite waiting list. If the resource has priority, the applicant will be sent a National Register packet, and the application will move to Step 3.

3. National Register Form: The applicant is responsible for completing a National Register form and returning it to the BHP. If no professional help has been involved to this point, it may be wise to invest in some here. An experienced consultant will produce a concise, convincing application and give advice about photos, floor plans, and other details. (The BHP will provide a list of consultants upon request.) Incomplete, technically deficient nominations are returned to the applicant for revisions. Complete, well-prepared nominations will be scheduled before the National Register Review Committee of the Historic Preservation Board.

4. Owner Notification: By law, the BHP must notify the owner of the nominated resource in writing between 30 and 75 days before the review

committee's meeting date. The owner may concur with or object (by written notarized statement) to the nomination. For the nomination of a historic district with more than 50 property owners, a general notice in one or more local newspapers will suffice. The BHP must also notify "local authorities" (the chief officials of the county and municipality) of its intent to nominate. If the owner or, in the case of a district, a majority of the owners objects, the nomination may still be reviewed by the review committee and recommended for national registration. The resource, however, may not be listed in the register over the objections of its owner. Instead, it may be determined eligible.

5. National Register Review Committee: Generally, the committee meets six times per year to review nominations. Normally there is a minimum 60-day wait from the time the BHP receives a satisfactory nomination until it is put on the agenda. Even that period can vary according to the nomination's priority, the geographic distribution of applications, and the committee's caseload.

The committee may request additional information before it can reach a final decision. Nominations that it finds eligible will be forwarded (along with any written comments or notices of objection submitted to the BHP) to Washington for review by the National Register Division. Applicants and owners of properties the committee finds ineligible are so notified.

6. National Register Review: A notice of the nomination's pending review and a 15-day commenting period is published in the *Federal Register*. If the National Register Division finds the resource eligible, it will be included in the National Register within 45 days of receipt. Eligible resources for which objections were filed will be given a determination of eligibility (DOE), a notice of which shall be published in the *Federal Register*.

7. Notification of Listing: The National Register Division notifies the local legislator and the BHP of a resource's listing. The BHP, in turn, notifies the applicant, the owner, and the chief local public official and forwards a certificate of acceptance.

Except for extraordinary situations—as when a nationally significant resource is in immediate danger—listing a building on the National Register can be complicated and time consuming. At the same time, registration is in itself no guarantee that a resource will be preserved. Private owners are still free to deal with their properties as they please, although government agencies must endeavor to avoid harming registered (and eligible) resources. A listing in the National Register of Historic Places is, nevertheless, to be valued. It gives a historic property the recognition it deserves and may awaken public respect for its preservation.

NATIONAL REGISTER CRITERIA

The quality of significance in American history, architecture, archeology, engineering, and culture is present in districts, sites, buildings, structures, and objects that possess integrity of location, design, setting, materials, workmanship, feeling, and association, and:

A. that are associated with events that have made a significant contribution to the broad patterns of our history; or

B. that are associated with the lives of persons significant in our past; or

C. that embody the distinctive characteristics of a type, period, or method of construction, or that represent the work of a master, or that possess high artistic values, or that represent a significant and distinguishable entity whose components may lack individual distinction; or

D. that have yielded, or may be likely to yield, information important in prehistory or history.

Considerations

Ordinarily, cemeteries, birthplaces, or graves of historical figures, properties owned by religious institutions or used for religious purposes, structures that have been moved from their original locations, reconstructed historic buildings, properties that are primarily commemorative, and properties that have achieved significance within the past 50 years are not considered eligible for the National Register. Such properties will qualify, however, if they are integral parts of districts that do meet the criteria or if they fall within the following categories:

A. a religious property deriving primary significance from architectural or artistic distinction or historical importance; or

B. a building or structure removed from its original location but which is significant primarily for architectural value, or which is the surviving structure most importantly associated with a historic person or event; or

C. a birthplace or grave of a historical figure of outstanding importance if there is no other appropriate site or building directly associated with his productive life; or

D. a cemetery which derives its primary significance from graves of persons of transcendent importance, from age, from distinctive design features, or from association with historic events; or

E. a reconstructed building when accurately executed in a suitable environment and presented in a dignified manner as part of a restoration master plan, and when no other building or structure with the same association has survived; or

F. a property primarily commemorative in intent if design, age, tradition, or symbolic value has invested it with its own historical significance; or

G. a property achieving significance within the past 50 years if it is of exceptional importance.

Source: *The National Register Process in Pennsylvania*

Figure 4–1

*This barn, standing adjacent to the American Revolutionary quarters of General Duportail, a Frenchman on George Washington's staff during the 1777-78 Valley Forge encampment, was slated for demolition. Fortunately, a provision of Tredyffrin Township's Ordinance 206 (which established the township as the Tredyffrin Historical District) required that its demolition be reviewed by the Board of Historical Architectural Review. After the board recommended against issuing a demolition permit, months of negotiation followed, and a plan was devised to stabilize and restore the barn, rather than demolish it. The barn, which is signed and dated "The Federal Barn 1792" on its west gable, was listed in the National Register of Historic Places in 1980 and was subsequently rehabilitated with a grant from the Bureau for Historic Preservation with matching funds chiefly provided by the developer, the Fox Companies. This was all part of the ways and means of preservation.
(Right: John Conti, restoration specialist, pauses during his work on the barn.)*

Photos: Anne H. Cook

Chapter 5
THE WAYS AND MEANS OF PRESERVATION

You've walked by that wisteria-draped Queen Anne mansion and dreamed of garden parties by the gazebo. You've coveted the 18th-century stone cottage since happening upon it along a country road. You've marveled at the exquisite terra-cotta detail on an old office building downtown.

But these treasures may not endure for you or future generations to enjoy. The mansion could be sacrificed for a parking lot; the cottage eradicated by a fast-food restaurant; the office building replaced by a high-rise.

Fortunately, preserving resources like these is no mystery. It's a matter of education—knowing the techniques and how to apply them; of preparation—planning in advance and being ready to act when the time is right; and of commitment—by caring individuals and their communities.

This chapter explains some of the basic tools available for preservation: survey, planning, local regulation, negotiation and mediation, and funding. Because the preservation easement and the investment tax credit are more complex techniques, they are discussed in the two chapters that follow.

SURVEY

The historic survey can be an activity of far-reaching impact. At the local level, it can result in an increased public awareness of the community's historic resources, a historic registration effort, historic district designation, or revisions to the comprehensive plan and zoning ordinance.

Organizing and conducting the local survey according to state and national standards will increase its impact. The survey data can be more readily integrated into existing lists and plans for historic resource protection. The survey of Lansdowne Borough, for example, had a number of impacts.

Lansdowne house on Windermere Avenue in an area proposed for historic district designation.

A street scene in the Lansdowne business district at the turn of the century.

By the time Lansdowne Borough in Delaware County was incorporated out of Upper Darby Township in 1893, it had changed from a small crossroads farm village to an up-and-coming suburban community of 875 people. Located only six miles west of center-city Philadelphia, it was, by the mid-19th century, well served by road and rail. Two highways, the Darby Radnor Road (Lansdowne Avenue) and Baltimore Pike, intersected near its center. A railroad line between Philadelphia and West Chester roughly paralleled Baltimore Pike.

Like many of Philadelphia's outlying communities of that period, Lansdowne was something of a resort. Hotels and boardinghouses were built to accommodate travelers, while the rising middle class took up permanent residence in spacious Shingle-style houses on tree-shaded lots away from the crowded city. By the early 20th century, Lansdowne Borough, with its amenities ranging from comfortable housing to convenient transportation, had become an attractive place in which to live.

Lansdowne remained relatively stable until the 1970s; then its population started to drop. Between 1970 and 1980 the population fell to 11,891, a decrease of 15.6 percent. During the same period, in which a number of older houses were torn down or adapted for commercial uses, the number of housing units declined as well, by 3.3 percent. By 1981, enough of the borough's late-Victorian homes had been demolished or converted to cause some residents considerable alarm. Concerned about Lansdowne's future and eager to have a say in the planning process, they formed the Greater Lansdowne Civic Association in 1981. Many of its 200 or so members were newcomers to the borough, attracted by its old-fashioned atmosphere and good buys in housing, and interested in preserving those qualities.

With the association's endorsement, a volunteer committee embarked on a survey of Lansdowne's older buildings. Their goal, according to Susanna Morikawa, chairman, "was to educate, to increase the community's awareness of the value of the older homes. We also wanted input in the borough's comprehensive plan and zoning policies." The survey committee soon met with the Delaware County Planning Department's survey coordinator, Nancy Webster. She provided forms and film for the survey and recommended procedures approved by the Bureau for Historic Preservation, the state agency that oversees historic surveys in the Commonwealth. The committee adopted her suggestions and plunged into the project. With the survey firmly on track, borough council took notice and gave the group an official go-ahead. Council needed historical information for a comprehensive plan then in preparation. It was also interested in what the recommendations of the committee would be.

Now that the field work has been done, the volunteers have tallied their findings. Among the "gems" uncovered during the survey were a house lavishly decorated with literary allusions (the house belonged to an author and editor who originated a popular teddy bear series in 1906), a house owned by a countess and complete with a Roman bath, examples of prominent architects' work, and the makings of a historic district. The committee is now preparing a short survey history of Lansdowne to be published in two parts.

As shown in Lansdowne, surveys are a highly effective way to raise public and private awareness of community development, past and future. The historic survey, however, did not originate at the local level; organized efforts to identify historic resources began with the federal government.

Federal Surveys

Historic survey as an activity of the federal government was inaugurated in 1933 with the Historic American Buildings Survey (HABS). Then a relief program for unemployed architects, draftsmen, and photographers, the HABS program viewed the survey as a method of historical inquiry and documentation. HABS was administered by the National Park Service, an agency established in 1916 within the Department of the Interior. Under the Historic Sites Act of 1935, which gave the department the responsibility for national preservation policy and programs (including historic surveys), HABS became a long-range program, operating between 1933 and 1941. It was revived in 1957 and continues to the present, operating in cooperation with the Library of Congress, the American Institute of Architects, state preservation offices, and others. Gradually HABS's emphasis has shifted from recording buildings of national significance to collecting data on all construction types and use types from all historical periods and regions of the country. In 1969, a companion program, the Historic American Engineering Record (HAER), was begun within the National Park Service to document resources of industrial and engineering significance.

Strafford Railroad Station, Chester County. A property included in the Historic American Buildings Survey (HABS) and listed in the National Register in 1984.

Statewide Surveys

In the 1960s, surveys became more than a form of historical research; they became a part of the planning process. The preservation mandate given to the Department of the Interior in 1935 was expanded by the National Historic Preservation Act of 1966. The act established a "national register of districts, sites, buildings, structures, and objects" and authorized federal funding for comprehensive statewide historic surveys and plans. Under this program, federal funds are made available through state historic preservation offices on a matching percentage basis to fund surveys and other planning projects at the state and local levels. In Pennsylvania, the Bureau for Historic Preservation of the Pennsylvania Historical and Museum Commission administers the program. Funding levels, which are set annually by the federal government, have suffered in recent years from uncertainties and cutbacks. Although reduced somewhat in scope, federally sponsored surveys in Pennsylvania and other states continue. Besides surveying state-owned resources such as bridges and park buildings, the bureau funds local surveys. It is estimated that more than 40 percent of the Commonwealth, including parts of Philadelphia, Pittsburgh, and numerous counties, has been surveyed through this program.

Local Surveys

Local surveys, like the one undertaken in Lansdowne, have been completed or are underway throughout the nation. To maximize their effect and regularize their procedures, most are coordinated with state or county preservation offices, which in turn operate under federal aegis.

The motives behind surveys, and their results, vary considerably. Concord Township (Delaware County), having already registered several houses and two districts, is working on a survey to supplement a new township history; the West Whiteland Township (Chester County) Historical Commission participated in the Chester County Historic Sites Survey (1979–82) and then, in one comprehensive application, nominated more than 50 properties and one historic district to the National Register of Historic Places; the Bucks County Conservancy began its first survey in 1972 and three years later established the Bucks County Register of Historic Places to recognize and promote public awareness of the county's historically or architecturally significant buildings; a survey by architectural historian Alice Schooler, commissioned in 1978 by the West Chester Borough (Chester County) Board of Historical Review, is proving invaluable to the borough in its comprehensive planning; design guidelines were drafted for Norristown Borough (Montgomery County) in conjunction with a survey undertaken there in 1980.

"Hillcrest" in Berwyn, Pennsylvania. Another building surveyed by HABS.

Surveys also provide a basis for the public to protect endangered resources. Hastily conceived, last-minute attempts to save historic buildings are more easily avoided if their historical and architectural significance have been assessed previously in official surveys. If, for example, a proposed development threatens an old farmhouse, its inclusion in an official survey may lead to negotiations with the developer or to the exploration of options for preserving it. On the other hand, last-ditch efforts mounted to halt construction plans that have been developed over a period of months, or even years, often result in bitter, credibility-damaging battles. A community that has both surveyed *and* prioritized its resources is better equipped to make intelligent decisions about public expenditures to preserve those resources.

Along with lessening, if not eliminating, the hit-or-miss approach toward preservation, comprehensive surveys tend to bring to light previously overlooked resources. All too often, valuable but lesser-known buildings have been lost while attention is focused on a few well-liked and obvious ones. Recent surveys, for example, have included (besides the ever-popular Colonial and Georgian houses) industrial structures, agricultural complexes, and early-20th-century buildings.

Organizing the Survey

As shown above, local surveys vary according to the needs and resources of individual communities. Certain concerns and procedures, however, are common to each undertaking. Most important, local surveys should be organized to complement, supplement, and coordinate with the survey programs administered by the various state historic preservation offices. This is not to discredit the importance or effectiveness of local efforts; rather, surveys are more useful in the long run if their methods, data collection, analysis, photography, and mapping adhere to an accepted standard. The bureau sets forth the Commonwealth's standards in its *Guidelines for Historic Resource Surveys in Pennsylvania* (October 1982). The book discusses procedures developed in accordance with national standards and criteria for surveys. A more general introduction to historic surveys is provided in a U.S. Department of the Interior publication, *Guidelines for Local Surveys: A Basis for Preservation Planning* (November 1977).

Within this framework, local surveys can be tailored to fit a community's objectives. They can be comprehensive (recording every historic resource about 50 years old or older); thematic (working around themes like those suggested in Figure 5-1); or preliminary (only locating and mapping resources, with research and setting priorities to follow at some future date). Regardless

THEMES AND RESOURCES FOR HISTORIC SURVEYS

THEME	HISTORIC RESOURCES
Architecture	buildings by well-known architects, buildings of exceptional architectural merit
Art	structures associated with artists, museums, theaters
Commerce	office buildings, warehouses, stores, diners
Community Planning	planned communities, parks, gardens
Early Settlement	log structures, forts
Education	schools, universities, libraries
Government	post offices, courthouses, city halls
Industry	mills, furnaces, factories
Military	arsenals, forts, battle sites
Religion	churches, meetinghouses, synagogues
Residences	houses, apartments, hotels
Science and Medicine	hospitals, clinics, laboratories
Technology	bridges, dams, tunnels
Transportation	railroad stations, canals, gas stations, locomotives, lighthouses

Source: *Guidelines for Historic Resource Surveys in Pennsylvania*

Figure 5-1

of scope, local surveys usually use a survey form for recording data and observations. The official state survey form is found in Appendix C. In the course of the Chester County Historic Sites Survey, the Brandywine Conservancy developed the four-page survey form shown as Figure 5-2. This "Architectural Inventory Form" has proven handy for field work and site visits, both for that survey and for subsequent ones. Information recorded on the form (site plan, building shape, roof profile, type and location of chimneys, and so forth) can be extracted and transferred with little difficulty to the more formal state survey form mentioned above.

While it is clear that surveys require substantial effort, organization, and funding, it is also clear that their value at the local level can be considerable. For example, consider that house in Lansdowne decorated with literary allusions. As a result of Lansdowne's survey, the civic association and borough council have been alerted to its existence; a description and photo of it are on file with the Delaware County Planning Department; and the Bureau for Historic Preservation and federal planners will see it on their lists when working on a project in the Lansdowne area. Remember that all of this began with the enthusiasm of a few volunteers, who couldn't bear to lose another historic landmark.

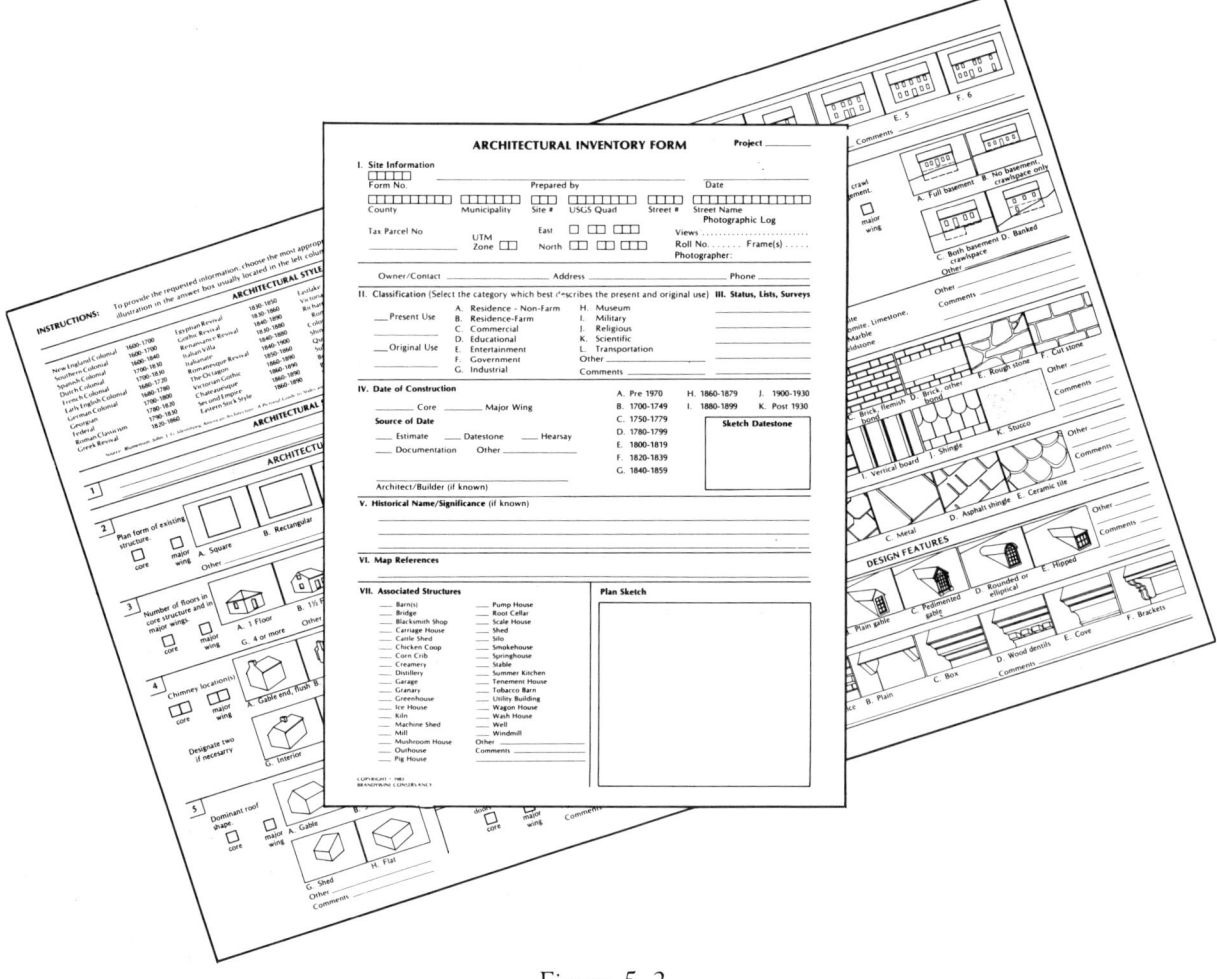

Figure 5-2

Oley Township's historic character is tied closely to its farmland.

PLANNING

Historic surveys and community planning go hand in hand. Obviously, each is individually useful; when coordinated, though, their benefits to the community can be multiplied. Once its resources worthy of preservation have been identified, the community is in a strong position to plan strategies to preserve them. Along the way, some tough choices may be confronted. The importance of saving certain buildings may need to be weighed against other factors, such as improving traffic patterns, saving agricultural land, providing a mix of housing opportunities, or minimizing the threat of flooding. The local comprehensive planning process can serve as a useful forum for all interest groups—preservationists, businessmen, farmers, developers—to have their say and to work together in charting a reasonable course for the future. In an open, broadly participatory planning program, reconciliation of seemingly irresolvable positions often can be achieved without severely jeopardizing any single objective.

Main Street in the Village of Oley.

Seldom is a community that cares about its historic resources in the enviable position that Oley Township, Berks County, was in 1980. In that year, a survey that identified 300 historic resources (primarily farmsteads) was completed by the Berks County Conservancy in cooperation with Pennsylvania's Bureau for Historic Preservation. In the same year, the National Trust for Historic Preservation selected the township as one of two communities in the nation for its Rural Project, a demonstration study for rural resource conservation. One of the outcomes of that study was the listing of the entire township in the National Register of Historic Places in 1983.

With these two important projects accomplished, the township then undertook a planning study to identify ways it could protect and enhance its historic resources. The planning study also focused on ways to preserve farmland; with 80 percent of the 24 square miles in Oley used for agriculture, the character of the historic landscape was rooted strongly in the continuation of farming. Policies were also devised to protect water and geologic resources and to guide future land use.

By the conclusion of the planning study, the project steering committee had become quite specific in its recommendations concerning historic resources. Using categories of significance established in the National Register nomination, the study recommended that the township direct its energies toward preserving resources in the top three groups, with maximum protection and incentives reserved for the first, or "exceptional" resources, category. The study proposed that the township (1) adopt a delay-of-demolition ordinance geared to the relative significance of its buildings; (2) institute architectural review of changes to buildings located in its one compact village area; (3) consider an advisory architectural review procedure for certain other "landmark" buildings; (4) develop standards in the zoning and subdivision/ land development ordinances to lessen the visual impact of new construction on certain buildings; (5) provide incentives for adaptive reuse of the "exceptional" resources; (6) implement or suggest a public education effort about these preservation policies; and (7) encourage and help its owners of historic properties to use tax incentives for historic preservation.

Although such a comprehensive list of policies may be difficult, perhaps impossible, to fully implement in the near future, the blueprint is there. Priorities among these actions have been proposed, and the preservation recommendations have been offered in the broader context of comprehensive planning goals.

LOCAL REGULATION

Local government's role in historic preservation is growing. In communities where there has been a tradition of citizen involvement—evidenced by an active historical society, for example—that role may be minimal. Increasingly, however, municipalities are taking a more active stance by planning for preservation or sponsoring historic surveys and registrations. Some local governments also use their regulatory powers for historic preservation. Local regulation can take several forms. It can be a direct exercise of the government's "police powers," as with the historic district ordinance; or regulation can provide incentives for historic preservation, through special zoning provisions, for instance. While local regulation is one of the most seldom used and most frequently controversial methods of preservation, it can be one of the most effective.

Historic Districts

Historic district laws have been the most visible form of local regulation. Although these laws vary from state to state and, within each state, from municipality to municipality, they have a common purpose: to regulate building activity, alterations to (and especially demolitions of) historic buildings, and new construction in historic districts. "Historic district" in these ordinances does not necessarily mean district in the National Register sense; rather, it refers to the area regulated by the ordinance. Some districts under local ordinance are also in the National Register.

The first historic district law in the United States was enacted in 1931 in

Charleston, South Carolina. Six years later, the Commission Council of New Orleans passed a historic district ordinance regulating the city's famous Vieux Carré (French Quarter). These first city historic district laws were followed by various state historic district laws. Pennsylvania enacted a statewide historic district law, Act 167, in 1961. Act 167 authorizes all municipalities (except Philadelphia, the state's only first-class city) to create historic districts within their boundaries and appoint boards of historical architectural review to oversee the "erection, reconstruction, alteration, restoration, demolition, or razing" of buildings within the districts. Since 1961, more than 35 Pennsylvania municipalities have adopted historic district ordinances in accordance with Act 167. Only one, the Borough of Upland (Delaware County), has since rescinded its ordinance. Lower Merion Township (Montgomery County), in contrast, has added two districts since designating its first, the Harriton Historic District, in 1962.

In truth, Lower Merion's creation of the Harriton Historic District in 1962 by Ordinance No. 1373 was probably not essential to that district's preservation. There is only one significant building—the Harriton House—in the small, 16½-acre historic district. Furthermore, it is township property, and the Harriton Association, which had formed in the 1960s to help raise funds for the acquisition, restoration, maintenance, and operation of the house, looks after it. Harriton House, built in 1704, was once the home of Charles Thomson, who served as Secretary of the Continental Congress from 1774 to 1789. Although the ordinance established a board of historical architectural review (HARB) to review changes to the house, rarely was there reason for the board to meet. Lower Merion's experience with historic district regulation, however, proved to be an asset in a later and far more ambitious undertaking.

Bicentennial fever gripped the Delaware Valley in 1975. Residents of Lower Merion, imbued with its 300 years of history and magnificent architecture, ranging from the 1690 John Roberts House to late-19th-century architectural tours de force at Bryn Mawr College, were not spared. When resident Betty Brockett proposed that the Gladwyne Civic Association pursue historic designation for Gladwyne and the area around Mill Creek, the association set up a committee to investigate further. Under chairman Edward D. Lewis, the committee researched the subject and concurred with Brockett's suggestion. The committee presented its findings to the township commissioners and was told to dig a little deeper. In May 1979, the Gladwyne Civic Association hired Gloria Becker, fresh out of graduate school with a master's degree in American civilization, as a consultant.

Over the next 12 months, at a desk provided by the township planning department, Gloria worked toward the registration of the two districts and revision of Ordinance No. 1373. The proposed Gladwyne, or Merion Square, Historic District encompassed over 100 buildings, some of which dated back to the 1790 crossroads village of Merion Square; others were products of the early 20th century. The Mill Creek district, in contrast, contained 7 or 8 houses, and its 23.8-acre size was roughly one third that of the Gladwyne district.

According to Gloria, getting the two districts on the National Register was easier than convincing their residents to accept the local historic district ordinance. They didn't like the idea of needing approval for exterior changes to their houses. Stormy public hearings were followed by special meetings,

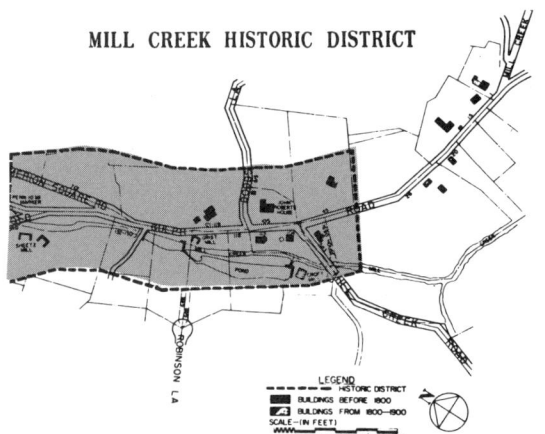
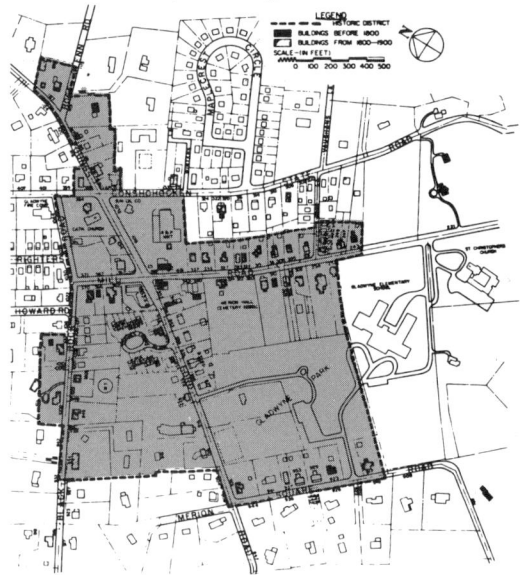
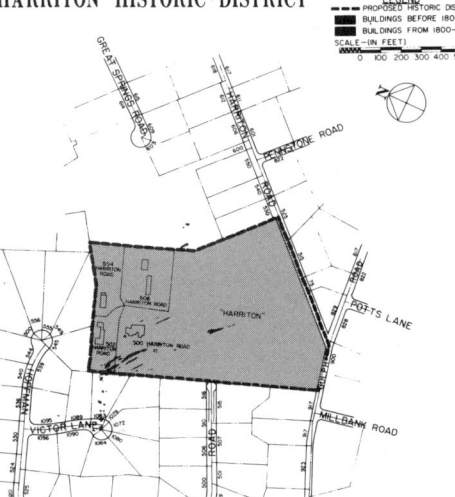

Maps: Lower Merion Township Planning Commission

Photos: Board of Historical Architectural Review (HARB), Lower Merion Township

Lower Merion Township's three historic districts.

flyers, notices, and more hearings. Finally, on April 16, 1980, feeling that community opposition had ebbed significantly, Lower Merion's Board of Commissioners amended the existing ordinance in its entirety with Ordinance No. 1902, "Historic Districts." This ordinance applies to all three of Lower Merion's historic districts: Gladwyne, Mill Creek, and Harriton.

Not surprisingly, since that night in April, work has picked up for members of HARB. They now have regularly scheduled monthly meetings. A member of the planning department usually sits in. Even though the current chairman and vice-chairman are both architects, there are problems with design review, especially of new construction in the Gladwyne Historic District. Recently the board published a brochure, "Guide for Property Owners within the Historic Districts," which explains how the ordinance works. A manual on design-review guidelines is in the offing.

From regulation of a one-building historic district to three districts encompassing more than 150 buildings, the township's active role in historic preservation has expanded significantly in the past 20 years. Lower Merion is not alone; its willingness to assume a regulatory function in historic preservation is shared by Lancaster, York, Media, Harrisburg, Gettysburg, Allentown, Reading, and numerous other municipalities across the state and the nation. (See Appendix C for a Philadelphia-area listing.)

While historic district ordinances must be tailored to each municipality's needs, in Pennsylvania they all adhere to the basic framework established in Act 167. (See Appendix C for a model ordinance.)

1. The ordinance creates and defines one or more historic districts. Whether by map reference or by legal description, the ordinance establishes the area to be regulated. The ordinance does not take effect until the historical significance of the district is certified by the Pennsylvania Historical and Museum Commission. (Procedures for obtaining this certification are similar to those for nominating a district to the National Register.)

2. The ordinance requires that the governing body appoint a board of historical architectural review (HARB). Act 167 stipulates that HARB have among its minimum of five members a building inspector, a licensed real estate broker, and a registered architect. The act also sets general rules for HARB's conduct of business.

3. HARB is charged with the review of proposed changes in the district and must counsel the governing body on the appropriateness of those changes. Proposed changes include the "erection, reconstruction, alteration, restoration, demolition, or razing" of any building in the district. Only changes affecting those architectural features which can be seen from "a public street or way" can be evaluated for appropriateness. HARB's review is activated by an application for a building permit for one or more of these activities in the historic district. It must hold a meeting to review those changes and then advise the governing body of its findings.

4. Taking into consideration HARB's recommendations, at a public meeting the governing body issues or denies a certificate of appropriateness for the proposed changes. Because HARB's powers are purely advisory, the governing body is not bound by its recommendations. If the governing body denies the application, it must indicate what changes in the plans and specifications would make them acceptable. Act 167

Sketches of three progressive changes to the facade of one building from Old Allentown Houses: Design Guidelines for an Historic District *(Allentown, Pennsylvania, 1979).*

provides for appeals by the applicant, and it states that the governing body can enforce the district regulations as it would any "other building, zoning or planning legislation or regulations."

Historic district ordinances are arguably the strongest form of local regulation for historic preservation. Because they permit the governing body to regulate the appearance of private property, these ordinances can lead to controversies. There is a small body of Pennsylvania case law on Act 167 historic district ordinances. One case involved the demolition of a building in the city of York (*First Presbyterian Church of York v. City of York,* 1976) and another involved the demolition of a building in Harrisburg (*Cleckner v. Harrisburg,* 1979). In each case, the governing body refused to issue a certificate of appropriateness for the demolition of a building in its historic district, and in each case the decision was upheld in court.

In 1978 the U.S. Supreme Court handed down an opinion that recognized the constitutional authority of municipal governments to preserve historic buildings through regulation. In the case of *Penn Central Transportation Co. v. New York City,* the Court affirmed the right of New York City's Landmark Preservation Commission to deny the owners of Grand Central Terminal a permit to construct a 53-story building on top of this architectural landmark. Although the *Penn Central* decision involved a landmark rather than a historic district, it set a national precedent for the exercise of municipal "police power" over historic properties. In their review of architectural changes to historic buildings, many local governments, like Lower Merion, use published design guidelines. Some design guidelines used in Pennsylvania are included in For Further Reading at the back of the book.

Zoning for Historic Preservation

The primary objective of an Act 167 historic district ordinance is to impose architectural and aesthetic controls over existing buildings and, in many cases, future construction. While such controls are frequently fraught with problems of subjective judgment as to the appropriateness of designs or paint colors, the establishment of historic districts frequently overlooks much more important questions about the appropriateness of the underlying zoning code to the achievement of historic preservation objectives. Should commercial or industrial zoning be permitted within residential areas of a district? Should buildings that served commercial or industrial uses in an earlier era be permitted to continue those zoning classifications when present-day commercial or industrial uses would have substantially different environmental impacts on neighboring residential uses? Off-street parking is a necessity for such uses, and yet frequently an impossibility in historic districts. In addition to the parking difficulties that some commercial uses cause for neighborhood residents, some uses (bars, for example) may attract people who have little respect for the properties or the sleeping patterns of neighborhood residents.

There is an important distinction between the Act 167 historic district ordinance and historic zoning. In establishing a historic district under the authority of Act 167, a municipality does not zone the area in the sense of permitted uses, lot sizes, dimensions, and so forth. Rather, an Act 167 district acts as an "overlay" on the existing, or base, zoning map. The historic district provisions concerning physical changes to the exteriors of buildings (including demolition) do not affect the base zoning of the area. For ease of administration, however, Act 167 ordinances frequently are included within a municipality's general zoning ordinance.

Under the Pennsylvania Municipalities Planning Code (Section 605(2) [vi]), local governments can enact zoning tailored to "places having unique historical or patriotic interest or value." In this kind of zoning district, the use and area regulations might be drafted to ensure compatibility between present-day activities and the historic nature of the area. For example, the nationally registered crossroads village of Dilworthtown (Birmingham Township, Chester County) is zoned for "colonial inns, . . . cottage industries, . . . museum(s), . . ." and small commercial uses that will not detract from its historic character. The township's zoning ordinance contains a general prerequisite for review, which states: "The proposed use shall be compatible with the preservation and protection of areas and buildings of unique and historic interest in the Township, and with commercial purposes consistent with their historic significance and early use."

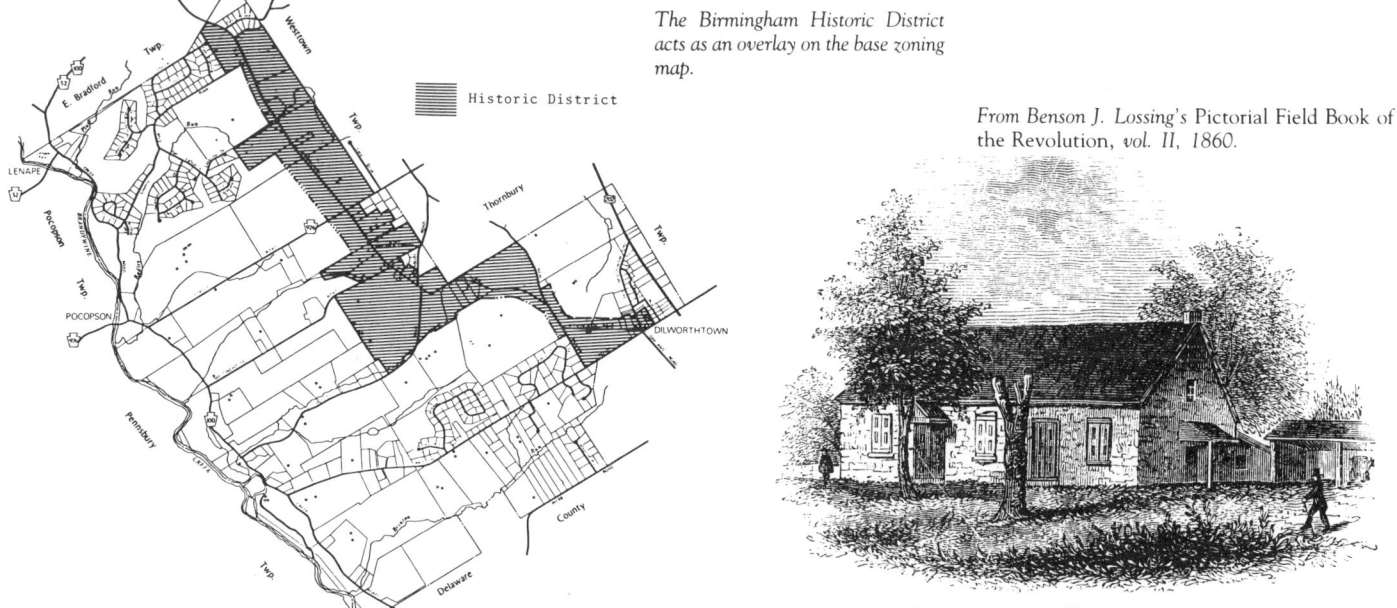

The Birmingham Historic District acts as an overlay on the base zoning map.

From Benson J. Lossing's Pictorial Field Book of the Revolution, vol. II, 1860.

BIRMINGHAM MEETING-HOUSE.[2]

Figure 5–3

In addition, area and bulk regulations for Dilworthtown reflect the configuration of the village; lots can be quite small, with minimal front, side, and rear yards, and no building can exceed two stories in height. Outside the village, the base zoning permits the more usual residential and commercial uses and larger lot sizes. But both the village and the corridor along Birmingham Road to the north (see Figure 5-3) are governed by Act 167 historic district provisions. The base zoning of this Birmingham Historic District, then, varies from Historic Commercial to Residential-Agricultural to Residential-1 and Residential-2 land.

Protecting Landmarks

Not all historic buildings, of course, lie within historic districts. Exceptional buildings, or "landmarks," may be found scattered throughout a municipality. Frequently they are intruded upon by new development or incompatible uses; some are threatened with integrity-damaging alterations.

While historic neighborhoods in cities and towns often have problems relating to permissive zoning codes that allow overly intensive use of buildings, a different problem frequently arises in suburban communities when older mansions, or landmarks and their grounds, are undergoing change. A nonresidential use that would permit restoration of the buildings and grounds with only minimal impact on the neighborhood might not be permitted by right or by discretion in the zoning code. Similarly, where the only economically feasible means to restore a white-elephant mansion is by splitting it into several dwelling units, zoning regulations may prohibit conversions of this type, and neighbors may oppose a zoning variance even though they wish to see the house preserved.

Part of the problem in both of the above examples is that historic pres-

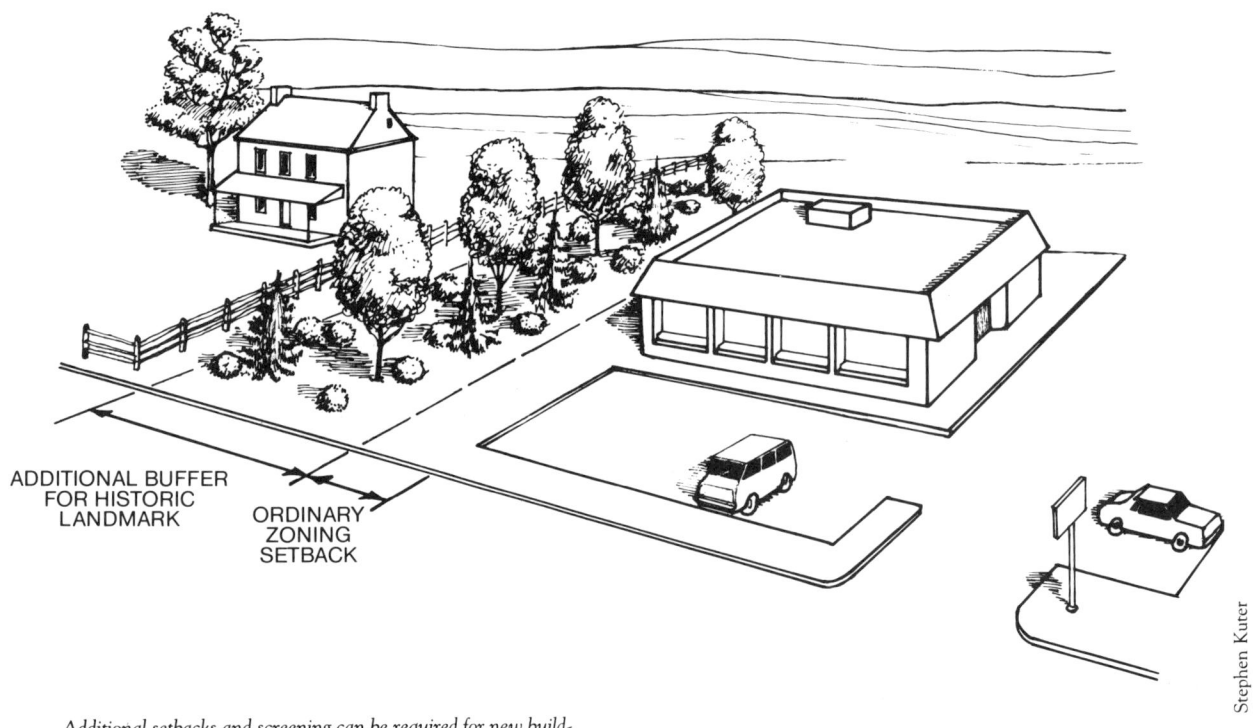

Additional setbacks and screening can be required for new buildings located close to existing landmarks.

ervation has rarely been addressed in suburban and rural areas in the zoning code revision process. As a consequence, municipal officials are often reluctant to permit changes to accommodate a particular property owner when there is inadequate time to consider long-term ramifications. If historic surveys were reviewed during the updating of comprehensive plans and of zoning codes—and the special problems of the community's historic buildings were carefully evaluated—appropriate zoning regulations could then be drafted.

Although there is strong interest in protecting landmarks in Pennsylvania, there is no specific enabling legislation like Act 167 (for historic districts) which applies to landmarks. Given the U.S. Supreme Court's precedent-setting *Penn Central* decision, however, local governments can initiate local landmark regulation with considerable confidence.

One avenue might be to adopt an official "Historic Resources Map," which would identify all the landmarks warranting special consideration. To ward off charges of "arbitrariness," this map should use information obtained from a comprehensive historic survey. Then the building code and zoning, subdivision/land development, and other ordinances can be tailored to maximize protection of these identified resources. For example, the subdivision ordinance might require extra screening and buffering when a new development falls within a certain distance of a landmark. The zoning ordinance might permit landmarks a greater diversity or intensity of uses than normally allowed, provided there is no negative impact on their architectural integrity or the surrounding neighborhood. There are dozens of ways local governments can tailor their regulations to protect landmarks. A comprehensive survey, priorities for preservation, and an informed and willing governing body are the minimum prerequisites.

Delay of Demolition

By adopting what is known as a delay-of-demolition ordinance, municipalities can "buy" time for historic buildings slated for demolition. The provisions to delay demolition can be adopted as a separate ordinance or as an amendment to the building code. Usually the delay process is activated by an application for a demolition permit. If the building to be demolished is on a list or map of protected properties, the demolition permit would not be issued until a certain period of time had elapsed. This delay would permit an authorized party (the local historical commission, perhaps) to discuss alternatives to demolition with the property owner. If the building to be demolished sits on a tract proposed for subdivision or land development, negotiations during this period might lead to site design revisions that would eliminate the need for demolition. A property owner apprised of the tax incentives for rehabilitation (see Chapter 7) might find them attractive enough to save the building and rehabilitate it. If no agreement or compromise solution has been reached by the end of the designated period of delay (which might range from 30 to 90 days), the demolition could proceed. There is no authority under current Pennsylvania law for municipalities to prohibit the demolition of landmarks.

New Castle County, Delaware, has an ordinance (see Appendix C) that allows a 10-day delay of demolition for all buildings older than 75 years and an additional 60-day delay for those the Historic Review Board finds to be of "historic significance." A maximum 6-month delay of demolition is permitted for all buildings appearing on or eligible for the New Castle County Register of Historic and Architectural Heritage (which includes all state and nationally registered buildings). Richard Jett, the county's historic preservation planner, has nevertheless noticed a trend away from demolition: "We are getting more applications for historic zoning and for buildings to be retained instead of being torn down. This reflects in part the availability of federal tax incentives for rehabilitation."

NEGOTIATION AND MEDIATION

As litigation costs rise and as courts are increasingly incapable of resolving complex environmental disputes, parties to such disputes are becoming more open to negotiating or mediating their differences. (Mediation is negotiation with the help of a neutral intermediary.) Negotiation and mediation are conflict resolution techniques that can be used to balance historic preservation objectives against other social and economic objectives. Instead of tying up the parties in a protracted and embittered court battle, in which someone else (the judge) makes the decisions, negotiation or mediation allows the parties to hash out their own creative remedies to the real issues at hand. For those weary of the "public hearing–agency decision–court challenge" syndrome, negotiation and mediation can offer a welcome relief *and* better decisions.

A case in point: In Charlottesville, Virginia, a negotiation involving neighbors, preservationists, and hospital officials prevented some 19th-century houses from being demolished for a parking lot. The negotiated agreement, unlike a litigated settlement, could be an inventive one: The proceeds from the sale of the preserved houses would help pay for the parking lot. Where and how would the lot be located? In the combined back yards of those same houses.

Negotiated solutions to disputes are not new to the historic preservation arena. Thomas F. King, director of the Office of Cultural Resource Preservation of the Advisory Council on Historic Preservation, points to the Section 106 consultation process in a 1984 article in the journal *Social Impact Assessment*. Under this process, any federal agency engaging in an activity potentially damaging to a historic site must sit down with the state historic preservation officer, other relevant parties of interest, and the Advisory Council to try to reach an agreement on ways of avoiding or minimizing the damage. The council assumes an impartial stance in these negotiations, much like a mediator. (Although council staff members are largely preservation experts, under Section 106 they explicitly view themselves as balancers of preservation and development interests.)

King points to several examples of mediation under the Section 106 process, one involving the Colorado Fuel and Iron industrial complex in Trenton, New Jersey. Eligible for the National Register and slated for demolition, the complex was to be replaced with a new supermarket and shopping center. The neighboring community strongly opposed the project. Writes King in the *Social Impact Assessment* article: "The Advisory Council's process brought all sides 'to the table,' initially with Council mediation, later by themselves. The result was redesign of the project to reduce the extent of demolition, preserve and rehabilitate part of the complex for use by the community for shops, food marketing keyed to local needs, and neighborhood services, and reorientation of the shopping center to fit more effectively into the existing street pattern and use of neighborhood space. These results were embodied in a Memorandum of Agreement, and the project is now proceeding with

Negotiation may sometimes be the best way to resolve historic preservation conflicts.

every evidence of satisfaction by all concerned."

The interest the Advisory Council has in negotiation and mediation is shared by the National Trust for Historic Preservation. In an interview for this book, Gary Wilburn, former assistant general counsel at the trust, explained: "The trust believes that preservationists and developers are finding more common ground, for example in the rehabilitation of historic structures. In this context, negotiation and mediation are useful tools that everyone should know about and that should be tried in appropriate circumstances. The trust intends to spread the word through written material, conference presentations, and so on."

Historic preservation disputes are particularly suitable for negotiation, since they characteristically involve a range of bargaining points and great potential for creative solutions. The Institute for Environmental Negotiation in Virginia has explored the idea extensively, and states in the Spring/Summer 1982 issue of *The Mediator:* "Successful negotiation depends upon the development of a number of alternative proposals and possible trade-offs. . . . Given the possibilities of re-design, adaptive use and transfer of development rights, the effort to combine preservation with compatible development provides an excellent opportunity for exploring creative alternatives."

What does all this mean for the local preservationist who is searching for a way to preserve a threatened historic site or district? First, negotiation or mediation works only when all parties are willing to compromise and each has some leverage on the others. It does not work when a legal precedent is needed, when one party feels it can win in court and intends to "stay the course" regardless of cost or delay, or when non-negotiable values or philosophical principles are paramount in any party's mind.

But in situations where negotiation or mediation is a feasible and attractive alternative, the opportunities are there. On the local level, for example, the Institute for Environmental Negotiation (in a May 1982 article in *Historic Preservation* by Elizabeth Waters) suggests: "Multi-party negotiation could

Collins Mill and race, 1974. The mill received a new roof under the "Jobs Bill" program.

also become part of the review process of local boards of architectural review. Particularly when faced with difficult decisions, boards could convene negotiating sessions to attempt to formulate responses acceptable to all. This, incidentally, would act to expand the influence and effectiveness of such boards considerably."

FUNDING

Sooner or later, most preservation organizations must grapple with the problem of funding—how to acquire enough money to get projects off the ground or keep them going. Foundation sources can be found in the *Foundation Directory* and similar reference publications available in local libraries. Corporations can also be excellent sources of support, and individual gifts can be solicited. Besides other fund-raising efforts, such as auctions, fairs, and house tours, there are a limited number of public funding sources to consider.

U.S. Department of the Interior

A major source of funding for historic preservation was established by the National Historic Preservation Act of 1966. Every year, federal moneys are allocated to each state from the National Historic Preservation Fund for surveys and planning and for the preservation, acquisition, or "development" (restoration and rehabilitation) of historic resources that are listed in or determined to be eligible for the National Register. In recent years, the grants have been given primarily for surveys (historic and archeological) and for planning activities like National Register nominations.

In Pennsylvania, the grants are administered by the Bureau for Historic Preservation (BHP). They can be awarded to both public and private applicants and are usually available on a 50 percent matching basis. Work done before the approval of the grant application is ineligible for funding. Application forms and detailed information about the process can be obtained from the BHP.

The year 1983 was unusual for preservation funding because for the first time in many years, federal grants were given for "bricks and mortar" work. Under the 1983 "Jobs Bill" (P.L. 98-8, March 24, 1983), $25 million was targeted for the National Historic Preservation Fund, and grants were then apportioned to each state. Only properties listed in the National Register could be rehabilitated, restored, or stabilized with "Jobs Bill" funds, which the recipient had to match. Working under a tight timetable, the BHP launched 16 projects in Pennsylvania under this program, among them a new roof and other improvements for the Collins Mill (see Chapter 4), the restoration and cleaning of 10 stained-glass windows in a mansion in Erie, and the rehabilitation of the 1883 Struther's Library Theater in Warren. Given the success of the "Jobs Bill" program, which in Pennsylvania created more than 250 full- and part-time jobs and stimulated more than $700,000 of private investment, similar programs may receive federal support in the future.

Community Development Block Grants

Public funding of historic preservation projects has been augmented in recent years through the Community Development Block Grant program (CDBG). This program was established under Title I of the 1974 Housing and Community Development Act. It is administered by the U.S. Department of Housing and Urban Development (HUD).

Eight-Arch Bridge. A CDBG-supported restoration effort by the Bucks County Conservancy. The 180-year-old bridge is to serve as the centerpiece for a passive recreational park along the Neshaminy Creek.

Eight-Arch Bridge. Reconstruction work on a severely deteriorated bridge footing.

Designed as a flexible funding tool for community development, the CDBG uses "block" rather than "categorical" grants. Funds can be allocated in numerous ways, but they must be used for at least one of the program's three main objectives: (1) to benefit low- and moderate-income households and neighborhoods; (2) to eliminate slums or blight; and (3) to answer an immediate threat to the health and welfare of the community. Under these guidelines, historic preservation can be an eligible activity.

CDBG funds can be used for neighborhood preservation (including housing rehabilitation) in historically significant areas, such as historic districts. Individual historic properties, either "blighted" or threatened by deterioration, can be acquired and restored or rehabilitated with CDBG funds. Properties listed in the National Register are in the strongest position to attract these grants. The funds can also be used to match other federal or state grants for activities such as preservation plans and historic surveys. The list of CDBG-supported preservation projects in the lower Delaware Valley includes work done on the Thomas Massey house, the outbuildings at the Thomas Leiper house, and the Old Central School in Delaware County; the Gunkle Mill, the Wisner-Rapp and Barns-Brinton houses, and the Birmingham Octagonal School in Chester County; the Bolton Mansion, the Moravian Tile Works, and the Eight-Arch Bridge in Bucks County; and the Pennypacker Mansion, Loller Academy, and Dewees Tavern in Montgomery County.

CDBG grants can be obtained by state, county, and local governments and can be passed on to nonprofit organizations. Unlike the Department of the Interior grants (discussed above), the CDBG grants do not require a local match.

Revolving Funds

A revolving fund can be one of the most timely and flexible sources of preservation funding. Money from the fund can be tapped in an emergency (for example, when a local landmark is suddenly slated for demolition), and—depending upon how the fund is organized—can be spent in a variety of ways, from the purchase of an option to outright acquisition. Money expended for a property's preservation is returned to the fund after the property's resale; this is usually contingent upon the new owner's agreeing to preserve or restore the building. In essence, money in the fund revolves in and out, facilitating the preservation of many more properties than could be preserved through any single expenditure.

Pennsylvania's first statewide preservation revolving fund was established in 1982. Based on successful models in other states (particularly the Historic Preservation Fund of North Carolina) and within Pennsylvania that of the Pittsburgh History and Landmarks Foundation, the Preservation Fund of Pennsylvania was incorporated as an independent, private, nonprofit fund with seed money from the General Assembly and the U.S. Department of the Interior.

The fund assists in preserving historic, archeological, and maritime properties that meet its criteria. Properties must be (1) listed in or eligible for the National Register; (2) endangered (i.e., threatened by demolition, neglect, vandalism); (3) significant to the community's preservation and revitalization; (4) capable of attracting local support for their preservation; and (5) able to be purchased and marketed for resale.

By June 1984, after one year of operation, the Preservation Fund had assisted directly in five preservation projects across the state. According to Bogue Wallin, executive director of the fund, the first completed project involved the 1855 Peter Herdic house in Williamsport. In 1983 the fund purchased an option on the house from its owner, a local preservation organization that had begun to rehabilitate it. By April 1984 the fund had sold that option to a partnership that agreed to finish the rehabilitation and then operate the house as a restaurant.

National Trust for Historic Preservation

The National Trust for Historic Preservation can be both a direct source of funding for special preservation projects and a source of information for funding alternatives. The National Trust is a private, nonprofit organization chartered by Congress in 1949 to "help protect America's historic and cultural heritage by preserving and interpreting elements from the past." Financial support for the trust comes from U.S. Department of the Interior grants, other grants and gifts, membership dues, and several other sources. Besides owning and administering many historic properties, the trust offers a wide range of programs and services. In 1983 it provided $677,424 in financial assistance to other groups through six special-purpose funds. The projects ranged from the preparation of technical reports and studies all the way to the acquisition and rehabilitation of historic buildings.

Because the trust's financial resources are limited, it cannot respond with funds to every plea for assistance. But it can help in other ways, such as identifying other funding sources, providing technical information on various programs, or recommending local organizations from which to seek suggestions.

Cliveden. Home of the National Trust for Historic Preservation's Mid-Atlantic Regional Office.

Two other preservation tools, easements and tax incentives, are covered in the next two chapters.

This house is restricted by a preservation easement. Any changes to its exterior must not significantly detract from the public's view of it along a well-traveled scenic roadway.

Chapter 6
PRESERVATION EASEMENTS

On the surface, the Alden Park Manor apartment complex in Philadelphia and the 1820 Carter-Worth farmhouse and barn in rural Chester County appear to have little, if anything, in common. The apartment complex is home to several hundred residents; the farmhouse, to a family of four. The complex comprises several buildings ranging from 9 to 14 stories tall; the farmhouse is 2½ stories with an attic. The complex is located in the historic community of Germantown in Philadelphia; the farmhouse is in the rolling hills of the Brandywine Valley. Both properties, however, are listed in the National Register of Historic Places for their architectural significance. And the architectural integrity of both is guaranteed by the same technique—the preservation easement.

Since gaining recognition in federal law in 1976, the easement has become an effective preservation tool. Simply defined, an easement is a legal agreement in which certain rights, or interests, in property are conveyed from one party (the donor) to another (the recipient). Negative easements, which remove certain rights from property and grant the recipient the right to enforce the restrictions, have long been applied in land conservation efforts to protect scenic vistas and open spaces by restricting them from development. Easements are now also used to ensure the architectural integrity of historic buildings over time by controlling physical changes to facades or entire structures. The use of easements to preserve both land and old buildings has been encouraged by recent developments in federal tax laws, which, under certain conditions, treat easements as tax-deductible charitable contributions. The Internal Revenue Service calls them "qualified conservation contributions."

Current law makes no distinction between an easement for land conservation and one for historic preservation. It uses the term conservation easement to describe any easement for a recognized "conservation purpose." The law recognizes the "preservation of a historically important land area or certified historic structure" as a "conservation purpose," just as it recognizes the preservation of certain natural habitats, open spaces, and land areas for outdoor recreation to be conservation purposes. Although viewed as conservation easements or restrictions under federal law, easements affecting historic buildings are commonly called preservation easements.

As a charitable contribution, an easement donation can provide relief from federal income, estate, and gift taxes and is available to owners of large and small, urban and rural, commercial and noncommercial "certified" historic properties. (See Certified Historic Structure later in this chapter for a complete explanation of the historic certification requirement. Generally, it applies to properties listed individually in the National Register or located in a registered historic district and certified to be significant to the district.) The tax incentives, combined with the flexibility and effectiveness of easements, have encouraged the use of easements for historic preservation, benefiting both the property owner and the surrounding community. Witness that apartment complex, Alden Park Manor in Germantown.

ALDEN PARK MANOR—ON A GRAND SCALE

Alden Park Manor, consisting of three multitowered apartment buildings—Manor, Cambridge, and Kenilworth—and accessory structures, looms over 37 acres of prime land in Germantown. It was built between 1923 and 1928 from plans by Edwyn Rorke (1890–1960) in the neo-Gothic style. According to Sandra Tatman, architectural librarian at the Athenaeum (and a resident of Alden Park), Rorke even designed two much-admired Alden Park "clones"—one in Detroit and the other outside Boston—modeled after the Philadelphia original.

Long inhabited by older people, the complex in recent years has attracted many younger families with children, students at nearby colleges, retirees, even preservationists. In the opinion of Michael Scholnick, executive vice-president of the Philadelphia Historic Preservation Corporation, Alden Park was, and still is, "an apartment of social and aesthetic value to the community."

In 1979 Alden Park Manor and its 630 apartments were for sale. A group of prospective buyers saw an opportunity to donate an easement for historic preservation and employed George Thomas's Philadelphia-based Clio Group to research the complex and nominate it to the National Register of Historic Places. When the nomination was approved in August 1980, the interested buyers could be sure that an easement on the property would constitute a "qualified conservation contribution." They bought it.

The next year the new owners, Alden Park Associates, conveyed to the nonprofit Philadelphia Historic Preservation Corporation an easement on the facade and 26 of the 37 surrounding acres. The easement grants the corporation a permanent interest in Alden Park's architecture and grounds. Without the corporation's written consent, the present (and future) owners of Alden Park may not alter the complex's exterior. Moreover, they must maintain the property in "good repair"—no small task, considering that Alden Park's annual operating costs exceed $3 million. The easement gives the corporation the right (and the responsibility) to see that any violations are eliminated and that the property is restored to its original condition.

Preservation Easements / 97

Alden Park Manor facade.

Alden Park Manor towers.

Carter-Worth house.

The easement document detailing Alden Park's current appearance and the permanent restrictions took nearly a year to prepare. The facades of the three major buildings, garages, swimming pools, and summer houses required painstaking documentation. In sum, a staggering total of 77 principal facades were identified, 67 of them ranging from 9 to 14 stories tall.

The appraisal of the easement's value took into consideration the property's fair market value both before and after the granting of the easement. Because of Alden Park's location and commercial use and the permanent restrictions on development, the easement's appraised value was high. The portion of its value removed by the easement restrictions was deductible from federal income taxes as a charitable contribution. Although refusing to divulge the easement's exact appraised value, Scholnick acknowledged that it was "well in excess of $1 million."

With the easement completed, Alden Park Associates began another major project at Alden Park—a gradual conversion to cooperative ownership. Whatever its ownership arrangement, however, the residents of Germantown can at least be sure that Alden Park will always look the same and will be maintained in good repair.

Although such a large contribution value for preservation easements is out of the ordinary, owner-occupants of smaller historic properties may also benefit financially by donating easements. More important than any possible financial benefit, however, they should derive satisfaction from knowing that the integrity of their properties will be permanently protected. Unlike investment tax credits for rehabilitation (see Chapter 7), which are available only to owners of income-producing properties, preservation easements may be used for private homes. In fact, preservation easements offer the only federal tax incentive available to owner-occupants of certified historic buildings. For many of these people, such as the owners of the Carter-Worth house in Chester County, that was an opportunity to be seized.

CARTER-WORTH HOUSE AND BARN

The Carter-Worth property was first encumbered with an easement in 1976. That easement, for land conservation, restricted from development

Carter-Worth house and barn.

3.8 acres of gentle slopes adjacent to the historic farmhouse. The green-serpentine stone dwelling, built about 1820 by Emmor Carter and enlarged in 1850 by Samuel Worth, overlooks the slopes, as does a massive stone bank barn. After the house and the barn were listed in the National Register in 1977, the owners donated an easement on both buildings and six more acres. These first two, and subsequent, charitable contributions have helped the owners acquire additional land adjacent to the main complex. Gradually, they are reassembling the original farm tract and protecting the setting. And their neighbors are delighted with the permanent open space and preservation of historic buildings guaranteed by the easements.

The use of easements to restrict open space and historic buildings from further change and development holds much appeal. But no preservation technique is flawless or universally applicable. Successful easements need willing donors and capable recipients. Nor is preservation accomplished by the mere signing of papers. By definition, preservation is a commitment to protect and maintain for the future. It is, as any old-house owner or preservation organization will acknowledge, an ongoing responsibility.

A preservation easement places weighty obligations on both the donor and the recipient. It requires the donor and his successors in title to the property to abide by restrictions, and it requires the recipient to enforce them. For a conservation or preservation easement to constitute a tax-deductible charitable contribution, the easement period must be *forever*. Thus the donor obligates himself and all future owners to comply with the easement's terms; the recipient, in turn, promises to enforce those terms—permanently. As a result, recipients tend to be highly selective about the easements they will agree to accept. They must decide whether the restrictions are reasonable and effective and can be feasibly enforced. Furthermore, most recipient organizations must require endowments from donors to cover the long-term costs of managing the easements. Prospective donors, too, must carefully weigh the advantages and disadvantages of an easement's permanent restrictions.

Easements offer no magical solution to problems of historic preservation. In certain situations, they are suitable. An understanding of the legal issues is important in determining their utility.

LEGISLATION

Legal Theory

As established by centuries of common law, real property consists of a bundle of rights, the sum of which constitutes "fee simple" ownership. An easement is a legally recorded instrument used to transfer partial ("less than fee") rights or interests in property. Traditionally, an easement gives another party a "non-possessory" right to a specific use of real property, such as a right of way for driveways, pipelines, or utilities. An agreement of this type is known as an "affirmative easement." On the other hand, when an owner surrenders his right to the full use of his property (by restricting development or prohibiting timbering, for example) and gives another party no rights except the enforcement of those restrictions, he creates a "negative easement." Agreements like Alden Park's, which also stipulate a certain level of

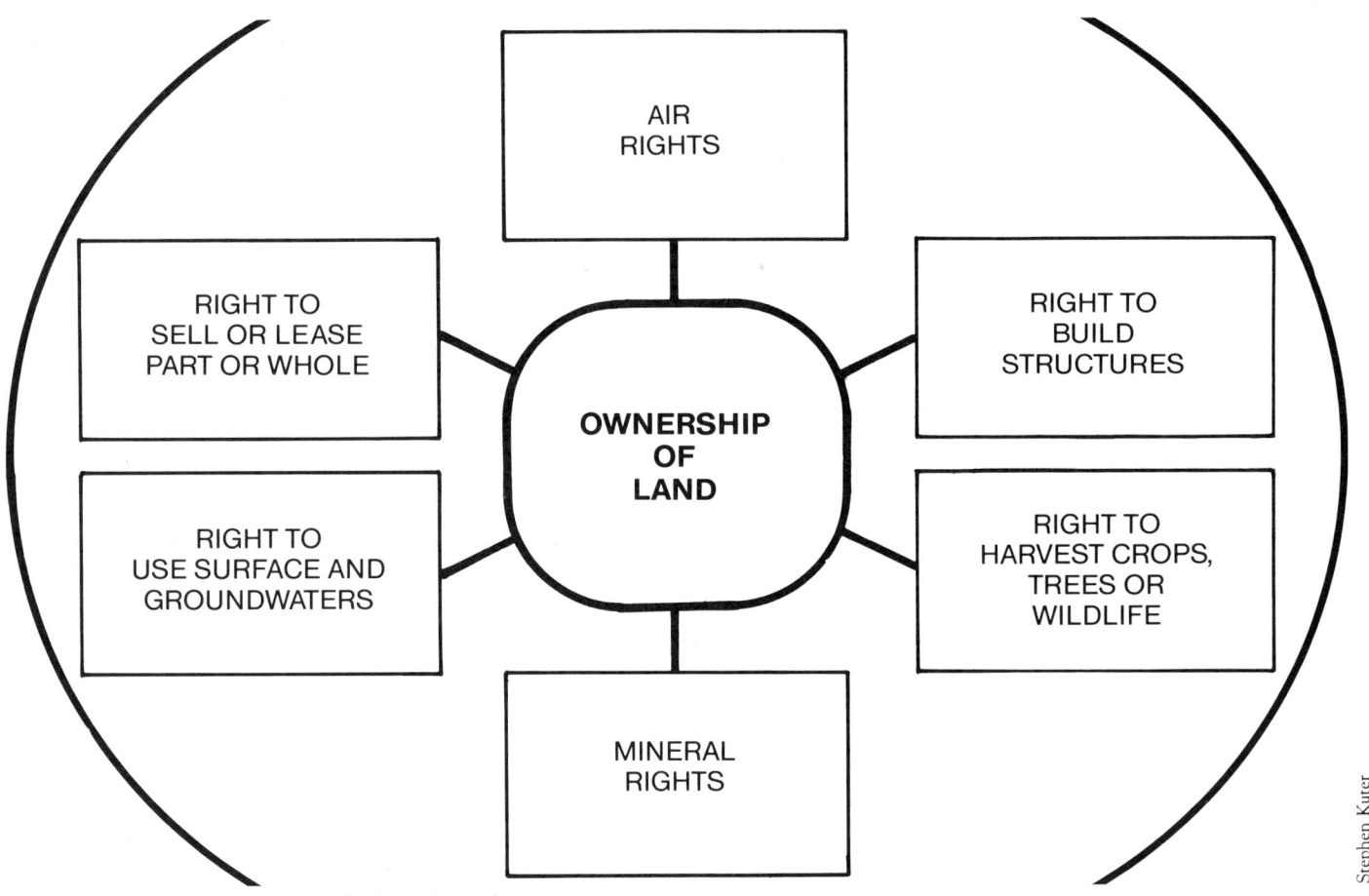

The "bundle of rights" concept is shown in this chart. Municipal, county, and state laws may place restrictions on some of these rights.

maintenance and other responsibilities to be enforced by the recipient, have both negative and affirmative aspects.

One of the earliest uses of negative easements for land conservation involved about 2,500 acres of land along the Blue Ridge Parkway in Virginia and North Carolina. In the 1930s, the National Park Service, with assistance

Natchez Trace, site of one of the earliest "negative" easements.

from state highway officials, launched an easement program to protect the road's scenic qualities between two national parks. At about the same time, 7,000 acres along the old Natchez Trace in Tennessee were protected through a similar program.

Not until the 1950s, however, was the possibility of allowing tax deductions for landowners granting easements explored. In a landmark ruling in 1964 (Revenue Ruling 64-205), the Internal Revenue Service (IRS) allowed tax deductions for scenic easements donated to qualified organizations. The IRS publicized the ruling in a news release the next year. This development, coupled with growing public concern about the natural environment (manifested in such legislation as the National Environmental Policy Act of 1969), greatly encouraged the use of easements. The 1969 Tax Reform Act and its 1972 regulations reaffirmed the 1964 ruling.

Although concerned primarily with open space, many early easements had salutary effects on historic properties. In some cases they restricted the development of open space around historic buildings. The easement around the William Twaddell house, for example, achieved several objectives.

That the William Twaddell house, a banked, stone Federal-style mansion from the late 18th century, reposes in splendid solitude at the Big Bend of the Brandywine River is no accident. In 1969, its owner placed 53 acres of surrounding woodland and flood plain under easement with the Brandywine Conservancy in Chadds Ford. The gift does more than protect the isolated setting of the handsomely restored house; it protects in perpetuity the banks along the scenic river beloved by canoeists and artists alike. Additionally, it restricts from development the site of an ancient Lenape Indian village, Queonemysing, as well as the archeological traces of an early iron and paper industry. The example set by this landowner acted as a catalyst for other donations in the area. Eventually, more than 1,000 acres in the area were placed under easement, and now a dozen historic buildings reap the rewards.

Deed Restrictions and Covenants

Deed restrictions and restrictive covenants also are used to protect historic buildings. They were, in fact, favored by historical societies and preservation organizations before preservation easements were recognized in federal law as charitable contributions. When a tax deduction is not desired or the term of the restriction is less than perpetuity, they are still the most appropriate preservation techniques. Simple deed restrictions are clauses contained in deeds to real property restricting it in certain ways, such as against further development or subdivision. Because deed restrictions usually do not require enforcement by another party (although they can be upheld by court action), their permanent enforceability is questionable. Restrictive covenants are more like easements because they are generally agreements between two parties. In the common law, they are viewed as "promises" not to do certain things with real property, such as altering a building's facade or building an addition. Easements, on the other hand, concern "interests," or "rights," in real property with legal rights of enforcement. If restrictive covenants and deed restrictions are established in perpetuity to be enforced by a qualified organization, they may, like preservation easements, be considered "qualified conservation contributions."

Tax Reform Act of 1976

Although the 1969 congressional tax package was the first legislative recognition of easements as charitable contributions, it did not explicitly cover easements on historic buildings. As Stephen J. Small pointed out in his often-cited article "The Tax Benefits of Donating Easements on Scenic and Historic Properties," after that act and a revenue ruling in 1975, easements protecting historic structures followed the form of open space easements. The easement was still not widely used for historic preservation. Many preservation organizations continued to rely on deed restrictions and covenants without a recipient steward to control changes to facades of old buildings, despite problems with the enforcement of the restrictions and a lack of tax incentives.

Ambiguities about a preservation easement's eligibility as a charitable contribution were somewhat clarified by the Tax Reform Act of 1976. This act required that an easement satisfy one of several "conservation purposes." These purposes were defined to embrace not only the protection of scenic land areas and environmental systems, but also the preservation of "histor-

William Twaddell house, south elevation after restoration.

ically important land areas or structures." As a result, landowners could execute preservation easements with some assurance that they would qualify as charitable donations. (Although the IRS never, for this act, promulgated regulations defining a "historically important land area or structure," donors were advised that the historic significance of their properties should be readily demonstrable, such as being listed in the National Register of Historic Places or the Historic American Buildings Survey. The most important feature of the 1976 act was that it provided for 30-year easements, a provision much desired by historic preservationists who felt that the preservation of a building beyond 30 years was difficult to ensure.)

Tax Reduction Act of 1977

Because of an error in the final bill presented for passage, the 1976 Tax Reform Act's provisions on 30-year easements carried an expiration date of June 14, 1977, rather than the June 14, 1981, date extended to other provisions of the act. When attempts were made in the Tax Reduction and Simplification Act of 1977 to extend that provision to 1981, the 30-year

Brandywine River flowing near the William Twaddell property; the easement on this property protects the scenic river banks as well as the house itself.

An urban townhouse under easement, also located in a National Register historic district.

requirement for easements was modified to read "in perpetuity," as advocated by the Treasury Department. As a result, since 1977, preservation organizations have had to draft and enforce perpetual restrictions on old buildings.

Tax Treatment Extension Act

By the Tax Treatment Extension Act of 1980, the easement provisions set to expire in 1981 were made permanent. The qualifying criteria for tax-deductible easements were made more specific, and "conservation purposes" were more explicitly defined. To qualify, a preservation easement must be seen as fulfilling the fourth conservation purpose: ". . . the preservation of a historically important land area or a certified historic structure." The certification procedures are identical to those for the investment tax credit, detailed in Chapter 7. The 1980 act firmly established easements for historic preservation in federal law and set a national standard for qualifying properties. Efforts to standardize state laws regarding easements have not, to date, been as successful.

State Legislation and Property Taxes

A "Uniform Conservation and Historic Preservation Easement Act" was proposed in 1979 by a committee of the American Bar Association and endorsed in 1981 by the National Conference of Commissioners on Uniform State Laws. To become effective, however, it must be acted upon by individual states. The act attempts to clarify easement terminology, enforceability, and other issues. Several states have adopted the act, among them Arkansas, Nevada, Oregon, and Wisconsin, while others have enacted different easement legislation.

Besides setting uniform standards and practices for easements, state easement legislation could clarify their effect on property tax assessments. By permanently restricting the use (including the development potential) of their properties, easement donors are entitled, in theory, to a reduction in their land's fair-market-value assessment. In Pennsylvania, some property tax relief is available through Act 319 ("Clean and Green" Act) and Act 515, which authorize reduced assessments on lands restricted against development for 10 years. Many easements, however, especially those with facade controls

Historic property under a facade easement.

on historic buildings, affect properties of less than the minimum 10 acres required by the two Pennsylvania acts, leaving their owners saddled with unadjusted tax bills despite the restrictions. Thus far, most local assessment boards have resisted lowering assessments on historic buildings encumbered with facade easements.

Landowners must also take into account the possible ramifications of a request for reassessment. In areas where assessments have not been periodically updated, a reassessment on a property under easement might result in *increased* taxes, because of an overall rise in fair market values in the community. In addition, other property owners might resent an increased tax burden on them brought about by a reduced tax base.

BENEFITS

The benefits deriving from an easement are felt by both the donor and the surrounding community. For the donor, an easement is a flexible tool. The restrictions are set by agreement between the donor and the recipient. Within this framework and the requirements set by federal law, there is room for negotiation. For example, a donor may wish to retain the right to build an addition or an accessory structure on his historic property, or even to develop a portion of it. The easement can be designed to allow such options, provided that the recipient organization agrees to them and that the easement's "conservation purpose" is not jeopardized. A well-written easement will specify the procedures and criteria for using such options. If an easement permits an addition, it should specify the maximum size, general location, design, and materials. It is advisable, as well, to include in or attach to the easement the procedure by which the donor may submit plans for such changes and by which the recipient organization reviews them. The more planning for contingencies done in the easement-drafting stage, the less likely the chance of disagreement in the future.

Besides providing for reasonable changes to the property, the easement may be designed to accommodate the donor's tax situation. After due consideration of the tax consequences and other factors, some property owners prefer to "stage" their easements. That is, they restrict portions of their properties as they are able. A first easement could restrict the main facade

Restrictions can be drafted to permit the construction of additions.

of a house. The grounds or outbuildings could be covered in a later easement. Thus the charitable contributions could be spread out over a number of years. If phasing is used, it may be essential to also provide for completion of all phases in the event of death. An easement by codicil to the donor's will can ensure that all of the land and buildings will be afforded protection.

An easement assures an owner that his property will not be improperly altered and will be maintained and appropriately used in the future. The technique epitomizes the concept of land and property stewardship. It is particularly attractive to individuals who, having painstakingly restored a site, are concerned for its preservation beyond the term of their ownership.

Another benefit to the donor is financial. Not only can the appraised value of an easement be claimed as a charitable donation for federal income tax purposes; by reducing or limiting the property's fair market value, an easement can reduce federal gift and estate taxes. But the appraisal of a preservation easement is a highly complex matter that must take into account a broad spectrum of issues, including land values, forgone opportunities to alter a building for greater income or value, and height limitations. As a result, the IRS has tended to view these appraisals very critically. A good appraisal will require careful attention to comparable sales and must rigorously document the position taken on issues such as those noted, and others.

An easement benefits both the donor and the community by keeping the property in private ownership, thereby fostering private responsibility for historic preservation. Because only partial interests are transferred, the owner retains his use and enjoyment of the property (subject, of course, to the easement's restrictions). Although an easement may require that a property be opened for public visits (particularly if the recipient is a public agency), such visits are generally only a few times per year. In any case, continued public visual enjoyment of the site is guaranteed without burdening the public with outright acquisition.

Significant historic properties under preservation easements are thus protected at no direct expense to the local taxpayer; and because they remain in private hands, they are kept in use and on the tax rolls. In addition, they will not be permitted to deteriorate: it is the recipient organization's permanent responsibility to enforce an easement's maintenance provisions.

Easements can augment a community's planning efforts and become a focus of public advocacy. Without requiring special legislation, a coordinated easement program can complement a community's zoning, protect its natural and historic resources, and reflect its planning goals. An example is Willistown Township in Chester County.

Located on the southwestern fringes of the Main Line and bordered by Malvern Borough, Willistown is one of the few municipalities in eastern Chester County that have retained their rural character in the face of strong suburbanizing forces. Despite some development in a few areas of the township, fox hunting is still a favored pastime and beagling is a close second. Willistown is the home of a Main Line institution, the Radnor Hunt. And the work of R. Brognard Okie (1875–1945), restoration architect par excellence of Pennsylvania stone farmhouses, is everywhere.

Cherishing their distinctive environment, and aware of the federal tax incentives for conservation, a group formed in 1980 to promote easements. Organized as a special program of the Brandywine Conservancy, the Willistown Area Conservation Program approached landowners about donating

Outbuildings like this springhouse can also be placed under conservation easement.

easements. By 1982, a base of some 970 acres of preserved land had been established, including most of the 18th-century village of White Horse. According to the program's coordinators, Bonnie Van Alen and Cathe McCoy (both longtime residents), educating their fellow citizens about the use of easements has been one of their most important goals. Originally the residents "expressed gloom and doom about the future, believing it's too late to preserve what's here," said McCoy. "But now that we've had some success, the movement is snowballing." Although the program is financed primarily through private fund-raising efforts, the township supervisors demonstrated their interest by adopting a resolution of support in 1981 and by funding the preparation of a map of areas of "critical concern." The program's plans include more open space easements and the certification and restriction of important historic buildings.

Conservation easements for natural and historic resources permanently remove or severely limit their potential for most development. Unlike land use controls, which are often at the mercy of court decisions and political whims, easements are forever. Community planning can encourage, reflect, and reinforce these permanent restrictions by designating (for example) historic, open space, or agricultural districts in areas where easements are desirable or in place.

CRITERIA—THE THREE TESTS

For an easement to be considered a "qualified conservation contribution" by the Internal Revenue Service (IRS), it must satisfy the three tests cited in Section 170(h) of the 1954 Internal Revenue Code, as amended:
1. It must be granted in perpetuity.
2. It must be donated to a "qualified organization."
3. It must be given exclusively for at least one of the "conservation purposes" stated in the Tax Treatment Extension Act of 1980.

Perpetuity

By IRS definition, an easement must be perpetual. In its regulations on easements, the IRS uses the terms "easement," "conservation restriction," and "perpetual conservation restriction" interchangeably. The legislation behind this requirement was briefly reviewed earlier in this chapter.

Of course, an easement may be donated for a shorter period if the donor is not concerned with qualifying for a federal tax deduction.

Qualified Organization

A qualified organization, the eligible recipient, is a governmental unit or a publicly supported charitable (nonprofit) organization under Section 501(c)(3) of the Internal Revenue Code, authorized to accept easements. Finding a suitable and willing recipient can be a formidable problem. Relatively few organizations specialize in, much less accept, preservation easements. Although there are dozens of active open space and conservation groups, rarely do their chartered purposes include accepting easements on old buildings. Those that do usually prefer to work near their home base, for both ease of enforcement and efficiency. For the same reasons, and to maximize the effectiveness of easements, most organizations find it desirable to acquire easements in a limited area. (See Appendix A for a list of organizations in Pennsylvania equipped to accept easements.)

White Horse Village in Willistown Township, Chester County, protected by conservation easement.

Conservation Purposes

The requirement that easements satisfy conservation purposes was first proposed in the 1976 Tax Reform Act. The purposes, which were redefined and elaborated upon in the Tax Treatment Extension Act of 1980 and which amend Section 170(h) of the Internal Revenue Code, are:

(i) the preservation of land areas for outdoor recreation by, or the education of, the general public,

(ii) the protection of a relatively natural habitat of fish, wildlife, or plants, or similar ecosystem,

(iii) the preservation of open space (including farmland and forest land) where such preservation is—
   (I) for the scenic enjoyment of the general public, or
   (II) pursuant to a clearly delineated Federal, State, or local governmental conservation policy, and will yield a significant public benefit, or

(iv) the preservation of an historically important land area or a certified historic structure.

This last purpose, concerning historic properties, requires additional explanation.

Historically Important Land Area

IRS regulations (proposed in May 1983 and not final as this book went to press) define a "historically important land area" as:

(A) An independently significant land area (for example, an archaeological site or a Civil War battlefield) that substantially meets the National Register Criteria for Evaluation . . .

(B) Any building or land area within a registered historic district (except buildings that cannot reasonably be considered as contributing to the significance of the district); and

(C) Any land area adjacent to a property listed individually in the National Register of Historic Places (but not within a registered historic district) in a case where the physical or environmental features of the land area contribute to the historic or cultural integrity of the structure.

In other words, land listed in the National Register and land not listed in it could both be eligible for easements.

One of the "conservation purposes" under the 1980 Tax Treatment Extension Act is the preservation of a historically important land area or structure.

Certified Historic Structure

In contrast to the fairly loose definition of historically important land, Section 170(h) of the Internal Revenue Code defines a "certified historic structure" for "qualified conservation contributions" as:

> any building, structure, or land area which—
> (i) is listed in the National Register, or
> (ii) is located in a registered historic district . . . and is certified by the Secretary of the Interior to the Secretary [of the Treasury] as being of historic significance to the district.

According to Section 48(g) of the code, a "registered historic district" is—

> (i) any district listed in the National Register, and
> (ii) any district—
> (I) which is designated under a statute of the appropriate State or local government, if such statute is certified by the Secretary of the Interior to the Secretary as containing criteria which will substantially achieve the purpose of preserving and rehabilitating buildings of historic significance to the district, and
> (II) which is certified by the Secretary of the Interior to the Secretary as meeting substantially all of the requirements for the listing of districts in the National Register.

Easements are available for historic properties whether or not the properties are income producing, and it bears repeating that an easement is the only federal income tax incentive for preservation available to owner-occupants of certified historic structures. Easements can, of course, also be used by owners of historic commercial properties, as evidenced in Alden Park. If a commercial property has also undergone certified rehabilitation to qualify for the maximum investment tax credit, the tax deductions can increase.

As a result of the 1980 act's explicit criteria, any doubts about a historic structure's eligibility for a preservation easement have been or can be answered through the U.S. Department of the Interior's registration and certification process. If the property is already listed individually in the National Register, no additional certifications are required. But, for the prospective easement donor who owns a not-yet-certified building (in a registered historic district or complex, for example), or a building lacking any registration status whatsoever, the burden becomes one of documentation and timing.

Preliminary determinations of eligibility, such as those available for the tax credit, may not be used for preservation easements. The structure must be on the National Register or certified for significance by the due date of the tax return for the year of the donation (generally April 15 of the next year, unless an automatic three-month extension is requested). Interested donors are therefore urged, in the words of Emma Jane Saxe of the National Register office, "to consider carefully the timing of the gift." Despite the statutory time limits for processing applications for registration and certification (as a rule, within 45 days of receipt by the federal agency), improperly prepared or incomplete applications can flounder for months. It is best to plan all aspects of the easement, particularly the certification procedures, well in advance. Many preservation organizations recommend that at least a year be allowed for completing an easement, especially when certification or registration is required.

THE STRUCTURE OF AN EASEMENT

While easements are tailored to individual properties, certain features are standard. Even these, however, vary somewhat. For discussion, easements may be regarded as consisting of three parts:

1. Statement of facts
2. Restrictions and duties
3. Provisions for enforcement

Viewing an easement in this way will make understanding the sample easement on pages 112 and 113 a little easier.

Statement of Facts

An easement's statement of facts tells the who, when, where, what, and why. In essence, it shows how the easement satisfies the three IRS tests for a charitable contribution.

Who—means the donor and the recipient. The *grantor* (donor) is the fee-simple owner. The donor may be looking to shelter income or may be motivated by purely altruistic considerations or probably a little of both. The *grantee* (recipient) must be a "qualified organization," such as a governmental unit or publicly supported, tax-exempt charity authorized to accept easements.

When—is the term of the easement. As noted previously, easements must be given in perpetuity; they run with the land as a "binding servitude" upon the premises of the donors, their successors, and assigns. The recipients (and their successors and assigns) are also obligated to enforce the easement forever.

Another "when" is the easement's date of execution and recording. Both must be completed by the end of the donor's tax year, usually December 31 of the year for which the tax deduction is taken.

Where—is the location of the area under easement and its boundary description in metes and bounds. If the easement affects an entire tract (as happens often), the easement's metes and bounds will match those on the deed. Where an easement takes in just a portion of a property, it may be possible to establish new metes and bounds from an existing plot plan (a scale drawing of the property). The more costly alternative for the donor is to commission a new survey, which could, depending on the size of the property, cost several thousand dollars. Altering the boundaries of an executed easement is nearly impossible. Property owners contemplating subdivision are advised to complete the subdivision (at least in theory or design) before executing an easement or to plan the one to complement the other.

What—refers to the type of easement: general exterior, facade only, interior, and (when the easement overlaps with a conservation easement), scenic open space.

An easement should be exact in defining the features it covers. It could list all exterior features, the way this 1974 easement to Historic Denver, Inc., does:

> Outside walls, cornice; stained or cut glass windows; location, shape and size of windows; style, coloration of building materials, paint color; location, shape and size of doors, portals, stairs, pediments, towers, fences and any other element of exterior or facade of any improvement or structure on the described real estate including trees and landscaping.

An easement on a building's exterior should carefully note the location, shape, and size of windows on each wall.

Or it can define them broadly:
> the exterior surfaces of improvements (including, without limitation, the exterior walls, roofs and chimney).

An easement can also include interior features worthy of preservation; this excerpt from an agreement against alterations for a house on Water Street in Ipswich, Massachusetts, mentions both exterior and interior:
> The front and side facades of the original 1690 building, including specifically the wooden roof shingles and wooden wall clapboards; The central frame including primary and secondary members; The feather edged paneling in the first floor right front room of the original 1690 building; The wooden architectural elements including, if any, paneling, mantlepieces, doors and other molded detail on the inner walls of the two second story bedrooms of the original 1690 dwelling.

Photos (dated and with views indicated) of the features' current appearance should be appended to the easement. Measured drawings and floor plans document the way the house is at the time the easement is made.

How—explains how the property's easement qualifies as a "conservation purpose" defined in the Tax Treatment Extension Act of 1980.

Preservation easements are given for certified historic structures, as explained earlier. If a property is listed individually in the National Register, it is enough to state its date of acceptance and official listing (the way it was entered in the *Federal Register*). For properties located in registered historic districts and certified as significant, the official notice and the number of the certification should be attached.

If the easement also satisfies other conservation purposes, such as the preservation of a natural habitat or open space, additional explanation and proof are required.

Restrictions and Duties

The heart of an easement is what it requires a landowner to do or not to do. (These restrictions and responsibilities run with the land and, accordingly, apply to succeeding landowners.) Typically, a preservation easement forbids any actions that would damage the historic structure's integrity, possibly including, but not limited to—

1. Construction, alteration, or remodeling, or "any other thing . . ." without the express written permission of the recipient
2. Inappropriate uses, such as changes from single-family to commercial or industrial use
3. Subdivision
4. Additions
5. New structures
6. Dumping or open storage of rubbish
7. Signs, billboards, or advertisements, with some exceptions
8. Quarrying, excavation, or removal of rocks

Not all these restrictions can be applied to every site, and some may be modified to reflect the wishes of the donor and the recipient. Physical changes to the structure, such as additions and remodelings, for example, are not always prohibited. Easements can be drafted to provide for limited changes with the approval of the recipient. For example, an easement written for a farm complex in northern Chester County, Pennsylvania, permits the construction of additional silos, sheds, and other farm buildings consistent with

Dumping of rubbish is typically forbidden on a property under easement.

(continued on page 114)

GRANT OF EASEMENT AND DECLARATION OF RESTRICTIVE COVENANTS

THIS GRANT OF EASEMENT AND DECLARATION OF RESTRICTIVE COVENANTS, hereinafter referred to as the "Grant and Declaration," made this _____ day of _____ in the year of our Lord One Thousand Nine Hundred and Eighty _____.
BETWEEN _____ and _____ of _____ Township, _____ County, Commonwealth of Pennsylvania, parties of the first part, hereinafter called the "Grantors,"

AND

BRANDYWINE CONSERVANCY, INC., a non-profit corporation of the State of Delaware, party of the second part, hereinafter called the "Grantee":

WITNESSETH:

WHEREAS, Grantors are the owners of a certain tract of ground in _____ Township, _____ County, Commonwealth of Pennsylvania, containing approximately _____ acres of land, being the same more or less, and improvements, hereinafter referred to as the Property, as shown on a survey attached hereto as Exhibit A, and described by legal description attached hereto as Exhibit B, and prepared by _____, Registered Land Surveyor, and including the _____ depicted in photographs and described by the accompanying narrative which are attached hereto and made a part hereof as Exhibit C; and

WHEREAS, the Property is located within the _____ National Register Historic District and the United States Department of the Interior has certified that the Property contributes to the significance of said district; and

WHEREAS, the _____ is highly visible from _____, a well-traveled scenic road which passes numerous resources listed in the National Register of Historic Places; and

WHEREAS, Grantors desire to preserve the natural, scenic, and historic state of the Property; and

WHEREAS, Grantee is a publicly supported charity, recognized as such under Section 170(h)(3) and Section 2522(a) of the Internal Revenue Code, organized for the purpose of preserving historic sites, natural areas, and areas important to the management of water resources.

NOW THEREFORE, Grantors, for and in consideration of the sum of FIVE DOLLARS ($5.00), lawful money of the United States of America, the receipt whereof is hereby acknowledged, and intending to be legally bound, hereby grant, declare, and covenant as follows:

1. Grantors hereby unconditionally and absolutely grant and convey unto Grantee, its successors and assigns a perpetual Easement in Gross, to have and to hold the same for the purpose of perpetually conserving and protecting in accordance with this Grant and Declaration from any actions by Grantors, their successors and assigns which would adversely affect the historic, scenic, and natural resource values of the Property subject to the qualifications hereinafter set forth.

2. In order to accomplish the intent of the Grant and Declaration set forth in paragraph 1 above, and the restrictions and covenants referred to therein, Grantors hereby declare and impose the following restrictions upon the use and enjoyment of the Property.

   A. No industrial activities shall be conducted or permitted on the Property.

   B. No building shall be placed, built or maintained on the Property, other than the existing structures which may be maintained as provided for in paragraph 3.

   C. No signs, billboards or outdoor advertising structures shall be placed, erected or maintained on the Property other than signs not exceeding twelve inches by eighteen inches for each of the following purposes:

   (i) to state the name of the Property and the names and address of the occupants;

   (ii) to advertise an activity permitted under the provisions of this Grant and Declaration;

   (iii) to post the Property against activities either prohibited or not specifically permitted under the provisions of this Grant and Declaration; and

   (iv) to advertise the sale or lease of the Property.

   Provided, however, that this sub-paragraph C shall not limit the right of Grantee to display on the Property at its discretion such signs as it may customarily use to identify lands under conservation easement or agreement to Grantee and the terms of such easement or agreement.

   D. No quarrying, excavation, or removal of rocks, minerals, gravel, sand, topsoil or other similar materials from the Property shall occur.

   E. No depositing, dumping, or abandoning of any solid waste or junk shall occur on the Property.

   F. No cutting or removing of trees is permitted excepting those which are fallen, dead, diseased, or dangerous.

   G. No subdivision of the Property shall occur.

   H. No construction or placement of any structures or works thereon including sheds, public or private roads, driveways, parking lots, pipelines, poles, any other facilities normally used in connection with supplying utilities or removing effluent, or any other impervious surfaces shall occur.

3. In addition to the restrictions and covenants imposed on the use and enjoyment of the Property by paragraph 2, supra, and in order to accomplish the intent of the Grant and Declaration as set forth in paragraph 1, Grantors declare to impose forever the following restrictions and covenants upon the use and enjoyment of the _____, except with the prior written approval of the Grantee, its successors or assigns, which approval shall be given only to the extent that the intent of the Grant and Declaration as set forth in paragraph 1 and prior sections of this document is not violated:

   A. No construction, alteration, or remodeling or any other activity shall be undertaken or permitted to be undertaken on the _____ which would affect either the exterior surfaces herein described, or increase the height, or alter the exterior street facades (including, without limitation, exterior walls, roofs and chimneys) or the appearance of the building located thereon, insofar as they are depicted in photographs and described in accompanying narratives in Exhibit C, or which would adversely affect the structural soundness of the _____. Provided, however, that this sub-paragraph A shall not limit the reconstruction, repair, repainting or refinishing of presently existing parts of elements of the _____, damage to which has resulted from casualty loss, deterioration, or wear and tear, without the prior written approval of Grantee, provided that such reconstruction, repair, repainting or refinishing is performed in a manner which will not alter the appearance of those elements of the buildings subject to this Grant and Declaration as they are as of this date.

   B. No sandblasting or other forms of abrasive cleaning shall be undertaken on the exterior of the _____. Any other cleaning process must be approved by Grantee prior to the employment of the process on the exterior of the _____.

   C. No paint of a quality or color significantly different from that presently existing shall be used on the exterior trim of the _____. Provided, however, that Grantor may restore to its original condition and appearance the exterior trim and woodwork, to the extent that the original condition and appearance can be determined.

   D. In the event of damage resulting from casualty loss to an extent rendering repair or reconstruction of the existing _____ impracticable, erection of a structure of the same size, bulk and design as the damaged structure, the design of which shall be subject to prior approval by Grantee, shall be permitted.

4. Grantors agree at all times to maintain the lot and structure herein described, and the exterior appearance of the _____ ____ (including, without limitation, the exterior walls, roofs, and chimneys of the buildings located thereon) in a good and sound state of repair, subject to the casualty loss provisions in sub-paragraph D of paragraph 3, supra.

5. Nothing herein shall be construed as a grant to the general public or to a person or persons other than Grantee, its servants, successors or assigns or its duly authorized agents, of the right to enter upon any parts of the Property. Grantors reserve unto themselves and their successors in title to the Property, all rights, privileges, powers and immunities in respect to the Property, including, without limitation, the right of exclusive possession and enjoyment subject only to the restrictions and easements herein set forth, and the terms and covenants of this Grant and Declaration.

6. Grantee shall have the right to enter upon the Property set forth herein to inspect for violations of the aforesaid provisions; to remove or eliminate any such violations; and to perform such restoration as may be deemed necessary to restore the land and the _____ ____ to their prior condition after removal of said violations. Grantee shall have the right to seek any legal action or remedy at law or in equity to enforce the provisions set forth herein and granted hereunder, including, without limitation, by the remedies of specific performance or injunction. In the event Grantors are found to have violated any of the obligations, Grantors shall reimburse Grantee, its successors or assigns for any costs or expenses incurred in connection therewith, including court costs and attorney's fees.

7. Grantee shall be under no obligation to maintain the Property or pay taxes or assessments hereon.

8. Grantors hereby agree to request in writing at least thirty (30) days prior to the closing of any sale or transfer of legal title to the Property, or the commencement of the term of any long term (ten years or more) lease of the Property, a written instrument from Grantee stating that Grantors are in compliance with the terms and conditions of this Grant and Declaration, or if Grantors are not in compliance with this Grant and Declaration, stating what violations of this Grant and Declaration exist. Grantee agrees in such cases or at any other time to execute, acknowledge and deliver to Grantors, to any mortgagee, transferee, purchaser or lessee and to any title insurance company issuing policy of title insurance with respect to any estate or interest in or lien upon the Property, a written instrument concerning compliance within thirty (30) days of written request from Grantors. Grantors shall provide a copy of Grantee's compliance statement dated not more than ninety (90) days preceding the date of execution and delivery of any agreement of sale, long term lease or mortgage with respect to the Property, to the purchaser, mortgagee or long term lessee hereunder and shall advise the Grantee in writing at least ten (10) days in advance of the closing of any transfer of legal title to the Property or the commencement of the term of any long term lease of the Property. Any reasonable costs incurred by the Grantee in determining compliance and advising Grantors as to compliance, all of which shall be billed to Grantors simultaneously with the delivery to Grantors of Grantee's compliance statement, and costs, if any, incurred as a result of Grantors' failure to notify Grantee of transfer, sale, assignment or long term lease of the Property shall be paid by the Grantors, their heirs and assigns. Grantors and each subsequent owner of the Property shall have no personal liability for the observance or performance of the covenants and obligations of Grantors hereunder after such party has conveyed his, her, its or their interest in the Property.

9. Grantee, and any succeeding assignee of Grantee's interest herein, as provided for in paragraph 11 hereof, shall have the right to assign, either wholly or partially, its right, title and interest hereunder to any public agency having and performing governmental functions, or to any publicly supported charitable organization described in Section 170(h)(3) and Section 2522(a) of the Internal Revenue Code.

10. If at any time any organization, agency or person having rights or duties hereunder as Grantee, whether as a party either original or succeeding as hereinafter set forth, shall fail to fully enforce the easement and restrictions set forth in this Grant and Declaration, Grantor or any governmental unit of _____County shall have the right to bring suit against Grantee for specific performance.

11. In the event Grantee shall cease to be an organization described in both Section 170(h)(3) and Section 2522(a) of the Internal Revenue Code, then its rights and duties hereunder shall succeed to, and become vested in and fall upon the following named entities to the extent they shall evidence acceptance of and fully enforce same, in the following order:

A. _____
B. _____
C. or such other organization having similar purposes

to which such rights and duties shall be awarded under the doctrine of *cy pres* by a Court of competent jurisdiction; provided however, that at the time of such acceptance, such entity shall be either an organization described in Section 170(h)(3) and Section 2522(a) of the Internal Revenue Code or a public agency performing governmental functions.

12. The provisions hereof shall inure to and be binding upon the heirs, executors, administrators, devisees, successors and assigns, as the case may be, of the parties hereto and shall be covenants running with the land.

IN WITNESS WHEREOF, and again stating their intention to be legally bound hereby, the said parties have hereunto set their hands and respective seals the _____ day of _____.

_____ _____
Witness   Grantor

_____ _____
Witness   Grantor

BRANDYWINE CONSERVANCY, INC.

By: _____
                        President

Attest: _____
                        Secretary

(continued from page 111)

the "historical and environmental qualities of the property" in consultation with the recipient. Most preservation easements require donors wishing to change paint color to get approval from the recipient.

Preservation easements also require the recipient to enforce certain positive actions by the landowner. Again, both parties must have agreed on the duties, which are not necessarily included in every preservation easement. A typical list includes:

1. Maintaining the property in good repair
2. Repair, refinishing, and so on, in the event of damage, deterioration, or wear and tear
3. Restoration if applicable

Easements generally provide that in the event of catastrophic damage, a replacement structure of comparable bulk and general design, and not necessarily a replica, *may* be built. A new structure, however, is not mandated.

Enforcement

The proper enforcement of an easement is a key to its effectiveness. Although the burden of upholding the easement's terms falls on the donor, the recipient accepts the responsibility of enforcement. A well-drafted easement includes provisions for enforcement. It gives the recipient the right of entry to inspect for violations. Periodic inspections are essential. Besides maintaining regular contact with the donor, inspections help spot problems before they cause irreversible damage. Some easement organizations add to their files annually with photos, notes, drawings, and maps.

If terms of the easement are violated, the easement gives the recipient the right, after notifying the landowner, to file an injunction requiring the restoration of the property to its former condition. As an alternative, the recipient may enter the premises, correct the violation, and hold the landowner financially responsible with legal remedies. An easement may include other provisions relating to enforcement, such as right of first refusal for purchase, notification of change in ownership, or a compliance statement (explained below).

The right of first refusal offered to the recipient at the time of the property's sale is generally a courtesy. Most preservation organizations lack the funds to acquire and maintain the historic structures on which they hold easements. A right of first refusal does alert the recipient to a possible change in ownership. Some organizations may even look for a suitable buyer when necessary. Some easements stipulate that the recipient be notified of a transfer in title or the drawing up of a long-term lease. Besides keeping the organization's records up to date, a notice of sale or lease helps the organization contact the new owner and explain the responsibilities of the owner and the preservation organization.

Easements accepted by the Brandywine Conservancy require the property owner to request, at least 30 days before closing a sale, a written statement from the conservancy certifying whether or not the property owner is complying with the easement. This assures the new landowners that they are not assuming responsibility for violations of the easement resulting from negligent actions by the previous owners.

Another aspect of enforcement concerns the recipient's ability to carry out its responsibilities "in perpetuity." What assurance do the donors, their successors, and assigns have that the easement will be enforced if the recipient ceases to exist or for some other reason fails to fulfill its obligations?

The recipient should approach this serious issue in two ways:

1. Establish a restricted endowment fund for enforcing easements and require that each easement donor (or parties interested in easements) contribute sufficient endowment to cover expected enforcement costs.

2. Include in the easement an assignment clause to protect the landowner, the community (which may have given some form of tax relief), and the sanctity of the charitable contribution for which the U.S. Treasury has granted a tax deduction. The clause might name organizations that have agreed to assume responsibilities from the recipient organization if it ceases to exist, name others who might assume the burden, authorize the recipient to assign its responsibilities to another organization with similar purposes, and (as a last resort) indicate that assignment may be made by the courts under the judicial doctrine of cy pres. This is a legal method used to determine how the charitable purpose of a grant or gift may be continued once the original recipient ceases to exist.

FINANCIAL CONSIDERATIONS

Costs

Easements involve direct costs to donors and recipients. Depending on the nature of the easements and the parties involved, those costs can include legal, mapping, surveying, photographic, and appraisal fees and endowment contributions. Most recipient organizations require the donor to assume most, if not all, of these expenses and to reimburse the organization for staff involvement. Costs to individual donors can sometimes be reduced if the recipient accepts several easements in a given area; this might lead to the donors' sharing the services of a lawyer, surveyor, and appraiser.

An endowment fund is established to cover the recipient organization's ongoing costs of monitoring and enforcing the easement. Although it is sometimes difficult for an organization to persuade an easement donor (or others) to fund an endowment, the long-term ability to enforce the easement should be a preeminent concern of the donor and the recipient. Since many preservation easements affect properties restored for commercial purposes, and since investment tax credits for them are generous and future obligations on the recipient are substantial, an endowment in such cases is necessary and appropriate. The endowment amount may be a flat fee, a percentage of the easement's appraised value, or established according to a formula reflecting projected costs of monitoring and enforcement. When a donor is truly strapped to provide a contribution at the time of a donation, deferred-contribution arrangements can be worked out (for example, the donor could make annual payments or give the endowment donation when he sells the property). All costs incurred for an easement donation are tax deductible as expenses related to the donation.

Valuation

To calculate tax savings, the value of the easement must be determined. Because easements are seldom sold in the marketplace, their values are arrived at by appraisal.

Appraisals of properties under easement take into account the restrictions imposed and the workings of the real estate market. According to an expert on appraising historic properties, Judith Reynolds, in a study for the National

Easements on farmsteads often permit construction of additional silos and other farm buildings if they do not conflict with the property's historic quality.

Trust for Historic Preservation and the Land Trust Exchange, "Precedent has established the before and after appraisal process as appropriate." The Internal Revenue Service also recognizes this method as the accepted method of appraisal. It first calculates the property's fair market value before the imposition of the easement (including potential for subdivision, expansion, demolition, altered use, and so on). Then the "after" value is calculated; it reflects the restrictions imposed by the easement and, as a rule, is lower than the value of the unburdened property.

The loss in value depends largely on the type of restrictions. Easements on properties with strong development potential tend to receive the highest valuations. For example, the fair market value of raw land capable of development may be $10,000 an acre; if an easement permanently restricts development, the land value may sink to less than $5,000 an acre. Generally, the highest appraisals for preservation easements are given to properties in cities where "air rights" are involved. For example, placing an easement on a 2-story townhouse in an area zoned for 12-story buildings drastically reduces the property's development potential and argues for a high easement value, particularly if there is a strong market for such buildings in the area. The same principle applies to easements on commercial buildings. The $5 million appraised value of preservation easements given in 1982 on the Alaska (1904) and Arctic (1916) buildings, two early skyscrapers in Seattle, was based primarily on the loss of value after the easements, which surrendered the right to construct higher-density buildings. In contrast, restricting just the facade of a rowhouse in a residential district may reduce the property's fair market value by only 5 or 10 percent. Similarly, easements on buildings in other types of residential areas that have little potential for commercial development may be lightly valued for tax purposes but may nonetheless be valuable to community preservation efforts.

Unusually aggressive appraisals tend to invite Internal Revenue Service audits. A donor is strongly advised to choose a professional appraiser experienced in valuing easements. Generally, the recipient organization can recommend appraisers with such experience.

Taxes

The value of a preservation easement given to a qualified organization, and the costs of preparing an easement, can be claimed as a charitable contribution on the donor's federal income tax return. Prospective donors will need to consult a tax attorney. The deduction is limited, as with any other charitable contribution, to 50 percent of the taxpayer's adjusted gross income for the tax year. Any value beyond that amount may be carried forward for a maximum of five tax years. (See Figure 6-1.)

Because the donation is made to a charitable organization, there is no gift tax liability for easements that comply with the federal law and IRS regulations. If the IRS proves that the easement is not a "qualified conservation contribution," however, the donor could be subject to gift taxes, the deductions claimed for the granting of the easement could be denied, and back taxes (and penalties) could be assessed. For overvaluations in excess of 150 percent, a penalty of 30 percent could be imposed. In cases where the donor is determined to have made a good-faith investigation of the value, the IRS has the authority to waive the penalty.

Easements can also reduce estate and gift taxes. These taxes are levied on an easement-protected property at its present, or "after," value. Accordingly, heirs or those who receive gifts avoid paying taxes on the portion of the appraised value assigned to the easement.

The foregoing is a broad discussion of how easements affect personal taxes. Landowners seriously interested in donating easements should work closely with a tax attorney through the entire process.

Despite all their benefits—to the individual, to the community, to the cause of preservation—easements are a complex method of preservation, not entered into lightly. While substantiating the validity of an easement donation and its value is difficult, often the real challenge is to find donors and recipients who have compatible objectives and are willing to make this permanent commitment to preservation.

ILLUSTRATION OF FEDERAL INCOME TAX BENEFIT FROM EASEMENT DONATION ON FACADE AND 15-ACRE HISTORIC PROPERTY

Assumptions

a. Taxpayer's annual adjusted gross income: $100,000.
b. Taxpayer's other annual deductions: $15,000.
c. Appraised "Before value" of property (without easement): $260,000.
  Appraised "After value" of property (with easement): $200,000.
  Appraised value of easement donation: $60,000.
d. Taxpayer's income and donations remain the same over the life of the easement donation deductions.
e. Federal taxes based on Schedule Y (joint return) of the 1984 Tax Rate Schedule.
f. Tax calculation based on 30% limitation.*
g. The $60,000 charitable contribution of the easement is distributed evenly over two years with a deduction of $30,000 each year.

Tax Year	Federal Tax Paid/No Easement Donation	Federal Tax Paid/ Easement Donation	Federal Tax Saved Due to Easement Donation
1	$25,668	$13,268	$12,400
2	25,668	13,268	12,400
Total Taxes Paid	$51,336	$26,536	

Total Savings $24,800

*Note: The taxpayer *must* deduct that portion of the appraised valuation of the donation representing 30% of the taxpayer's adjusted gross income in the year of the gift. The remaining donation value may be allocated over five successive tax years provided each annual deduction is 30% of adjusted gross income.

Figure 6–1

Thompson house, north elevation before rehabilitation.

Chapter 7

TAX INCENTIVES FOR HISTORIC BUILDINGS

AN OLD HOUSE

In 1798, Daniel Thompson, a cartwright from Mill Creek Hundred, Delaware, bought two adjoining tracts of land that straddled the boundary between Pennsylvania and Delaware. Thirty-five years later, his grandson, Ezra Thompson, built a six-room brick farmhouse on the Pennsylvania side, in London Britain Township, Chester County. The house stood on a 90-acre tract in the hills below Landenburg, about a mile north of the Mason-Dixon line.

Constructed well within the conservative Quaker tradition prevailing in rural Chester County, the farmhouse did have refinements. Like other noteworthy houses in the area, such as Lunn's Tavern and the Whann house in Strickersville, and the London Britain Friends Meetinghouse, it featured a double-string brick cornice and a brick facade laid in Flemish bond. It also had a Federal-style stairway, wide hallway, beehive oven, back-to-back corner fireplaces, and a kitchen wing. Water was originally pumped from a spring by a hydraulic ram, and later from a 40-foot-deep stone-lined well dug near the beehive oven within the "summer kitchen."

In 1857, Ezra and his wife, Mary Thompson, built a four-room addition. It had a new kitchen on the first floor and three bedrooms on the second. A most unusual feature was a hand-hewn 20-foot-long lintel above a door on the south side of the house bearing the painted letters "EMT," for Ezra and Mary Thompson, and below that the date 1857.

In 1878, Mary Thompson, by then a widow, sold the house and 77 acres to Ross D. Pierson. Pierson's son, Ross W., married and lived in the house with his wife until 1960. That year both of them died. For years after that the house had no occupants, although the attic was filled with trunks, a rocking horse, old sewing machines, and black clothes; an upright piano, a

Thompson house, south elevation before rehabilitation.

square piano, and a stove remained in the parlor; and a 19th-century iron stove sat in the kitchen. Dozens of pieces of farm equipment, including a manure spreader and some hand plows, sat in the cavernous stone barn.

Edwin Pierson, Ross W. Pierson's son, lived on an adjoining property and continued to raise cattle on the farm.

In 1972, Robert and Faye Young moved with their three children from Houston and built a house across the street from the old farmhouse. Bob worked for DuPont; Faye ran the family framing business, Youngcraft Customs, Inc., out of their house. She was the president; he the vice president.

For 10 years they lived across from the empty house; for 10 years they admired it and "wished it was ours." They thought it would be a perfect place to live and to carry out the business, which was growing too big for their own house. "But we never expected to get it," said Mrs. Young, "because we never thought it would go on the market."

Edwin Pierson, who owned it with his brother, felt a great sentimental attachment to the place. Four generations of Piersons had lived there. In 1982, Edwin's brother died, and his sister-in-law pressed him to sell. Pierson, 72, resisted but eventually gave in. He sold his 35 head of cattle and offered the Youngs the first option on the farmhouse and 10 of the property's 77 acres.

"It took a lot of negotiating to get the terms," said Mrs. Young. "No one had lived in the house for 20 years. Here we were talking about buying it, and I had never even been in it." Pierson and the Youngs did come to terms. The property, including the house, the barn, a chicken coop, farm machinery, and 10 acres, passed into their hands on April 19, 1982.

The Youngs became only the fourth family to own the property since John Chambers purchased it in 1720. Long interested in old houses, they began delving into the nuts and bolts—and dollars and cents—of rehabilitation.

Thompson house and barn, distant view.

TAX INCENTIVES FOR HISTORIC PRESERVATION, 1976–80

While the farmhouse was standing vacant, the federal government began offering tax incentives to encourage people to spend money on fixing up historic buildings.

The first incentives came with the Tax Reform Act of 1976. Its most important provisions were a five-year amortization of qualified rehabilitation costs, and accelerated depreciation for "substantial rehabilitations" (explained below). Both allowed you to write off costs much faster than regular depreciation, which lasted for the useful life of the improvements.

The 1976 law also established tax deductions for the donation of easements for charitable purposes, and tax penalties for demolishing certified historic buildings.

The Revenue Act of 1978 instituted an investment tax credit of 10 percent for rehabilitating commercial and industrial buildings at least 20 years old (whether they were historic or not). A credit is subtracted directly from taxes owed, whereas amortization and depreciation reduce the income on which taxes are calculated.

The 1980 Tax Treatment Extension Act extended provisions of the earlier acts beyond their original 1981 expiration dates and tightened the criteria for easement donations.

Sweeping changes came with the Reagan administration's overhaul of the tax laws in 1981. Section 212 of the Economic Recovery Tax Act (ERTA), which President Reagan signed on August 13, 1981, offers even stronger incentives for rehabilitation than previous laws. It became effective on January 1, 1982, and, with some modifications enacted in August 1982, is the law that applies as of press time.

(Please note that the descriptions here summarize complex laws and are intended only as a summary. You should consult an accountant and an attorney before doing any rehabilitation.)

All the tax incentives for historic rehabilitation have applied only to income-producing, that is, depreciable, properties. They have had no bearing on owner-occupied housing, except when portions of a house are used for business.

The 1976 law, said Bill Brookover, an architect with the National Park Service's regional office in Philadelphia, marked "the first time that accelerated depreciation was allowed for existing buildings. For new buildings, accelerated depreciation had been allowed since World War II. The 1976 law was an attempt to put old and new buildings on equal footing. The 1981 law perhaps even pushed old buildings ahead."

ECONOMIC RECOVERY TAX ACT OF 1981

The main incentive of this law is an investment tax credit (ITC) based on a building's age and historic significance. The law has a three-tier ITC:

— 15 percent ITC for rehabilitating a building between 30 and 40 years old

— 20 percent ITC for a building at least 40 years old

— 25 percent ITC for a "certified rehabilitation" of a "certified historic structure"

According to the Department of the Interior's final regulations on historic preservation certifications, published in the *Federal Register* of March 12, 1984, a certified historic structure is a depreciable "building (and its structural components) which is either (a) individually listed in the National Register or (b) located in a registered historic district and certified by the Secretary [of the Interior] as being of historic significance to the district."

A registered historic district is a National Register district or a state or local district certified by the Secretary of the Interior.

The law has other criteria. At least 75 percent of the existing exterior walls must remain in place in the rehabilitation. The 15 and 20 percent credits apply only to nonresidential (industrial and commercial) buildings. The 25 percent credit applies to both nonresidential and residential.

Thus you cannot take a credit for rehabilitating the house you live in (regardless of its age) unless it is certified historic and you (1) rent it out or (2) use at least part of it for business. You could then qualify for a prorated credit according to the portion of the house you rent out or use for business.

Another criterion is that the rehabilitation must be "substantial." To be substantial, your rehabilitation costs over a 24-month period (60 months for phased projects) must exceed the higher of these figures: (1) $5,000 or (2) the property's "adjusted basis." The adjusted basis is the cost of the building plus capital improvements, minus any depreciation you've taken while you've owned it. Adjusted basis does not include land costs.

To qualify if you rehabilitate, say, an office building that cost $75,000—of which $15,000 was land cost—you would have to spend at least $60,000 on the rehabilitation.

Not only must the building be certified historic; the rehabilitation itself must be certified as being consistent with the historic character of the building or of the district in which the building is located. All applications are evaluated against the Secretary of the Interior's Standards for Rehabilitation (see Figure 7-1).

If the Secretary of the Interior determines that your building is not significant to the district, you can still take an ITC—15 percent if the building is between 30 and 40 years old; 20 percent if it is at least 40 years old. On the other hand, you cannot choose to bypass the rehabilitation certification requirement if your building is certified as historic either individually or in a district. You rehabilitate according to the secretary's standards and take a 25 percent credit, or else are allowed no credit.

Besides the ITC, you can take a 15-year straight-line depreciation on the adjusted basis of the building. For the 15 and 20 percent ITC's, the amount you can depreciate is the adjusted basis minus the value of the credit. Thus if you spend $50,000 to rehabilitate a 35-year-old building, you can take an ITC of $7,500 (15 percent of $50,000), but the amount you can depreciate is $7,500 less than $50,000, or $42,500.

> **SECRETARY OF THE INTERIOR'S STANDARDS FOR REHABILITATION**
>
> The Standards shall be applied taking into consideration the economic and technical feasibility of each project; in the final analysis, however, to be certified, the rehabilitation project must be consistent with the historic character of the structure(s) and, where applicable, the district in which it is located.
>
> 1. Every reasonable effort shall be made to provide a compatible use for a property which requires minimal alteration of the building, structure, or site and its environment, or to use a property for its originally intended purpose.
> 2. The distinguishing original qualities or character of a building, structure, or site and its environment shall not be destroyed. The removal or alteration of any historic material or distinctive architectural features should be avoided when possible.
> 3. All buildings, structures, and sites shall be recognized as products of their own time. Alterations that have no historical basis and which seek to create an earlier appearance shall be discouraged.
> 4. Changes which may have taken place in the course of time are evidence of the history and development of a building, structure, or site and its environment. These changes may have acquired significance in their own right, and this significance shall be recognized and respected.
> 5. Distinctive stylistic features or examples of skilled craftsmanship which characterize a building, structure, or site shall be treated with sensitivity.
> 6. Deteriorated architectural features shall be repaired rather than replaced, wherever possible. In the event replacement is necessary, the new material should match the material being replaced in composition, design, color, texture, and other visual qualities. Repair or replacement of missing architectural features should be based on accurate duplications of features, substantiated by historic, physical, or pictorial evidence rather than on conjectural designs or the availability of different architectural elements from other buildings or structures.
> 7. The surface cleaning of structures shall be undertaken with the gentlest means possible. Sandblasting and other cleaning methods that will damage the historic building materials shall not be undertaken.
> 8. Every reasonable effort shall be made to protect and preserve archaeological resources affected by, or adjacent to any project.
> 9. Contemporary design for alterations and additions to existing properties shall not be discouraged when such alterations and additions do not destroy significant historical, architectural, or cultural material, and such design is compatible with the size, scale, color, material, and character of the property, neighborhood or environment.
> 10. Wherever possible, new additions or alterations to structures shall be done in such a manner that if such additions or alterations were to be removed in the future, the essential form and integrity of the structure would be unimpaired.

Figure 7–1

With the 25 percent ITC, in contrast, you have to reduce the basis by only half the ITC. If you spend $50,000 on a certified rehabilitation of a certified historic building, you can take an ITC of $12,500, and the amount you can depreciate is $6,250 less than $50,000, or $43,750.

The adjustment-to-basis requirement for the 25 percent ITC, enacted in 1982, amends the 1981 law. Under that law you didn't have to reduce the basis at all with the 25 percent ITC. The new requirement applies to properties placed in service after December 31, 1982 (with some exceptions covered by a transition rule).

WHAT TO DO

To qualify for the maximum ITC, 25 percent, both the building and the rehabilitation must be certified by the Secretary of the Interior through the National Park Service (NPS). The NPS generally works with state historic preservation offices; in Pennsylvania that office is the Bureau for Historic

National Park Service

Pennsylvania Historical and Museum Commission

Preservation within the Pennsylvania Historical and Museum Commission (PHMC).

A building is automatically certified if it is listed in the National Register of Historic Places. If you don't know the status of a building you own or are interested in buying and rehabilitating, a call to the PHMC should elicit the answer. If the building is registered, you're spared a good part of the required procedures and can skip to the description under Part 2 below. A building located in a registered historic district must be certified as contributing to the significance of the district.

Historic Preservation Certification Application, Part 1

You can begin the certification process by completing Part 1 of the NPS's Historic Preservation Certification Application and submitting it to the PHMC. Part 1 concerns the building's historic or architectural significance (see Appendix C). In it you describe the building's exterior and interior appearance and architectural style and explain why it is historically or architecturally significant. The application calls for recent photos and a map.

The PHMC staff will review the application and forward it to the NPS with a recommendation. The application is evaluated against the National Register criteria. If the building is in a registered historic district, it is evaluated against the Secretary of the Interior's Standards for Evaluating Significance within Registered Historic Districts. If the NPS approves the Part 1 application, the building will qualify for the 25 percent credit once Part 2 of the application is approved. For a building not yet on the National Register (or not in a registered historic district), you can give up the idea of pursuing the 25 percent credit and take a lesser credit, or you can try to get the building placed on the register through the PHMC and the NPS in Washington (see Chapter 4).

After the state nominates a building to the National Register, the NPS has 45 days to list it on the register or to ask for more information. If the NPS doesn't ask, the building is automatically listed. Generally, said Patrick O'Bannon, formerly a historian in the PHMC's Division of Preservation Services, the NPS "doesn't deny. If there is a denial, it will be at our staff level or the state Review Committee level."

Getting a building on the register "can be a long process," O'Bannon said, "because they ask for very good documentation. A lot of people are hiring historians and architects to do the documentation."

Historic Preservation Certification Application, Part 2

Once the building is placed on the register or once the PHMC staff says it's eligible, you can submit Part 2 (see Appendix C). Part 2 describes the rehabilitation you intend to do.

The PHMC will review your plans for consistency with the Secretary of the Interior's Standards for Rehabilitation and make a recommendation to the NPS Mid-Atlantic Regional Office in Philadelphia. The standards cover such matters as exterior masonry, roofs, porches, and window sashes.

Sometimes applicants think the PHMC is overly bureaucratic in asking for detailed information, O'Bannon said. "When we want additional information, it's because we expect the National Park Service will ask for more. We want applications we send on to be complete. We try to work with applicants to get as good an application as possible."

If the PHMC recommends that the NPS approve the Part 2 application and the NPS does so, you will receive preliminary certification of the rehabilitation. You can then proceed knowing that the work meets the law's requirements. Final certification from the NPS comes after you do the work and the NPS reviews the rehabilitation itself.

If the NPS determines that your completed rehabilitation does not meet the secretary's standards, you will receive an explanatory letter. You can appeal the decision to the NPS's Chief Appeals Officer for Cultural Resources in Washington.

The NPS recommends that you submit Part 2 before beginning work. Work done before the building is certified historic and the rehabilitation is certified may be futile. Richard Tyler, a historian with the Philadelphia Historical Commission and a nationally recognized expert on historic preservation, said: "I tell the interested people, if you start from square zero and are a cautious investor, don't start work until the building is on the register. You're talking six months to a year to get it on the register.

"If you want to roll the dice—that is, file Part 1 and go forward with the hope of getting on the register—it's risky." Under IRS regulations written

Sears International Trade Headquarters in Washington, D.C. Formerly the Apex Building, this structure was restored using federal tax incentives for rehabilitation.

The Metropolitan (old YMCA building) in Philadelphia after conversion into apartments.

The Metropolitan after rehabilitation; facade detail from terrace.

for the 1976 law, the building must be placed on the National Register within 30 months of the time you take your first tax deduction for rehabilitation. Otherwise the IRS may disallow part of the tax benefits.

As for rehabilitating before getting certification, Tyler said, "You can file retroactively, but that's chancy too. I wouldn't recommend it. We had one project in Philadelphia where a guy applied for retroactive certification after tearing out part of the original fabric of the interior and throwing it away. The application was denied. He took it to court and lost. My recommendation: get your certification before driving a nail."

If your Part 1 and Part 2 applications are complete, and your building is on the National Register, and the rehabilitation gets preliminary certification, you can sign your contract and drive your nails. You can also bite your nails when the time comes to file your tax return.

CAN YOU BENEFIT?

Before you conclude that all of this is a lot of trouble, you should realize that you don't have to go through all of it to benefit from the tax incentives. They are available not only to people who rehabilitate their own properties but also to people who buy limited-partnership interests in large projects. Developers often raise capital for projects by syndicating limited partnerships to investors.

For example, Butcher and Singer, an investment banking firm in Philadelphia, has a division, Sovereign Realty, that finds promising historic rehabilitation projects and puts together syndications. In 1982 Sovereign syndicated three projects, including a conversion of the YMCA building in downtown Philadelphia to apartments and a $35 million rehabilitation in Chicago.

To participate in a Sovereign offering, though, "you have to be very wealthy." So said Robin Rosenfeld, who specializes in historic projects for Sovereign. "The unit size per investor is at least $100,000. Sometimes half units are available; it varies from deal to deal." Sovereign has "suitability requirements" for how much money an investor must have. "Normally," Ms. Rosenfeld said, "your net worth has to be three times the investment." Net worth here doesn't even include your house or its furnishings or your car.

If you're a doctor, lawyer, athlete, TV star, or other wealthy person, you might be able to invest in a Sovereign syndication. Sovereign has attracted lots of investors. Because of the 25 percent credit, Ms. Rosenfeld said, "it's one of the hottest items we offer."

Sovereign syndications are "private placements." Lower-priced limited partnerships can be had in "public offerings." For those, you don't need nearly as much money. A firm could, for example, divide a $1 million rehabilitation into 100 limited-partnership investments worth $10,000 each. You could then take the $2,500 tax credit, depreciation, and other benefits, on your $10,000 investment.

Whether or not that investment, or any other rehabilitation, makes sense financially depends on your income and your tax situation, on how much money you have to invest and to risk, your interest in history, and other factors. You have to sit down with an accountant, a lawyer, or both, and figure out whether the investment is worth it to you.

Said John Lacy, a certified public accountant in Center Square, Montgomery County, "You have to have a lot of income to benefit—probably in the 45 percent tax bracket or above. You should be in that range if the tax benefits of historic rehabilitation are to compete with less troublesome tax shelters, such as shopping centers or oil and gas wells."

On the other hand, Lacy said, "If you're interested in rehabilitation incentives because of a love of history rather than as a tax shelter, they do offer a stimulus. If you can get a building at a low price, make authentic improvements, and put some love and money into it," he said, "it could be a good investment. You need knowledge, and a desire to do it right, and an income above $50,000 a year to afford it."

WHAT'S BEING DONE

A *Preservation News* supplement published by the National Trust for Historic Preservation in November 1981 reported that applicants using tax incentives "tend to fall into three categories: individuals with an interest in preservation who undertake relatively small, residential rental projects (be-

John Milner Associates

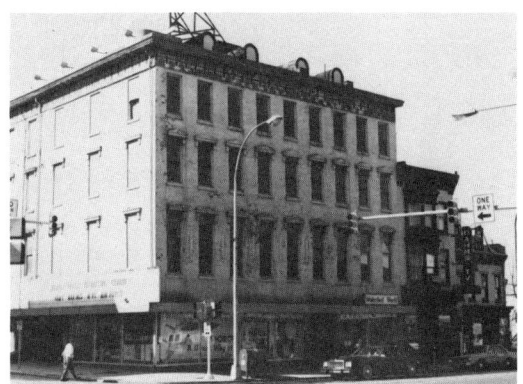

American House in Reading, Pennsylvania, before and after rehabilitation using federal tax incentives.

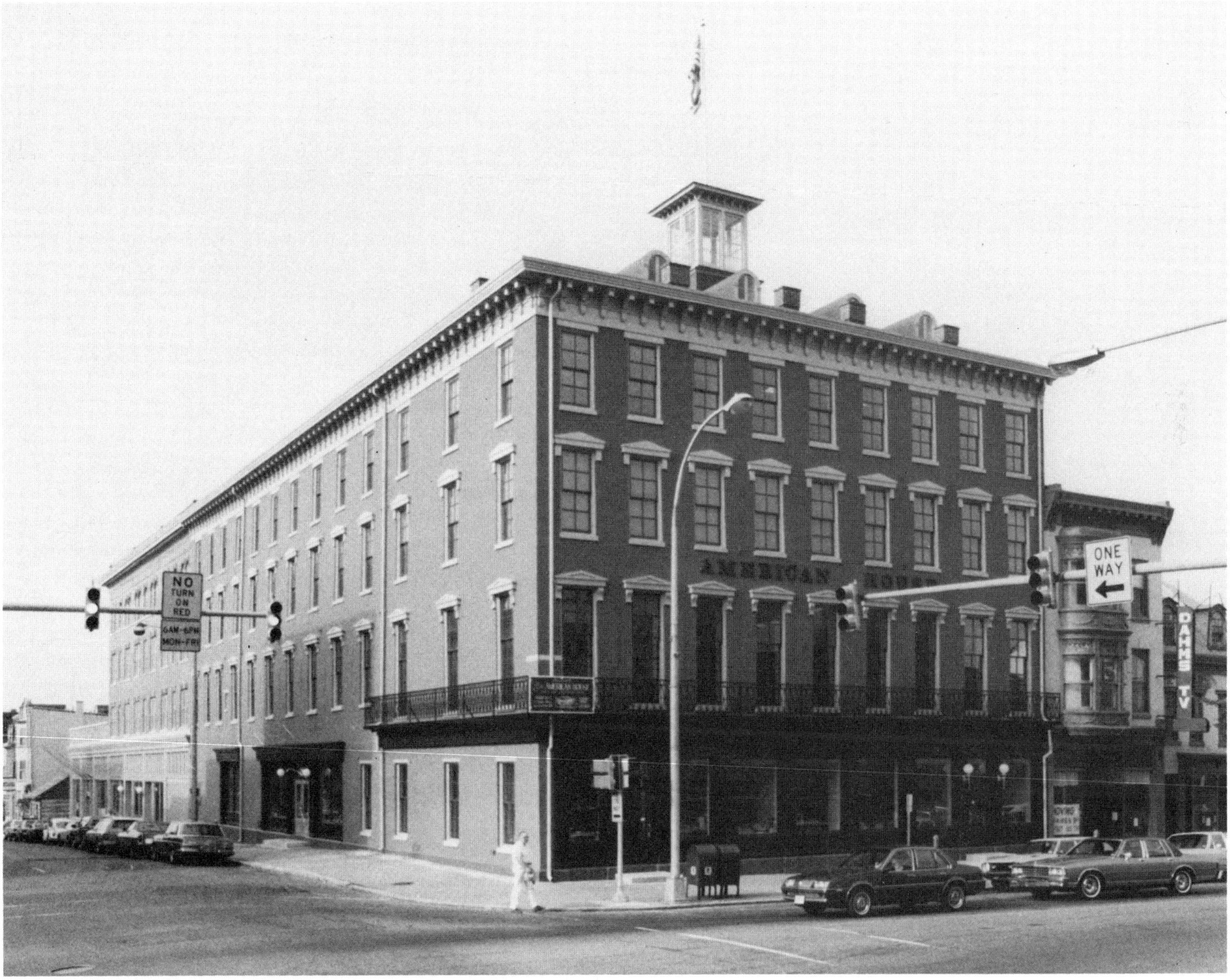

John Milner Associates

tween $50,000 and $150,000 total investment); organizations, such as law firms and banks, needing additional office space (spending under $1 million); and large-scale investors who, as limited partnerships, typically undertake such projects as multi-million dollar conversions of historic mills into housing or renovations of major office buildings or hotels."

A National Park Service "Information Update" on tax incentives, dated June 30, 1984, reported that since the passage of the Tax Reform Act in 1976, more than 9,984 projects nationwide had qualified for incentives. They amounted to more than $6.24 billion. Fifty percent of the projects were residential; 21 percent were for mixed use; 16 percent were for office space; 8 percent were for commercial enterprises; and 3 percent were for hotel rehabilitations. About 49,530 housing units had been involved in those projects, including more the 30,615 new housing units, of which 13,666 were intended for low- and moderate-income families.

Some people have said that the current law tends to shut out small projects. The reason is the "substantial rehabilitation" test. Kirk Cordell, of the NPS Atlanta office, was quoted in the April 15, 1982, issue of *Urban Conservation Reports* as saying: "We're seeing larger projects than we've seen before—and more money. There are fewer projects in which the old family homestead is being renovated."

But O'Bannon of the PHMC said, "Here in Pennsylvania I don't think that's true. In Philadelphia, for example, we're seeing a lot of $40,000 Federal-style rowhouses being rehabilitated and rented out."

Across the state, O'Bannon said, "we're getting a wide range of projects—from small industrial housing to big corporate projects. We see a lot of limited partnerships formed for medium-to-large projects. We can get some guy redoing an old rowhouse for an office, and then we see a $17.9 million project to redo a railroad station in Pittsburgh."

Big houses, O'Bannon said, "are tailor-made for insurance company and law offices."

Regardless of the size of projects, O'Bannon said the 1981 law attracted much attention. After it went into effect in January 1982, "the number of applications skyrocketed."

The state doesn't keep a precise breakdown by area. O'Bannon said, however, "most applications come from cities. The heaviest action is in Philadelphia and Pittsburgh. Then Allentown, Reading, Lancaster, and York, and a smattering in other areas."

The four counties around Philadelphia have had relatively few projects, O'Bannon said. "Generally what you have in the suburbs is owner-occupied housing. That's just not eligible." Another reason is that the suburbs have far fewer buildings on the National Register, and fewer historic districts, than cities. Having buildings on the register or in certified districts makes it much easier to get certification. Also, a lot of people in the suburbs resist putting buildings on the register.

Said John Milner, president of John Milner Associates in West Chester: "People here tend to be suspicious of creating a historic district. They tend to think they'll have so many restrictions that they'll be tied down. The residents get the wrong information and they rebel. So they resist the National Register."

Richard Tyler said not enough energy is being expended to take advantage of the tax law—in the city or, especially, in the suburbs. "A substantial part

Strickler Insurance offices in Lebanon, Pennsylvania, after restoration (formerly the Cornwall-Lebanon Railway Station).

of West Chester," Tyler believes, "is eligible for the National Register. My suggestion is to get it on the register. In suburban downtown Main Streets, the tax act would help the merchant. Chester County is a wealthy part of the world. People of affluence don't want to go to Exton Mall. Why can't West Chester become the Chestnut Hill of Chester County?"

Milner's firm, which includes architects, archeologists, and planners, was founded in 1968 and has always specialized in historic preservation. The firm has done plans for many projects under the tax laws. One, rehabilitated partly under the old laws and partly under the current law, is the Cornwall and Lebanon railroad station in Lebanon, a Victorian building converted to insurance company offices. Another project is the Fidelity Mutual Life Insurance segmental building across from the Art Museum in Philadelphia. Another is the former St. Marks Hotel in Washington, a late-Victorian building converted to offices. "It would never fly if not for the tax incentives," Milner said. "The construction costs would be too high. But with the incentives, the numbers work and it can be done."

"The credits won't make a sow's ear into a silk purse," said Jay Nathan, who rehabilitated the Drexel building at 15th and Walnut Streets, Philadelphia, under the old laws. "If a building is not well located or doesn't have the special ingredients to make a project realistic, the credits won't work. Where they become critically important is a building on the borderline, or better. With a building on the borderline, one that might or might not work, the credits can clearly push it over into the positive."

"A developer has to have a measure of appreciation for old buildings," said Milner. "He has to be creative, because historical projects are not easy to do."

The Drexel building, with its huge banking floor, marble floors and walls, and mahogany paneling, had been vacant for more than 20 years. "Everybody had looked at it and thrown up their hands," Nathan said. "They said it had great bulk but not much square footage. The first floor was 40 feet high; the second was 20. You couldn't rent it as regular office space: it had only 35,000 square feet.

"Tax law or not, 35,000 feet couldn't work. The question was how to create more space without raping the building. It shocked me what some fancy architects put their names on. One said, 'Here's a 40-foot space; insert another floor.' Clearly that would have destroyed the space. I said, 'The essence of this room is the unobstructed expanse of the great ceiling. I want to stand in the middle, look up, and see the expanse.'"

Nathan installed two mezzanines, adding 8,000 square feet. "It isn't as nice as if that hadn't been done," Nathan said, "but it had to get to the point of making sense."

"Purity is nice," said Philadelphia historian Tyler, "but you lose a lot of buildings being pure."

REHABILITATING THE OLD HOUSE

Bob and Faye Young investigated the tax laws by reading articles, speaking with PHMC staff people in Harrisburg, and attending seminars. After they bought the 1833 farmhouse in April 1982, they set out to have it placed on the National Register.

They hired Susan Herr of Landenburg to research the deeds, wills, and other sources to document the building's historical significance.

"The main significance," said Ms. Herr, "is the unusual brick construction features, such as the huge, barnlike arched opening on the south wall and the cantilevered second-floor bedroom. Other nice features are the double-brick cornice and the flat brick arches over the windows."

Added Young: "A great thing about this house is that nobody tried to do anything before. The house had minimal heating and electricity and no plumbing. Most old houses have been so tampered with that it's almost impossible to redo them without going down to the walls. This is a jewel, mainly because Edwin Pierson took good care of it. The mortised and pegged rafters are all oak, and in most places the wood is like brand new." Young crawled under the first floor to show some of the hand-hewn joists. "You could run a herd of elephants across it."

Young spoke with PHMC architect Alan Wolmer about the standards for rehabilitation. (They don't mention elephants.) He spoke with his tax lawyer in Wilmington and "had him look at a few things." Early on, the Youngs and Ms. Herr filled out the state's Historic Resource Survey Form (see Appendix C), from which the PHMC makes an early determination of whether a building has historical significance. The state said to proceed and fill out Parts 1 and 2 of the Historic Preservation Certification Application.

"We sent Part 1 to Harrisburg in June 1982," said Ms. Herr. "Pat O'Bannon said our chances looked good and to send in Part 2. We sent that in August."

In September 1982 the state said that the house appeared to meet National Register criteria for evaluation and was likely to be nominated to the National Register. The PHMC forwarded its recommendation to the NPS. The house was listed in the National Register on July 14, 1983.

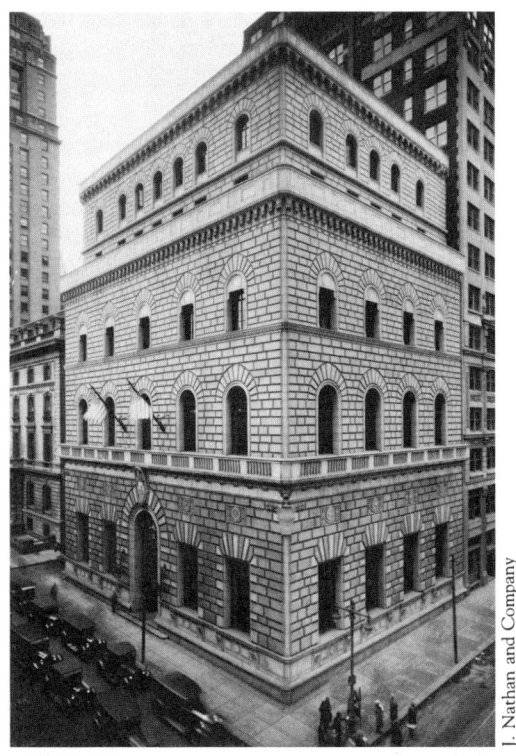

Drexel building, exterior.

Drexel building, interior ceiling.

Thompson house, with rehabilitation in progress.

Thompson house, interior stairway undergoing rehabilitation.

Meanwhile, the Youngs had drawn their plans for their new home and business and begun work on rehabilitating it.

They decided to use the original parlor as their studio. The first-floor hallway will be a gallery, with pictures displayed on the walls. The cellar will have woodworking tools and will be used to store glass and molding. Eventually the barn too will be used for storage. One upstairs bedroom will be used as the office.

The other parts of the house—the upstairs bedrooms, the old living room with the two pianos, the kitchen, and the old pump room—will be used as living space. Young estimated that about 50 percent of the house will be devoted to business and 50 percent to residence.

He rebuilt the makeshift enclosure around the old pump room (summer kitchen). Its beehive oven has been restored. He has lighted the 40-foot well from within and covered it with a $350 piece of lucite to show off the stonework.

The rehabilitation work, some of which has already been done, entailed hiring an electrician, a brick and stone mason, and a contractor for heating. It meant sanding the rust off 150-year-old hinges, and following the original roofline of a shed—and not the line of a later lean-to—for a frame addition.

Young has done much of the work himself. A crisp, late-October afternoon found him hammering new Canadian cedar shake shingles on the roof.

"We're taking our time," said Mrs. Young. "We want to do it right."

"When we started," she said, "there were a lot of things we didn't know. The first carpenter we talked to suggested tearing everything out, starting from scratch. I stood numb listening to him. Others wanted to fix it up like a new house. I said I didn't want a new house."

Young has taken some chances. He's serving as his own architect and doing much of the rehabilitation work himself. The value of his own labor can't figure in his rehabilitation costs, because the IRS won't let you deduct the

Thompson house, south elevation with rehabilitation completed.

value of your own labor. Also, he did a lot of work before sitting down with an accountant to figure out the costs, taxes, credits, and deductions.

He has, however, estimated the adjusted basis of the property and has determined that the rehabilitation costs will exceed them:

"We paid $90,000 for the house, barn, and 10 acres. We valued the house and barn at $60,000. We'll easily spend $60,000 just in restoring the house. Materials alone will be close to $60,000. Take this roof. The material is $4,000. If I had the roof done, it would cost me $10,000. I'm taking off from work and getting it done myself."

Going ahead with the rehabilitation before getting the house on the register and preliminary certification of the rehabilitation was also risky: If the house had failed to make the register, Young would have had to settle for a 20 percent tax credit instead of 25 percent. If the National Park Service had disapproved the rehabilitation, he'd have had to do things over again (if he could) or lose the tax credit altogether.

The PHMC, Young said, "has been efficient and helpful. They're interested in seeing our heritage saved.

"I'd recommend that others do this. If you get a house that has been well taken care of, it will probably last longer than a new house. This has financial advantages, and cultural advantages too. We've always wanted to fix up a house as it was years ago. The incentives give us tax benefits, and the house gives us a place to live and work."

Preservation is reaching far more people today than it did in the 1960s, said John Milner. Back then, "it was the specialty of a small group of people. Now it has evolved into something that affects many more people. They recognize that we have a significant architectural heritage.

"The reason for the change is the tax laws. They've made it advantageous to think about history."

FOR FURTHER READING

Chapter 2
Three Centuries of Delaware Valley Architecture: A Tour

Bennett, George Fletcher. *Early Architecture of Delaware.* New York, New York: Bonanza Books, 1932.

Blumenson, John J.G. *Identifying American Architecture: A Pictoral Guide to Styles and Terms, 1600-1945.* Nashville, Tennessee: American Association for State and Local History, 1977.

Detweiler, Willard S., Jr., Inc. *Chestnut Hill: An Architectural History.* Philadelphia, Pennsylvania, 1969.

Feaver, Jane. *Seventeenth Century Survivors.* Philadelphia, Pennsylvania: The Colonial Society of Pennsylvania, 1982.

Glassie, Henry. *Delaware Valley Folk Building.* Winterthur Portfolio. Winterthur, Delaware: Henry Francis duPont Winterthur Museum, 1972.

Glassie, Henry. *Pattern in the Material Folk Culture of the Eastern United States.* Philadelphia, Pennsylvania: University of Pennsylvania Press, 1968.

Maass, John. *The Victorian Home in America.* New York, New York: Hawthorn Books, Inc., 1972.

Marshall, Howard Wight. *American Folk Architecture: A Selected Bibliography.* American Folklife Center No. 8., 1981.

Poppeliers, John; Chambers, S. Allen; and Schwartz, Nancy B. *What Style Is It?* Washington, D.C.: Preservation Press, 1976-1977.

Raymond, Eleanor. *Early Domestic Architecture of Pennsylvania.* Princeton, New Jersey: Pyne Press, 1973.

Richie, Margaret Bye. *History of Bucks County Architecture.* pamphlet 1980.

Richman, Irwin, *Pennsylvania's Architecture.* Pennsylvania History Studies No. 10, University Park, Pennsylvania: The Pennsylvania Historical Association, 1969.

Schiffer, Margaret Berwind. *Survey of Chester County, Pennsylvania, Architecture.* Exton, Pennsylvania: Schiffer Publishing Ltd., 1976.

Tatum, G.B., *Penn's Great Town: 250 Years of Philadelphia Architecture Illustrated in Prints and Drawings.* Philadelphia, Pennsylvania: University of Pennsylvania Press, 1961.

Tatum, G.B. *Philadelphia Georgian.* Middletown, Connecticut: Wesleyan University Press, 1976.

Webster, Richard J. *Philadelphia Preserved: Catalog of the Historic American Buildings Survey.* Philadelphia, Pennsylvania, 1976.

Whiffen, Marcus. *American Architecture Since 1780: A Guide to the Styles.* Cambridge, Massachusetts: M.I.T. Press, 1969.

White, Theo B. *Philadelphia Architecture in the Nineteenth Century.* Philadelphia, 1953.

Chapter 3
Researching Historic Buildings

Abramson, Howard S. "Digging Up the Secret of Our Cities." *Historic Preservation*, vol. 34, no. 3, May-June 1982, pp. 32-37.

Association for State and Local History. *Nail Chronology As an Aid to Dating Old Buildings.* Nashville, Tennessee: Association for State and Local History, n.d.

Colflesh, Julia. "Pennsylvania and the 'Window Tax'" Ms., 1976.

Cremers, Estelle. "How to Research Old Houses." Transcript of speech. Pottstown, Pennsylvania: French and Pickering Creeks Conservation Trust, 1979.

Mercer, Henry C. *The Dating of Old Houses.* New Hope, Pennsylvania: Bucks County Historical Society, 1923 (reprinted 1976).

Old House Journal. *How to Date an Old House.* Brooklyn, New York: The Old-House Journal Corporation, 1977.

Schiffer, Herbert. *Early Pennsylvania Hardware.* Whitford, Pennsylvania: Whitford Press, 1966.

Vider, Elise. "Getting to Know Your House." *Historic Preservation*, vol. 34, no. 2, March-April 1982, pp. 22-25.

Welsh, Frank S. *Paintpamphlet: A Guide to Assist the Investigation of Original Paint Color in Old Houses.* Bryn Mawr, Pennsylvania: Frank S. Welsh, 1981.

Weitzman, David. *Underfoot, An Everyday Guide to Exploring the American Past.* New York, New York: Charles Scribner's Sons, 1976.

Chapter 4
The National Register of Historic Places

Greiff, Constance M. *The Historic Property Owner's Handbook.* Washington, D.C.: Preservation Press, 1977.

Pennsylvania Historical and Museum Commission, Bureau for Historic Preservation. *The National Register Process in Pennsylvania.* Harrisburg, Pennsylvania, 1982.

U.S. Department of the Interior, Heritage Conservation and Recreation Service. *Using the UTM Grid System to Record Historic Sites.* Washington, D.C.: Government Printing Office, 1980.

U.S. Department of the Interior, National Park Service, National Register Division. *How to Complete National Register Forms*. Washington, D.C.: Government Printing Office, 1977.

Weinberg, Steve. "Our Nation's Super List: Is it in Trouble?" *Historic Preservation*, July-August 1982, pp. 10-17.

Chapter 5
The Ways and Means of Preservation

Boasberg, Tersh. *A Primer on Historic Preservation Law in Pennsylvania*. Washington, D.C.: National Center for Preservation Law, 1982.

City of Lancaster. *A Design Guide: Lancaster, Pennsylvania*. Lancaster, Pennsylvania, 1977.

Delaware Valley Regional Planning Commission. *Inventory of Historic Sites*. Philadelphia, Pennsylvania, 1969.

Doylestown Borough Planning Commission. *Design Resources of Doylestown*. Doylestown Borough, Pennsylvania, 1969.

Dueriksen, Christopher J. Ed., *A Handbook on Historic Preservation Law*. Washington, D.C.: Conservation Foundation and National Center for Preservation Law, 1983.

Getzels, Judith N. *Recycling Public Buildings*. Planning Advisory Service Report No. 319. Chicago, Illinois: American Planning Association, 1976.

"Historic Preservation." *Urban Land*. July-August 1975.

"Historic Preservation in Small Communities." *Small Town*. vol. 5, no. 8, March 1975.

John Reynolds Design Associates. *Architectural Guidelines for Construction in the Historic District*. Birmingham Township, Chester County, Pennsylvania, n.d.

Miner, Ralph W. *Conservation of Historic and Cultural Resources*. Planning Advisory Service Report No. 244. Chicago, Illinois: American Society of Planning Officials, 1969.

Morrison, Jacob H. *Historic Preservation Law*. Washington, D.C.: National Trust for Historic Preservation, 1965.

National Endowment for the Arts. *Design Guidelines: An Annotated Bibliography*. Washington, D.C., n.d.

National Trust for Historic Preservation.
The Brown Book: A Directory of Preservation Information. Washington, D.C.: Preservation Press, 1983.
Information: A Preservation Sourcebook. Washington, D.C.: Preservation Press (annual supplements).
Old and New Architecture: Design Relationship. Washington, D.C.: Preservation Press, 1980.

Preservation Law Reporter. vols. 1-3, Washington, D.C., 1982-1984.

Old Allentown Preservation Association, Inc. *Old Allentown Houses: Design Guidelines for an Historic District*. Allentown, Pennsylvania, 1979.

Pennsylvania Historical and Museum Commission, Bureau for Historic Preservation. *Guidelines for Historic Resource Surveys in Pennsylvania*. Harrisburg, Pennsylvania, 1982.

Roddewig, Richard J. *Preparing A Historic Preservation Ordinance*. Planning Advisory Service Report No. 374. Chicago, Illinois: American Planning Association, 1983.

Chapter 6
Preservation Easements

Barrett, Thomas S. and Livermore, Putnam. *The Conservation Easement in California*. Covelo, California: Island Press, 1983.

Brenneman, Russell L. *Private Approaches to the Preservation of Open Land*. New London, Connecticut: The Conservation and Research Foundation, 1967.

Brenneman, Russell L. *Should "Easements" Be Used to Protect National Historic Landmarks? A Study for the National Park Service*. 3 vols. Hartford, Connecticut: Copp, Brenneman, Tighe, Koletsky and Berall, 1975.

Coughlin, Thomas. *Easements and Other Legal Techniques to Protect Historic Houses in Private Ownership*. Washington, D.C.: Historic House Association of America, 1981.

Fisher, Charles E.; MacRostie, William G.; and Sowick, Christopher A. *Directory of Historic Preservation Easement Organizations*. Washington, D.C.: U.S. Department of the Interior, National Park Service Technical Preservation Services Division, 1981.

Holmes, Robert J. "Conservation Easement: At Last, Preservation Pays." *Urban Land*, vol. 41, no. 11, November 1982, pp. 3-8.

Proceedings of the Conference on Voluntary Preservation of Open Space, March 9, 1974. Pottstown, Pennsylvania: French and Pickering Creeks Conservation Trust.

Reynolds, Judith, and Reynolds, Anthony. "Factors Affecting Valuation of Historic Property." Information sheet. National Trust for Historic Preservation, 1976.

Saxe, Emma Jane. "How to Qualify Historic Properties under the New Federal Law Affecting Easements." Washington, D.C.: U.S. Department of the Interior, National Park Service, National Register Division, 1981.

Silverman, Jane. "The Trade-Off That Pays Off." *Historic Preservation,* vol. 34, no. 2, March-April 1982.

Small, Stephen J. "The Tax Benefits of Donating Easements on Scenic and Historic Property." *Real Estate Law Journal,* vol. 7, Spring 1979, pp. 304-19.

U.S. Department of the Interior, Heritage Conservation and Recreation Service. *Land Conservation and Preservation Techniques.* March 1979.

Watson, A. Elizabeth. "Establishing an Easement Program to Protect Historic, Scenic, and Natural Resources." Information sheet no. 25. National Trust for Historic Preservation, 1980.

Chapter 7
Tax Incentives for Historic Buildings

Anthony, Aubra H., Jr. "Summary of Preservation Tax Incentives in Economic Recovery Tax Act of 1981." Information sheet no. 30. National Trust for Historic Preservation, 1981.

Lynch, Bruce E. "New Tax Credits No Preservation Cure-All." *Planning,* February 1982.

Oldham, Sally G., and Jandl, H. Ward. "Preservation Tax Incentives: New Investment Opportunities under the Economic Recovery Tax Act." *Urban Land,* March 1982.

"Rehab Tax Credits Attract Big Money, Shut Out Little Guys." *Urban Conservation Report,* vol. 6, no. 7, April 15, 1982.

"Tax Incentives: New Investment Opportunities: Economic Recovery Tax Act of 1981." *Preservation News* supplement, November 1981.

U.S. Congress, Staff of the Joint Committee on Taxation. *General Explanation of the Economic Recovery Tax Act of 1981.* Washington, D.C.: U.S. Government Printing Office, 1981.

U.S. Department of the Interior, Heritage Conservation and Recreation Service. *The Secretary of the Interior's Standards for Rehabilitation and Guidelines for Rehabilitating Historic Buildings.* January 1981.

U.S. Department of Interior, National Park Service. "Historic Preservation Certifications; Final Rule." *Federal Register,* vol. 49, no. 49, March 12, 1984.

APPENDIX A — Directory of Organizations Concerned with Historic Preservation

National and Pennsylvania

County and Local (Delaware Valley)

Easement Programs in Pennsylvania

The material contained in this appendix was compiled and updated to September 1984, with the help of the Delaware County Planning Department, the Bucks County Conservancy, the Chester County Historic Preservation Office, and the Montgomery County Historical Society. Telephone numbers are provided where available. Addresses may change regularly in some cases; for example, those of local historical societies and other smaller organizations can change when officers change.

National and Pennsylvania

Advisory Council on Historic Preservation
1100 Pennsylvania Avenue, NW
Washington, D.C. 20004
(202) 254-3967

American Association for State and Local History
708 Berry Road
Nashville, TN 37204
(615) 383-5991

American Institute of Architects, Philadelphia Chapter
Conservation and Historic Preservation Committee
Architects Building
117 South 17th Street
Philadelphia, PA 19103
(215) 569-3186

American Planning Association, Eastern Pennsylvania Chapter
c/o American Planning Association
1313 East 60th Street
Chicago, IL 60637
(312) 955-9100

Foundation for Preservation Technology
5619 Southampton Drive
Springfield, VA 22151

National Alliance of Preservation Commissions
1522 K Street, NW, Suite 500
Washington, D.C. 20005
(202) 783-3363

National Center for Preservation Law
2101 L Street, NW, Suite 906
Washington, D.C. 20037
(202) 466-8960

National Trust for Historic Preservation
1785 Massachusetts Avenue, NW
Washington, D.C. 20036
(202) 673-4000

    Mid-Atlantic Regional Office
    6401 Germantown Avenue
    Philadelphia, PA 19144
    (215) 438-2886

Pennsylvania Committee for the Preservation of Architectural Records
c/o The Athenaeum
219 South Sixth Street
Philadelphia, PA 19106
(215) 925-2688

Pennsylvania Historical and Museum Commission
Bureau for Historic Preservation
Box 1026
Harrisburg, PA 17120
(717) 787-4363/2891

Pennsylvania Trust for Historic Preservation
John Bowles House
Fairmount Park
West Park
Philadelphia, PA 19131

Preservation Action
1700 Connecticut Avenue, NW, Suite 400
Washington, D.C. 20009
(202) 659-0915

Preservation Fund of Pennsylvania, Inc.
2470 Kissel Hill Road
Lancaster, PA 17601
(717) 569-2243

U.S. Department of the Interior
National Park Service
18th and C Streets, NW
Washington, D.C. 20204
    Interagency Resources Division
    (202) 343-9500
        National Register of Historic Places Branch
        (202) 343-9536
        Survey and Planning Branch
        (202) 343-9505
        Natural Landmarks Branch
        (202) 343-9525
    History Division — National Historic Landmarks Program
    (202) 343-8163
    Preservation Assistance Division
    (202) 343-9573
        Technical Preservation Services
        (202) 343-9578
        Grants Administration Branch
        (202) 343-9573
        Curatorial Services Branch
        (202) 343-8153
    Historic American Buildings Survey/Historic American Engineering Record Division
    (202) 343-9606
    Regional Office: Mid-Atlantic Region, Cultural Programs
    National Park Service
    143 South Third Street
    Philadelphia, PA 19106
    (215) 597-2283

Victorian Society in America
c/o The Athenaeum
219 South Sixth Street
Philadelphia, PA 19106
(215) 627-4252

County and Local (Delaware Valley)

Bucks County

Bristol Historical Museum Society
417 Radcliffe Street
Bristol, PA 19007
(215) 788-8656

Buckingham Historical Commission
Box 413
Buckingham, PA 18912
(215) 794-8834

Bucks County Conservancy
11 North Main Street
Doylestown, PA 18901
(215) 345-7020

Bucks County Historical Society
Pine and Ashland Streets
Doylestown, Pa 18901
(215) 345-0210

Bucks County Tourist Commission
152 Swamp Road
Doylestown, PA 18901
(215) 345-4552

Citizens for the Preservation of Craven Hall
P.O. Box 2042
Warminster, PA 18974

Doylestown Community Association
218 East Court Street
Doylestown, PA 18901

Friends of Bolton Mansion
2 Honeysuckle Lane
Levittown, PA 19055

Friends of the Delaware Canal
P.O. Box 312
Point Pleasant, PA 18950

Growden Mansion Association
5408 Neshaminy Boulevard
Bensalem, PA 19020

Hilltown Historical Society
Box 79
Hilltown, PA 18927
(215) 822-1206

Historic Carversville Society
P.O. Box 41
Carversville, PA 18913

Historic Falsington, Inc.
4 Yardley Avenue
Falsington, PA 19054
(215) 295-6567

Historic Langhorne Association
160 Maple Avenue
Langhorne, PA 19047
(215) 752-2079

Historic Morrisville Society
Hillcrest and Legion Avenues
Morrisville, PA 19067
(215) 295-7209 or 4845

Historical Society of Bensalem Township
P.O. Box 1101
Bensalem, PA 19020
(215) 946-1744

Hulmeville Historical Society
300 Main Street
Hulmeville, PA 19047

Lower Makefield Historical Commission
1100 Edgewood Road
Yardley, PA 19067
(215) 493-3646

Lower Makefield Historical Society
P.O. Box 228
Yardley, PA 19067

Lower Southampton Historical Society
1500 Desire Avenue
Feasterville, PA 19047
(215) 357-9274

Middletown Township Historical
Preservation Committee
2140 Trenton Road
Levittown, PA 19056
(215) 943-0300

Milford Township Historical and
Preservation Society
c/o Dr. Roger and Carol Baldwin
The Spinner House
Box 66
Spinnerstown, PA 18968

New Britain Borough Historical Commission
56 Keeley Avenue
New Britain, PA 18901
(215) 348-4586

New Hope Historical Society
Box 41
New Hope, PA 18938
(215) 862-5652

Newtown Historic Association, Inc.
P.O. Box 303
Newtown, PA 18940
(215) 968-4004

Newtown Joint Historic Commission
P.O. Box 103
Newtown, PA 18940

Northampton Township Historical
Commission
55 Township Road
Richboro, PA 18954
(215) 357-6800

Northampton Township Historical Society
Northampton Township Building
55 Township Road
Richboro, PA 18954

Penndel Historical Committee
c/o James Blake
531 Julie Lane
Penndel, PA 19047

Pennsbury Society
400 Pennsbury Memorial Road
Morrisville, PA 19067

Perkasie Historical Society
629 Shadywood Drive
Perkasie, PA 18944

Plumstead Historical Society
R.D. #4
Doylestown, PA 18901

Quakertown Historical Society
26 North Main Street
Quakertown, PA 18951
(215) 536-3499

Radcliffe Cultural and Historical Foundation
P.O. Box 215
Bristol, PA 19007

Richland Historical Society
Richlandtown Pike
Quakertown, PA 18951
(215) 536-4508

Solebury Township Historical Society
Box 223
Solebury, PA 18963
(215) 297-8771

Springfield Township Historical Society
Box 21
Springtown, PA 18081
(215) 536-6814

Sellersville Borough Historical & Achievement Authori
140 East Church Street
Sellersville, PA 18960
(215) 257-5075

Tinicum Township Historical Society
R.D. #1
Box 60
Ottsville, PA 18942

Tyler Park Associates
c/o Tom Mayer
Silver Lake Road
Langhorne, PA 19047

Upper Makefield Historical Society
Box 1737
Washington Crossing, PA 18977

Upper Makefield Township Historic Commission
c/o Richard Walker
Route 532
Newtown, PA 18940

Upper Southampton Historical Advisory Commission
939 Street Road
Southampton, PA 18966
(215) 357-1582

Warwick Township Historical Commission
P.O. Box 364
Jamison, PA 18929
(215) 343-6100

Washington Crossing Foundation
P.O. Box 1976
Washington Crossing, PA 18977
(215) 493-6577

Wrightstown Historical Commission
P.O. Box 90
Wycombe, PA 18980
(215) 598-3313

Yardley Historical Association, Inc.
32 Canal Street
Yardley, PA 19067
(215) 493-3390

Chester County

Brandywine Conservancy, Inc.*
Environmental Management Center
P.O. Box 141
Chadds Ford, PA 19317
(215) 459-1900

Chadds Ford Historical Society*
P.O. Box 27
Chadds Ford, PA 19317
(215) 388-7376

Charlestown Historical Society
Valley Hill Road
Box 48, R.D. 1
Malvern, PA 19355
(215) 644-1809

Chester County Day Committee
Box 1
West Chester, PA 19380

Chester County Historical Society
225 North High Street
West Chester, PA 19380
(215) 692-4800

Chester County Historic Preservation Office
Courthouse Annex
17 North Church Street
West Chester, PA 19380
(215) 431-6917

Chester County Tourist Promotion Bureau
33 West Market Street
West Chester, PA 19382
(215) 431-6365

Coatesville Historical Commission
53 South First Avenue
Coatesville, PA 19320
(215) 384-0300

Downingtown Historical Commission
4 West Lancaster Avenue
Downingtown, PA 19335
(215) 269-0344

Downingtown Historical Society
P.O. Box 9
Downingtown, PA 19335

East Bradford Historical Commission
880 Brandywine Road
West Chester, PA 19380
(215) 269-1405

East Brandywine Historical Committee
1114 Horseshoe Pike
Downingtown, PA 19335
(215) 269-2938

East Fallowfield Historical Committee
RD 1, Box 387-A
Coatesville, PA 19320
(215) 383-7144

East Nantmeal Historical Commission
c/o East Nantmeal Township
R.D.1
Glenmoore, PA 19343
(215) 458-5780

East Whiteland Historical Commission
209 Conestoga Road
Frazer, PA 19355
(215) 648-0600

French and Pickering Creeks Conservation Trust
Box 360, RD 2
Pottstown, PA 19464
(215) 469-6287

Historical Society of the Phoenixville Area
P.O. Box 552
Phoenixville, PA 19460
(215) 933-8145

Historic Yellow Spring, Inc.
Art School Road
Chester Springs, PA 19425
(215) 827-7414

Kennett Township Historical Committee
P.O. Box H
Kennett Square, PA 19348
(215) 388-1300

New London Area Historical Society
R.D. 1 Box 352
Lincoln University, PA 19352
(215) 932-8936

North Coventry Historical Society
c/o Mrs. Peg Deegan
837 Temple Road
Pottstown, PA 19464
(215) 323-7744

Malvern Borough Historical Commission
P.O. Box 437
Malvern, PA 19355
(215) 644-2602

Octorara Valley Historical Society
c/o Kerry Glenn
807 West Third Avenue
Parkesburg, PA 19365

Old Caln Historical Society
P.O. Box 428
Thorndale, PA 19372

Pikeland Historical Society
c/o Centennial Lutheran Church
Kimberton, PA 19442

Primitive Hall Foundation
595 East Chestnut Street
Coatesville, PA 19320

Southeastern Chester County Historical Society
Box 394
Kennett Square, PA 19348
(215) 444-1930

Tredyffrin-Easttown History Club
1475 Russell Road
Berwyn, PA 19312
(215) 644-0982

Uwchlan Conservation Trust, Inc.
Box 212
Lionville, PA 19353
(215) 363-9726

Uwchlan Township Historical Commission
P.O. Box 255
Lionville, PA 19353
(215) 363-9450

Valley Forge Historical Society
P.O. Box 122
Valley Forge, PA 19481
(215) 783-0535

Wallace Township Historical Commission
P.O. Box 96
Glenmoore, PA 19343
(215) 942-2880

West Bradford Historical Committee
1535 Poorhouse Road
Downingtown, PA 19335
(215) 269-4174

West Chester Board of Historical Review
802 Goshen Road
West Chester, PA 19380
(215) 696-9311

West Nantmeal Historical Commission
Box 251, R.D. 2
Elverson, PA 19520

West Whiteland Historical Commission
Box 210
Exton, PA 19341
(215) 363-8091

Willistown Township Historical Commission
Box 67, R.D. 2
Sugartown Road
Malvern, PA 19355
(215) 647-5300

Delaware County

Bethel Township Historical Society
c/o Reece Thomas
1369 Naaman's Creek Road
Boothwyn, PA 19061
(215) 485-4888

Bishop Mills Historical Institute
The Colonial Pennsylvania Plantation
Ridley Creek State Park
Media, PA 19063
(215) 566-1725

Chester Heights Historical Committee
c/o John deCampi
Box 196, Valley Brook Road
Chester Heights, PA 19017
(215) 459-2118

Concord Township Historical Society
c/o Mrs. Harold DeNenno
278 Kirk Road
Boothwyn, PA 19061
(215) 459-3518

*Note: These two organizations technically are located inside the border of Delaware County, and while frequently thought of as Chester County institutions, also should be considered on the Delaware County list.

Delaware County Heritage Commission
c/o Delaware County Planning Department
350 North Middletown Road
Lima, PA 19037
(215) 891-5663

Delaware County Historical Society
Wolfgram Memorial Library
Widener University
Chester, PA 19013
(215) 874-6444

Delaware County Tourist Bureau
602 East Baltimore Pike
Media, PA 19063
(215) 565-3679

Haverford Township Historical Society
c/o Margaret E. Johnston
805 Lawson Avenue
Havertown, PA 19083
(215) 446-1026

Historic Upland
c/o Robert Singley
3727 Clearwater Lane
Upland, PA 19014
(215) 872-8580

Lansdowne Historical Committee
c/o Dr. C. William Miller
119 Gladstone Avenue
Lansdowne, PA 19050
(215) 626-5685

Marple Newtown Historical Society
Attn: President
P.O. Box 355
Broomall, PA 19008

Media Historic Preservation, Inc.
Box A
Media, PA 19063

Middletown Township Historical Society
Box 275
Lima, PA 19037

Okehocking Heritage Society
Box 64
Gradyville, PA 19039

Radnor Historical Society
c/o Mr. George W. Smith
12 Forest Road
Wayne, PA 19087

Scottish Historical Research Society
c/o James Ross
2137 MacLarie Lane
Broomall, PA 19008

Springfield Township Historical Society
c/o Mrs. Louise Wentz
P.O. Box 1686
Springfield, PA 19064
(215) 544-5289

Thornbury Historical Society
c/o Richard Lukenbach
Box 155
Cheyney, PA 19319

Tyler Arboretum
515 Painter Road
Lima, Pa 19063
(215) 566-5431

Upper Darby Historical Society
c/o George E. Cain
1205 Morgan Avenue
Drexel Hill, PA 19026
(215) 789-9266

Montgomery County

Central Perkiomen Valley Historical Society
Route 29, R.D. 2
Schwenksville, PA 19473
(215) 287-9150

Cheltenham Township Historical Commission
c/o Township Building
8230 Old York Road
Elkins Park, PA 19117
(215) 887-1000

Conshohocken Historical Society
c/o William F. Collins
2nd Avenue and Forest Street
Conshohocken, PA 19428
(215) 828-9576

Goschenhoppen Historians, Inc.
Red Men's Hall
Green Lane, PA 18054

Hatboro Borough Historical Commission
c/o Hatboro Borough
120 Montgomery Avenue
Hatboro, PA 19040
(215) 675-0129

Hatboro Horsham Historical Society
64 Meadowbrook Avenue
Hatboro, PA 19040
(215) 675-0677

Highlands Historical Society
7001 Sheaff Lane
Fort Washington, PA 19034
(215) 641-2687

Historical Society of Fort Washington
473 Bethlehem Pike
Fort Washington, PA 19034
(215) 646-6065

Historical Society of Montgomery County
1654 DeKalb Street
Norristown, PA 19401
(215) 272-0297

King of Prussia Historical Society
c/o Carl F. Schultheis, Jr.
491 Allendale Road
King of Prussia, PA 19406

Lansdale Historical Society
Box 293
Lansdale, PA 19446
(215) 855-8044

Lower Merion Historical Society
Box 51
Ardmore, PA 19003

Old York Road Historical Society
c/o Jenkintown Library
York and Vista Roads
Jenkintown, PA 19046
(215) 886-5763

Penickpacka Historical Society
165 Propert Drive
Huntingdon Valley, PA 19006
(215) 947-0763

Peter Wentz Farmstead Society
Box 240
Worcester, PA 19490
(215) 584-5104

Plymouth Meeting Historical Society
Box 167
Plymouth Meeting, PA 19462
(215) 275-2950

Pottstown Historical Society
P.O. Box 661
Pottstown, PA 19464
(215) 326-4392

Skippack Historical Society
3119 Ridge Pike
Eagleville, PA 19408
(215) 539-6221

Towamencin Historical Society
P.O. Box 261
Kulpsville, PA 19443

Trappe Historical Society
305 Main Street
Collegeville, PA 19426

Upper Providence Historical Society
Box 156
River Road
Oaks, PA 19456

Valley Forge Country Convention and Visitors Bureau
P.O. Box 311
Norristown, PA 19404
(215) 278-3558

Valley Forge Historical Society
P.O. Box 122
Valley Forge, PA 19481
(215) 783-0535

Wissahickon Valley Historical Society
c/o Virginia Zabriskie
24 Morris Road
Ambler, PA 19002

Worcester Historical Society
3354 Mill Road
Collegeville, PA 19426
(215) 489-4962

Easement Programs in Pennsylvania

This survey of organizations that will accept or presently hold preservation or facade easements was made by the Bureau for Historic Preservation in August of 1984. While it may not be totally inclusive, it covers the majority of such programs across the Commonwealth. This survey does not include Philadelphia. For information about facade easement donations within that city's limits, contact:

>   The Philadelphia Historic Preservation Corporation
>   One East Penn Square
>   Philadelphia, PA 19107
>   Phone: (215) 568-4210

1. Brandywine Conservancy
   Box 141
   Chadds Ford, PA 19317
   Phone: (215) 459-1900, Ext. 143
   Contact Person: Martha Wolf/Emily Hart

2. Berks County Conservancy
   960 Old Mill Road
   Wyomissing, PA 19610
   Phone: (215) 372-4992
   Contact Person: Dennis Collins

3. Bucks County Conservancy
   11 North Main Street
   Doylestown, PA 18901
   Phone: (215) 345-7020
   Contact Person: Robert Pierson

4. French and Pickering Creeks Conservation Trust
   Box 360, R.D. 2
   Pottstown, PA 19464
   Phone: (215) 469-6287
   Contact Person: Eleanor Morris

5. Historic Preservation Trust of Lancaster County
   123 North Prince Street
   Lancaster, PA 17603
   Phone: (717) 291-5861
   Contact Person: Jane Higinbotham

6. Historic York, Inc.
   P.O. Box 2312
   York, PA 17405
   Phone: (717) 843-0320
   Contact Person: Lynn Rozental

7. National Trust for Historic Preservation
   Mid-Atlantic Regional Office
   6401 Germantown Avenue
   Philadelphia, PA 19144
   Phone: (215) 438-2886
   Contact Person: Grace Gary

8. Pittsburgh History and Landmarks Foundation
   450 Landmarks Building
   1 Station Square
   Pittsburgh, PA 15219
   Phone: (412) 471-5808
   Contact Person: Louise King Ferguson

9. Preservation Fund of Pennsylvania, Inc.
   2470 Kissel Hill Road
   Lancaster, PA 17601
   Phone: (717) 569-2243
   Contact Person: F. Bogue Wallin

10. Western Pennsylvania Conservancy
    316 Fourth Avenue
    Pittsburgh, PA 15222
    Phone: (412) 288-2777
    Contact Person: Tom Schmidt

Source: Pennsylvania Historical and Museum Commission, Bureau for Historic Preservation, August 1984.

APPENDIX B—Research Libraries and Collections (Delaware Valley)

American Philosophical Society Library
105 South Fifth Street
Philadelphia, PA 19106
(215) 627-0706

American Swedish Historical Museum
1900 Pattison Avenue
Philadelphia, PA 19145
(215) 389-1776

Athenaeum
219 South Sixth Street
Philadelphia, PA 19106
(215) 925-2688

Bucks County Historical Society
Spruance Library
Pine and Ashland Streets
Doylestown, PA 18901
(215) 345-0210

City Archives of Philadelphia
Room 5
23 City Hall Annex
Philadelphia, PA 19107
(215) 686-2276

Chester County Archives
Chester County Courthouse
High and Market Streets
West Chester, PA 19380
(215) 696-5370

Chester County Historical Society Library
225 North High Street
West Chester, PA 19380
(215) 692-4800

Delaware County Historical Society
Wolfgram Memorial Library at Widener College
Chester, PA 19013
(215) 874-6444

Delaware County Institute of Science
11 South Avenue (Veteran's Square)
Media, PA 19063
(215) 566-5126

Eleutherian Mills Historical Library
P.O. Box 3630
Wilmington, DE 19807
(302) 658-2400

Francis Harvey Green Library—Special Collections Department
West Chester University
West Chester, PA 19383
(215) 436-3456

Franklin Institute Library
20th and Benjamin Franklin Parkway
Philadelphia, PA 19103
(215) 448-1227

Friends Free Library
5418 Germantown Avenue
Philadelphia, PA 19144
(215) 438-6023

Friends Historical Library
Swarthmore College
Swarthmore, PA 19081
(215) 447-7496

Free Library of Philadelphia
Logan Square
Philadelphia, PA 19103
(215) 686-1776

German Society of Pennsylvania
Joseph Horner Memorial Library
611 Spring Garden Street
Philadelphia, PA 19123
(215) 627-4365

Germantown Historical Society Library and Archives
5214 Germantown Avenue
Philadelphia, PA 19144
(215) 844-0514

Historical Society of Montgomery County Library
1654 DeKalb Street
Norristown, PA 19401
(215) 272-0297

Historical Society of Pennsylvania and
Genealogical Society of Pennsylvania
1300 Locust Street
Philadelphia, PA 19107
(215) 732-6200

Hopewell Village National Historic Site Library
R.D. 1, Box 345
Elverson, PA 19520
(215) 582-8773

Horace Willcox Library
Valley Forge National Historical Park
Valley Forge, PA 19481
(215) 783-7700

Library Company of Philadelphia
1314 Locust Street
Philadelphia, PA 19107
(215) 546-3181

Magill Library — Quaker Collection
Haverford College
Haverford, PA 19041
(215) 896-1161

Mennonite Library and Archives of Eastern Pennsylvania
Christopher Dock Mennonite High School
1000 Forty Foot Road
Lansdale, PA 19446
(215) 362-0304

National Trust for Historic Preservation
Mid-Atlantic Regional Office
6401 Germantown Avenue
Philadelphia, PA 19144
(215) 438-2886

Newtown Library Company
114 East Centre Avenue
Newtown, PA 18940
(215) 968-7659

Painter Library
Tyler Arboretum
515 Painter Road
Lima, PA 19063
(215) 566-5431

Philadelphia Historical Commission
Room 1313
City Hall Annex
Philadelphia, PA 19107
(215) 686-4543

Schwenkfelder Library
1 Seminary Street
Pennsburg, PA 18073
(215) 679-3103

War Library and Museum
1805 Pine Street
Philadelphia, PA 19103
(215) 735-8196

Washington Crossing Historic Park
Library of the American Revolution
Washington Crossing, PA 18977
(215) 493-5532

APPENDIX C—Pennsylvania Historic District Listings; Sample Documents and Forms; Local Ordinances

National Register Historic Districts Surrounding Philadelphia

Historic Districts Surrounding Philadelphia Certified by the Pennsylvania Historical and Museum Commission in Accordance with Act No. 167

Pennsylvania Historic Resource Survey Form and Instructions

Pennsylvania's Priorities for the Processing of National Register Nominations

Historic District Model Ordinance (under Pennsylvania Act No. 167)

Delay of Demolition Ordinance, New Castle County, Delaware

Historic Preservation Certification Application (U.S. Department of Interior, National Park Service)

National Register Historic Districts Surrounding Philadelphia

County	Name of District
BUCKS	Carversville Historic District
	Falsington Historic District
	Holingcong Village Historic District
	Newtown Historic District
	Shaw Historic District (Doylestown)
	Village of Edgewood Historic District
	Forest Grove Historic District
	Phillips Mill Historic District (Solebury Twp.)
CHESTER	Charlestown Village Historic District
	Coventryville Historic District
	Dilworthtown Historic District
	East Lancaster Historic District (Downingtown)
	Lionville Historic District
	Longwood Gardens District
	Kimberton Village Historic District
	Unionville Village Historic District
	Hatfield-Hibernia Historic District
	West Chester State College Quadrangle Historic District
DELAWARE	Chadds Ford Historic District
	Ivy Mills Historic District
	Concordville Historic District
	Chester Creek Historic District (Thornbury)
	Pusey-Crozier Mill Historic District (Upland)
MONTGOMERY	Bergy Bridge Historic District
	Bryn Mawr College Historic District
	Evansburg Historic District
	Plymouth Meeting Historic District
	Gladwyne Historic District (Merion Square)
	Mill Creek Historic District
	Cold Point Historic District

Source: Pennsylvania Historical and Museum Commission, Bureau for Historic Preservation, July 1984.

Historic Districts Surrounding Philadelphia Certified by the Pennsylvania Historical and Museum Commission in Accordance with Act No. 167

County	District/Location
BUCKS	**Village of Brownsburg Historic District:** Upper Makefield Township
	Village of Dollington Historic District: Upper Makefield Township
	Doylestown Borough Historic District: Borough of Doylestown
	Historic Newtown: Borough of Newtown
	Historic Radcliffe Street: Borough of Bristol
	Langhorne Borough Historic District: Borough of Langhorne
	Spring Valley Historic District: Buckingham Township
	New Hope Historic District: Borough of New Hope
	Carversville Historic District: Solebury Township
	Village of Fallsington: Falls Township
	Village of Edgewood Historic District: Lower Makefield Township
CHESTER	**Chester Springs Historic District:** West Pikeland Township
	Birmingham Township Historic District: Birmingham Township
	Village of Unionville: East Marlborough Township
	Coventryville Historic District: South Coventry Township
	Tredyffrin Historical District: Tredyffrin Township
	Charlestown Village Historic District: Charlestown Township

143

DELAWARE	**Media Borough Historic District:** Borough of Media	
MONTGOMERY	**Gladwyne (Merion Square) Historic District:** Lower Merion Township	
	Mill Creek Historic District: Lower Merion Township	
	Harriton Historic District: Lower Merion Township	
	Historical Lamott: Cheltenham Township	
	Plymouth Meeting Historic District: Plymouth and Whitemarsh Townships	
	Huntingdon Valley Historic District: Lower Moreland Township	

Source: Pennsylvania Historical and Museum Commission, Bureau for Historic Preservation, January 1984.

Pennsylvania Historic Resource Survey Form Instructions

1. COUNTY: Name of county in which resource is located.
2. MUNICIPALITY: Name of local governmental area (city, borough, township) in which resource is located.
3. SPECIFIC LOCATION: Street address or physical location of resource (not an RD mailing address).
4. SURVEY CODE: The three-part survey number for the resource.
5. PRESENT NAME: Current name of the resource (John Doe House, Cynthia's Carpet Cleaning).
6. HISTORIC NAME: Original name of resource. This may be the builder's or first owner's name. If original name is not known, specify original use of resource (tavern, hardware store, shirt factory).
7. LOCAL SURVEY ORGANIZATION: Name, address, and phone number of group conducting survey.
8. OWNER'S NAME AND ADDRESS: Current owner's name and address.
9. TAX PARCEL NUMBER: Local tax number of property.
10. GEOGRAPHICAL DATA: Name of USGS quad map showing location of resource and UTM coordinates of the resource.
11. STATUS: Name and date of any other survey or inventory that included the resource.
12. CLASSIFICATION: Check appropriate box.
13. DATE: Date of original construction and any major alterations to the resource.
14. PERIOD: Select appropriate period—before 1700-1749, 1750-1799, 1800-1824, 1825-1849, 1850-1874, 1875-1899, 1900-1924, 1925-1949.
15. STYLE: Note architectural style of structure (Federal, Italianate, Art Deco, etc.—see BHP Computerization Code Book for list*).
16. ARCHITECT OR ENGINEER: Name of individual or firm.
17. CONTRACTOR OR BUILDER: Name of individual or firm.
18. PRIMARY BUILDING MATERIAL: Principal material in structure (stone, log, brick, wood frame, reinforced concrete). This is not the siding material (stucco, clapboard, aluminum siding).
19. ORIGINAL USE: General description of original use of resource (factory, store, apartment house).
20. PRESENT USE: General description of present use (factory, store, apartment house).
21. CONDITION: What is the physical condition of the resource? Excellent, poor, deteriorated?
22. INTEGRITY: How does the present appearance of the resource relate to its historic appearance? Is it intact, altered, modified?
23. SITE PLAN: Sketch map showing location of resource in relation to nearest roads, streams, outbuildings, etc. Include north arrow.
24. PHOTO NOTATION CAPTION: Explanation of photo view (i.e. south facade, view of rear from northeast, etc.)
25. FILE LOCATION: Not applicable.
26. DESCRIPTION: Description of physical appearance of resource. Size, number of stories (spans), building materials, architectural style, etc.
27. SIGNIFICANCE: Must convey in concise terms, importance of resource. Not merely a history of the resource, this section should attempt to relate the structure to the broad historical trends identified for the survey areas by the historical research.
28. BIBLIOGRAPHY: List of sources consulted. Do not include general reference works unless they provided specific information on the resource. Use a standard bibliographic format listing author's full name, complete title, location of publication, publisher, date published, and page numbers (if applicable). Archival sources should be identified as to location, so that future researchers may consult the same sources.
29. COMPLETED BY: Name and address of person who completed the form and date of preparation.
30. DATE: Date form completed.
31. COUNTY: See codes list. If resource is in more than one county use general Pennsylvania code number (42).
32. STYLE: See codes list.
33. CONSTRUCTION MATERIAL: Code primary structure materials.
34. ROOF: See codes list.
35. DESIGN TYPE: Code if notable and appropriate to resource.
36. HISTORIC FUNCTION: See codes list. Be sure to indicate P, S, or A after each number. The letters P, S, and A relate to historic significance in the following manner:

    Use P when the resource was *primarily* important as a hotel, jail, department store, etc. This often is reflected in the resource being of a particular *type*, e.g. courthouse, railroad station although is not necessarily a building's first use.

    Use S when the resource had a use in its historic period additional to primary uses. This is often reflected in buildings which though built for one purpose may have housed something else (of lesser historical importance) during its historic period.

    Use A to *associate* the resource with a historical theme or function. For example, a house of a person important in chemical manufacture can be linked with that historical theme by choosing the appropriate 6 digit number for the chemical manufacture and following it with the letter "A".

37. CONSTRUCTION FEATURE: Code if notable and appropriate to resource.
38. EXTERIOR WALLS. Code primary present exterior wall materials.
39. PLAN. Code if notable and appropriate to resource.
40. FACADE WIDTH: Code if notable and appropriate to resource.
41. ROOF MATERIAL: Code primary present roof material.

42. STORIES: See codes list.
43. DEPTH: Code if appropriate to resource.
44. EXTERIOR DESIGN FEATURE: Code if notable and appropriate to resource.
45. INTERIOR DESIGN FEATURE: Code if notable and appropriate to resource.

*NOTE: Only BHP Survey Grantees are required to use the codes list.

Source: Pennsylvania Historical and Museum Commission, Bureau for Historic Preservation.

Pennsylvania's Priorities for the Processing of National Register Nominations

Pennsylvania's priorities were developed as an aggressive preservation strategy rather than a reactionary approach to the preservation and registration of our historic resources. These priorities will be applied by the Bureau for Historic Preservation staff in a professional and unbiased manner. The Bureau for Historic Preservation reserves the right to process nominations which may meet other interests and concerns; decisions will be made on a case by case basis.

The following priorities are listed in their order of importance. In all cases nominations must be of high quality and the property must meet the National Register criteria.

Priority will be given to properties:

(1) For which registration will significantly assist in their preservation from threats of alteration, neglect or demolition.
(2) Which demonstrate the importance of restoration, rehabilitation, and reuse of significant historic resources under federal tax provisions.
(3) Which possess national or state significance. Those buildings, sites, objects or districts which possess exceptional value or quality in illustrating or interpreting the history and architecture of our nation or state.
(4) Which have been identified as eligible from areas in which comprehensive historic site surveys have been completed.
(5) Which include the protection and registration of multiple historic resources as nominated in:

Historic Districts: a geographically definable area, urban or rural, possessing a significant concentration, linkage or continuity of sites, buildings, structures, or objects united by past events or aesthetically by plan or physical development.

Thematic Resource Nominations: a nomination which includes a finite group of resources related to one another by a clearly distinguishable theme.

Multiple Resource Nominations: a nomination which includes all or defined portion of the historic resources identified in a specified geographical area in which a comprehensive historic site survey has been completed.

Source: Pennsylvania Historical and Museum Commission, Bureau for Historic Preservation, 1982.

HISTORIC DISTRICT MODEL ORDINANCE: _____ TOWNSHIP[1]

(Under Pennsylvania Act No. 167, P.L. 282, June 13, 1961)

An ordinance[2] to create and define an historic district to be known as the "_____ Historic District" within the geographic limits of "_____ Township; providing for notification of the Pennsylvania Historical and Museum Commission of the adoption of this ordinance and for obtaining from said Commission a certificate as to the historical significance of said District; providing for the appointment of a Board of Historical Architectural Review to counsel the Board of Supervisors of _____ Township regarding the issuance of certificates of appropriateness in connection with the granting or refusal of permits for the erection, reconstruction, alteration, restoration, demolition, or razing of buildings or structures located within said District as defined herein; providing for appeals from such refusals and for changes in the procedure for the issuance of building permits necessary to carry out the provisions of this ordinance; imposing fines and penalties for violations.

The Board of Supervisors of _____ Township, under and by virtue of the authority granted by the act of June 13, 1961, P. L. 282, as amended, 53 P.S. Sec. 8001 et seq. (hereinafter referred to as the Act of June 13, 1961), entitled:

> "An Act authorizing counties, cities, boroughs, incorporated towns and townships to create historic districts within their geographic boundaries; providing for the appointment of Boards of Historical Architectural Review; empowering governing bodies of political subdivisions to protect the distinctive historical character of these districts and to regulate the erection, reconstruction, alteration, restoration, demolition or razing of buildings within the historic districts.

does hereby enact and ordain:

Section 1. Statement of Purpose.

It is the purpose of this ordinance to protect those historic buildings and areas within _____ Township which have a distinctive character recalling the architectural and historical heritage of the Township, of _____ County, and of the Commonwealth of Pennsylvania, and to promote the general welfare, education, and culture of the Township by encouraging an interest in its historical heritage.

Section 2. General Provisions

a. *Short title.* This ordinance shall be known and may be cited as the "_____ Township Historic District Ordinance."

b. *Definition of Historic District.* The boundaries of the _____ Historic District shall be as shown on the map attached hereto as Exhibit "A" and made a part of this ordinance, which map shall be known as the "Historic District Map of _____ Township." The provisions of this ordinance shall be applied to all land, buildings, and structures within the boundaries of the _____ Historic District.

c. *Compliance.* No structure shall hereafter be used and no structure shall hereafter be erected, reconstructed, altered, restored, demolished, or razed, in whole or in part, without full compliance with the terms of this ordinance and other applicable regulations.

d. *Repealer.* All ordinances inconsistent with this ordinance are hereby repealed to the extent of the inconsistency only.

e. *Severability.* The provisions of this ordinance shall be severable, and if any of the provisions hereof shall be held to be unconstitutional, invalid, or illegal

---

[1] "Township" is used throughout this model ordinance purely for convenience. Its provisions are applicable to boroughs, cities, and counties, as well.

[2] This ordinance can be enacted as a separate, discrete regulation or as an element of a municipal zoning ordinance, with the historic district acting as an overlay on the zoning map.

by a court of competent jurisdiction, such decision shall not affect the validity of any of the remaining provisions of this ordinance.

f. *Effective Date.* This ordinance shall not take effect until the Pennsylvania Historical and Museum Commission has been notified, in writing, of the ordinance and has certified, by resolution, to the historical significance of the _____ Historic District as defined in Section 2(b) hereof.

> Note: *Certification by the Pennsylvania Historical and Museum Commission is required by Sect. 2 of the Act, 53 P.S. Sec. 8002.*

Section 3. *Board of Historical Architectural Review.*

a. *Appointment.* Upon receipt of the certifying resolution of the Pennsylvania Historical and Museum Commission referred to in Section 2(f) hereof, the Board of Supervisors of _____ Township shall appoint a Board of Historical Architectural Review.

b. *Membership.* The Board of Historical Architectural Review shall consist of not less than five (5) members, of whom one shall be a registered architect, one shall be a licensed real estate broker, one shall be a building inspector, and one shall be a member of the Planning Commission of _____ Township. The remaining member or members shall have a knowledge of and interest in the preservation of historic districts. Three members of the Board must be Township residents. The initial terms of the members of the Board of Historical Architectural Review shall be as follows: One member shall be appointed for one year, one member for two years, one member for three years, one member for four years, and one member for five years. Annually thereafter, a member of said Board shall be appointed for a term of five years. An appointment to fill a vacancy shall be only for the unexpired portion of the term.

> Note: *An architect, a real estate broker, and a building inspector are required by Sect. 3 of the Act, 53 P.S. Sec. 8003.*

c. *Compensation.* The members of the Board of Historical Architectural Review shall serve without compensation, but may be reimbursed for direct expenses. The Board of Historical Architectural Review may, pursuant to appropriations authorized by the Board of Supervisors, employ secretarial assistance and incur such other expenses as may be necessary to the enforcement of this ordinance.

d. *Conduct of Business.* The Board of Historical Architectural Review shall elect its own chairman and vice-chairman and create and fill such other offices as it may determine. Officers shall serve annual terms and may succeed themselves. The Board of Historical Architectural Review may make and alter by-laws and rules and regulations to govern its procedures, consistent with the ordinances of _____ Township and the laws of the Commonwealth of Pennsylvania; shall keep a full record of its business; and shall make a written report of its activities to the Board of Supervisors by March 1 of each year. Interim reports may be made as often as may be necessary, or as requested by the Board of Supervisors.

e. *Duties.* The Board of Historical Architectural Review shall give counsel to the Board of Supervisors regarding the advisability of issuing any certificates which the Board of Supervisors is required to issue pursuant to this ordinance and the Act of June 13, 1961, and shall hold such hearings and render such reports as are required by Section 5 hereof. In determining the counsel to be given to the Board of Supervisors relative to the issuance of a certificate of appropriateness, the Board of Historical Architectural Review shall consider only those matters that are pertinent to the preservation of the historic aspect and nature of the buildings and structures located within the _____ Historic District, including:

1. The effect which the proposed change will have upon the general historic and architectural character and appearance of the District; and
2. The appropriateness of exterior architectural features and the general design, arrangement, texture, material, and color of the building or structure and the relation of such factors to the traditional architectural character of the District.

Board members are required to disqualify themselves from voting on any project in which their own financial interests or those of their immediate family are directly or indirectly involved.

Section 4. *Certificate of Appropriateness.*

a. *Permits and Certificate Required.* No person shall commence any work for the erection, reconstruction, alteration, restoration, demolition, or razing of any building or structure located in whole or in part within the _____ Historic District, without first obtaining a certificate of appropriateness with respect thereto from the Board of Supervisors as provided hereinafter.

b. *Duties of Zoning Officer.* The Zoning Officer of _____ Township, or such other person or agency charged by the Board of Supervisors with the issuance of permits for the erection, demolition, or alteration of buildings or structures subject to the provisions of this ordinance, shall issue no permit for any such building changes until a certificate of appropriateness with respect thereto has been received from the Board of Supervisors.

c. *Application for Permit.* The application for a building permit for any building changes with respect to any buildings or structures subject to the provisions of this ordinance shall be filed with the Zoning Officer of _____ Township together with the filing fee required under the schedule of fees then in effect. The application shall include a site plan at a scale of one inch to 40 feet, schematic architectural drawings of the proposed construction or changes at a scale of one foot to one-quarter (1/4) inch, and such other material and such number of copies thereof as may from time to time be required in accordance with the rules and regulations of the Board of Historical Architectural Review. Within three days after receiving such application for a building permit, the Zoning Officer shall forward the application, together with all plans and other documentation submitted therewith, to the office of the Board of Historical Architectural Review.

d. *Standards for determining appropriateness.* In determining whether or not any proposed work for the erection, reconstruction, alteration, restoration, demolition, or razing of any building or structure within the _____ Historic District is appropriate to the District, the Board of Historical Architectural Review and Board of Supervisors shall consider the following criteria, where relevant:

1. Mass (height, bulk, nature of roof line)
2. Proportions (height to width)
3. Nature of yard space
4. Extent of landscaped areas versus paved areas
5. The nature of facade openings (doors and windows)—their size, locations, and proportions
6. The type of roof (flat, gabled, hip, gambrel, mansard, etc.)
7. The nature of projections (porches, etc.)
8. The nature of the architectural details and style
9. The nature of the materials
10. Color
11. Texture
12. Ornamentation
13. Signs

Where the proposed work is to be done on an historic structure within the District, then the primary basis for comparison shall be the structure itself (in its then-existing state as compared to its state after the proposed work), and the secondary basis for comparison shall be the effect of the proposed work on the District as a whole.

> *Note: This list of criteria represents one suggestion; standards and emphases are likely to vary from one community to the next.*

Section 5. Hearing Before Board of Historical Architectural Review.

a. *Hearing.* Within thirty (30) days from the time said application for a building permit is received by the Board of Historical Architectural Review, a hearing shall be held by said Board to consider the recommendations which it will give to the Board of Supervisors. The person applying for the permit shall be given a minimum of ten (10) days' notice of the time and place of the said hearing and shall be invited to appear to explain his reasons for such application.

> *Note: The applicant must be given notice and opportunity to appear and explain his reasons; Sect. 4(g) of the Act, 53 P.S. Sec. 8004(c).*

b. *Findings after Hearings.* Within thirty (30) days following the conclusion of the hearing or hearings, the Board of Historical Architectural Review shall, by official written communication to the applicant, recommend either:

1. The issuance of a certificate of appropriateness authorizing a permit for the proposed changes as submitted; or
2. The issuance of a certificate of appropriateness subject to specified changes and conditions not included in the application as submitted, but which, in its opinion, would protect the distinctive historic character of the building, site, or area which is proposed to be changed; or
3. The denial of a certificate of appropriateness with respect to the proposed changes as submitted.

Failure of the Board of Historical Architectural Review to so act within the said period shall be deemed to constitute a recommendation for the issuance of a certificate of appropriateness with respect to the application as submitted. In the event that the recommendation for the issuance of a certificate of appropriateness is subject to conditions, the applicant may, within ten (10) days after receiving a copy of the official written communication from the Board of Historical Architectural Review, give notice of his refusal to accept all of the conditions, in which case the Board shall be deemed to have recommended against the issuance of a certificate of appropriateness. In the event that the applicant does not, within the said period, notify the Board of his refusal to accept all of the said conditions, conditional approval of the application with all conditions shall stand as granted.

c. *Report to Board of Supervisors.* Upon or before the expiration of the aforesaid forty (40) day period, the Board of Historical Architectural Review shall submit to the Board of Supervisors, in writing, its counsel concerning the issuance of a certificate of appropriateness to authorize a permit for the erection, reconstruction, alteration, restoration, demolition, or razing of all or a part of any building, site, or area for which an application for a building permit has been made in accordance with Section 4(c) hereof. The written report shall set out the following matters:

1. The exact location of the area in which the work is to be done.
2. The exterior changes to be made or the exterior character of the structure to be erected.
3. A list of the surrounding structures certified to have historical significance, with their general exterior characteristics.
4. An analysis of the appropriateness of the proposed work, taking into consideration the criteria specified in Section 4(d), hereof, where each such factor is deemed relevant.
5. The opinion of the Board, including any dissent, as to the appropriateness of the work proposed in regard to preserving or destroying the historic aspect and nature of the building, site, or area.
6. The specific counsel of the Board of Historical Architectural Review regarding the issuance of or refusal to issue a certificate of appropriateness.
7. Any changes in plans and specifications recommended by the Board of Historical Architectural Review.

Section 6. Public Meeting of the Board of Supervisors.

a. *Meeting.* Upon receipt of the written counsel of the Board of Historical Architectural Review, the Board of Supervisors shall consider, at the next regularly scheduled meeting of the Board of Supervisors, the question of issuing a certificate of appropriateness authorizing a permit for the work proposed by the applicant. The applicant shall be given ten (10) days' notice by the Township Secretary of the time and place of the meeting at which his application will be considered and shall have the right to attend and be heard regarding his application. All interested persons may appear and be heard at the meeting held by the Board of Supervisors.

> Note: The applicant must be given notice and opportunity to appear and explain his reasons; Sect. 4(c) of the Act, 53 P.S. Sec. 8004(c).

b. *Decision of Board of Supervisors.* Within fifteen (15) days following the conclusion of the aforesaid public meeting, the Board of Supervisors shall, by official written communication to the applicant, either:

1. Issue a certificate of appropriateness authorizing a permit for the proposed changes as submitted; or
2. Issue a certificate of appropriateness subject to specified changes and conditions not included in the application as submitted, but which would protect the distinctive historic character of the building, site,

or area which is proposed to be changed; or

3. Deny a certificate of appropriateness with respect to the proposed changes as submitted.

Failure of the Board of Supervisors to so act within the said period shall be deemed to constitute a decision in favor of the applicant and a certificate of appropriateness shall thereupon be issued. In the event that approval is granted subject to conditions, the applicant may, within ten (10) days after receiving a copy of the official written communication from the Board of Supervisors, give notice of his refusal to accept all of the conditions, in which case the Board shall be deemed to have denied a certificate of appropriateness. In the event the applicant does not, within the said period, notify the Board of Supervisors of his refusal to accept all of the said conditions, the approval, with all conditions, shall stand as granted.

c. *Resolution of Board of Supervisors.* The grant or denial of a certificate of appropriateness shall be in the form of a written resolution which shall include findings of fact related to the specific proposal and shall set forth the reasons of the grant, with or without conditions, or for the denial, referring to such of the criteria set forth in Section 4(d) hereof which were relevant to its decision. A copy of each resolution of denial shall be forwarded to the Pennsylvania Historical and Museum Commission. A copy of such resolution shall accompany the official written communication to the applicant as provided in this Section.

Section 7. Appeals.

Any decision of the Board of Supervisors under this ordinance, granting or denying a certificate of appropriateness or authorizing or refusing to authorize a modification in such certificate of appropriateness, shall be subject to review and appeal in the same manner and within the same time limitation as is provided for zoning appeals by the Pennsylvania Municipalities Planning Code, Act of July 31, 1968, P.L. 805, as amended, 53 P.S. Sec. 10101, et seq.

Section 8. Enforcement.

The building inspector (or such other person or agency charged by the Board of Supervisors with the enforcement of the provisions of this ordinance) shall review the progress and status of the proposed changes and render such reports thereon to the Board of Supervisors and to the Board of Historical Architectural Review as may be necessary to assure compliance with the provisions of this ordinance and the conditions of the certificate of appropriateness.

Section 9. Penalties.

For any and every violation of the provisions of this ordinance, the owner, general agent, or contractor of a building or structure where such violation has been committed or shall exist, and the lessee or tenant of an entire building or entire structure where such violation has been committed or shall exist, and the owner, general agent, contractor, lessee, or tenant of any part of a building or structure in which part such violation has been committed or shall exist, and the general agent, architect, builder, contractor, or any person who knowingly commits, takes part, or assists in any such violation or who maintains any building or structure in which any such violation shall exist, shall be liable on conviction thereof to a fine or penalty not exceeding three hundred dollars ($300) for each and every offense. Whenever such person shall have been officially notified by the building inspector (or such other person or agency charged by the Board of Supervisors with the enforcement of the provisions of this ordinance) or by service of a summons in a prosecution, or in any other official manner, that he is committing a violation of this ordinance, each day's continuance of such violation after such notification shall constitute a separate offense punishable by a like fine or penalty. Such fines and penalties shall be in addition to any other fines, penalties, and remedies provided by law for such cases and shall be collected in the same manner as is provided in the Second Class Township Code, Act of May 1, 1933, P.L. 103, as amended, 53 P.S. Sec. 65101, et seq.

Source: *Environmental Management Handbook*, Environmental Management Center, Brandywine Conservancy, 1982.

DELAY OF DEMOLITION ORDINANCE
New Castle County, Delaware

105.4 Demolition and Historic Structures. Demolition of any structure and re-construction of historic properties shall comply with the requirement of this subsection.

105.4.1 Historic Structures. The Building Official shall delay for ten (10) days the issuance of any demolition permit for any building or structure over seventy-five (75) years of age and refer the application for such a permit to the Historic Review Board of the County within two (2) working days of its receipt. If the Historic Review Board determines that the building or structure is of historic significance for reasons it shall state in a written opinion to the Building Official, the Historic Review Board may order an additional delay in the issuance of the permit up to sixty (60) days from the date of application for the permit. The issuance of a demolition permit for any building or structure appearing on or eligible for the New Castle County Register of Historic and Architectural Heritage may be delayed by the Historic Review Board for up to six (6) months from the date of application for the permit during which time it shall seek alternatives to demolition.

105.4.2 Penalties. Upon verification by the Historic Review Board that a building or structure of historic significance has been demolished prior to issuance of a demolition permit, the Building Official shall take immediate action for prosecution of said violation(s) with the intent of invoking the maximum penalties, as established in Section 117.0, against the person, firm or corporation responsible for the demolition.

105.5 Definition. *"Demolish"*—To alter a structure by rendering it unfit for use to such an extent that repair is not feasible or is so costly as to be economically prohibitive. Alterations within the scope of an approved building permit shall not be regarded as demolition as defined in this paragraph.

Source: Excerpt from New Castle County Ordinance 84-097, August 6, 1984.

HISTORIC PRESERVATION CERTIFICATION APPLICATION

National Park Service Regional Offices (Cultural Programs) Issuing Certifications

Alaska Region
Preservation Tax Incentives
National Park Service
2525 Gambell Street
Anchorage, Alaska 99503

Mid-Atlantic Region
Preservation Tax Incentives
National Park Service
600 Arch Street, Room 9414
Philadelphia, Pennsylvania 19106
(215) 597-2283

Rocky Mountain Region
Preservation Tax Incentives
National Park Service
655 Parfet Street
P.O. Box 25287
Denver, Colorado 80225

Southeast Region
Preservation Tax Incentives
National Park Service
75 Spring Street, SW
Atlanta, Georgia 30303

Western Region
Preservation Tax Incentives
National Park Service
450 Golden Gate Avenue
P.O. Box 36063
San Francisco, California 94102

NOTE:
To obtain the Certification Application forms and detailed instructions for completing them, contact the appropriate NPS regional office from list above.